Dan Lewis
personal copy
10/94

California Progressivism Revisited

California Progressivism Revisited

Edited by
William Deverell
and Tom Sitton

UNIVERSITY OF CALIFORNIA PRESS
Berkeley · *Los Angeles* · *London*

Mary Ann Mason's essay, "Neither Friends nor Foes," is based upon "California Progressive Labor's Point of View" in the Winter 1976 issue of *Labor History*, available from B. P. Ink, P.O. Box 1236, Washington, CT 06793.

George J. Sanchez's essay, "The 'New Nationalism,' Mexican Style," is based upon a chapter in his book *Becoming Mexican American: Ethnicity, Culture, and Identity in Chicano Los Angeles, 1900–1945*, published by Oxford University Press in 1993.

Jackson K. Putnam's essay, "The Progressive Legacy in California," is based upon an essay by the same title in the February 1992 issue of *Pacific Historical Review*.

University of California Press
Berkeley and Los Angeles, California

University of California Press, Ltd.
London, England

© 1994 by
The Regents of the University of California

Library of Congress Cataloging-in-Publication Data

California progressivism revisited / edited by William
    Deverell and Tom Sitton.
        p.   cm.
    Includes bibliographical references and index.
    ISBN 0-520-08469-1 (alk. paper). — ISBN 0-520-08470-5 (pbk.
    : alk. paper)
    1. California—Politics and government—1850–1950.
    2. Progressivism (United States politics)   3. Women—California—
    Political activity—History—20th century.   4. Afro-Americans—
    California—Politics and government.   I. Deverell, William
    Francis.   II. Sitton, Tom, 1949– .
    F866.C224   1994
    320.0794—dc20   93-11110

Printed in the United States of America
9 8 7 6 5 4 3 2 1
The paper used in this publication meets the minimum requirements of American National Standard for Information Sciences—Permanence of Paper for Printed Library Materials, ANSI Z39.48-1984. ∞

For our parents
William and Margaret Deverell
John and Dorothy Sitton

Contents

Acknowledgments

Our chief debt is to the John Randolph Haynes and Dora Haynes Foundation of Los Angeles, which generously underwrote the project. Thanks especially to Diane Cornwell of the Haynes Foundation and to the foundation's president, Haynes Lindley, Jr. We would especially like to thank Martin Ridge of the Huntington Library for his advice, encouragment, and help in getting this book off the ground. We also thank the Los Angeles County Museum of Natural History, particularly Janet Fireman, chief of the History Division, for supporting this project. We both feel lucky to have worked with Lynne Withey and Laura Driussi of the University of California Press. We are also grateful to copy editor Dorothy Conway and the two outside readers for UC Press, who all gave so much time and thought to the manuscript and helped make this a much better book.

CONTRIBUTORS

William Deverell received his Ph.D. from Princeton University in 1989. He is the author of *Railroad Crossing: Californians and the Railroad, 1850–1910* (Berkeley: University of California Press, 1994) and teaches history and urban studies at the University of California, San Diego.

Douglas Flamming is assistant professor of history at the California Institute of Technology. He is the author of *Creating the Modern South: Millhands and Managers in Dalton, Georgia, 1884–1984*, which won the 1993 Philip Taft Labor History Prize. He is now at work on a manuscript entitled "A World to Gain: African Americans and the Making of Los Angeles, 1890–1940."

Anne F. Hyde received her Ph.D. from the University of California, Berkeley. She is associate professor of history at the Colorado College and is the author of the award-winning *An American Vision: Far Western Landscape and National Culture, 1820–1920*, published by New York University Press in 1990.

Sherry Katz received her B.A. from the University of California, Santa Cruz, and her Ph.D. from the University of California, Los Angeles. She is an affiliated scholar of the Beatrice M. Bain Research Group at the University of California, Berkeley, and a lecturer in the Department of History at UCLA. Currently, she is completing a book on socialist women, social reform, and the emerging welfare state in Progressive Era California.

Mary Ann Mason received her Ph.D. from the University of California, Berkeley. She is an associate professor in the School of Social Welfare at the University of California, Berkeley, and is the author of a forthcoming study on the history of child custody in America.

Mary Odem is assistant professor of history and women's studies at Emory University. Her forthcoming book is entitled *Delinquent Daughters: Protecting and Policing Adolescent Female Sexuality in the United States, 1880–1920*.

Jackson K. Putnam is professor emeritus of history at the California State University, Fullerton, and the author of numerous studies of California politics. Among his most recent works is an examination of the decline of liberalism in California since the Second World War, forthcoming in a University of Oklahoma Press collection (Richard Lowitt, ed.).

Judith Raftery received her B.A. at the University of California, Berkeley, and her Ph.D. at the University of California, Los Angeles. She is associate professor of history at California State University, Chico, and is the author of *Land of Fair Promise: Politics and Reform in Los Angeles Schools, 1885–1941*, published in 1992 by Stanford University Press.

George J. Sanchez attended Harvard University and received his Ph.D. from Stanford University. He is associate professor of history at the University of Michigan and the author of *Becoming Mexican American: Ethnicity, Culture, and Identity in Chicano Los Angeles, 1900–1945*, published by Oxford University Press in 1993.

Tom Sitton is associate curator of history, Los Angeles County Museum of Natural History. He is the author of *John Randolph Haynes: California Progressive*, published by Stanford University Press in 1992.

Gerald Woods received a doctorate in history from UCLA in 1973. He is the author of *The Police in Los Angeles: Reform and Professionalization* (New York: Garland Publishing, 1993) and a forthcoming history of the Canadian federal penitentiary system. At present he is an independent consultant on criminal justice issues.

The Varieties of Progressive Experience

William Deverell

Politics, n. A strife of interests masquerading as a contest
of principles.

Ambrose Bierce

We know that imperialism and progressivism were closely
related crusades, and it seems clear that together they largely
banished gloom and anxiety in favor of an optimistic,
adventurous engagement in social change.

John Higham

Think of the words *progressivism* and *progressive:* siblings that carry
diverse and heavy burdens of meaning. The first staggers beneath
weighty baggage such as "a political movement" and "a social movement" and the unwieldy "worldview." The second stumbles as it simultaneously shoulders "an era" and the startling variety of individuals and
groups who seized or are subsequently allowed to claim the word as ad-
jective or noun, description of thought or behavior. The strain seems
to worsen every time the words undergo scholarly inspection. We dis-
cover progressivism in once-hidden places and hidden guises; we happen
upon progressives who—because of racial or ethnic identity, class or political stratification—were formerly excluded from the now-expanding
definition.

What only a decade ago was insightfully described by Daniel Rodgers
as a search for progressivism has now become a seemingly endless tale
of discovery.[1] As a result, the terms *progressive and progressivism* appear to have outlived their usefulness as meaningful expressions by

which to explain people, events, or periods in American history. Can a term elastic enough to characterize an entire era inform us of the component parts of a movement, if indeed there was such a thing as a progressive movement (or movements)? As Martin Sklar has succinctly observed in a provocative essay, "the term 'Progressive Era' no longer conveys a concept of interpretive precision; nor does 'Progressive Movement.' "[2] The terms are convenient and handy catchphrases, but they are growing increasingly unwieldy.

Yet an admitted lack of precision in terminology does not seem reason enough to dispense with the words altogether. This book is predicated in part on an assumption that there is some meaning left to be teased out of these two besieged words. What is more, the dilution of precision means only that scholars are busy adding new dimensions of complexity to our perceptions of the past. Precision, therefore, must come from those of us who use the terms in our writing and teaching. Though we remain attracted to the apparent simplicity of single-term descriptions of motives, goals, or historical eras, we must always be sure to emphasize the complicated nature of what we are describing. Such is true, surely, for all our neat "isms."

Another reason for retaining the terms—at least for now—is that to do away with them would be to close our eyes and ears to the past. Individuals, parties, and groups used the terms *progressive* and *progressivism* to define themselves, their work, and their outlook as the new century arrived. It would be unfair, not to mention historically invalid, to steal the word entirely away from those people.[3] Of course, their definitions need not be our own. In the single state under scrutiny here, "progressive" does describe California's vehicle of Republican party insurgence, the Lincoln-Roosevelt League, at least insofar as it was offered as self-description by those actors themselves. But there was much more to reform and, as this book argues, much more to progressivism than a single-party housecleaning.

The authors of the following essays take seriously an obligation to study the historical context within which the terms *progressive* and *progressivism* were borrowed, taken, utilized, even invented. Before we decide at last that these terms mean nothing, we must first admit that they once meant something.

The essays in *California Progressivism Revisited* represent an attempt to broaden our historical understanding of an era and its actors. We seek to include groups and individuals traditionally left out or underrepresented in the progressive profiles of older historiography, and we add conceptual depth to a previously narrow casting of the ethos. We focus on a single state during a single critical period partly for convenience. In many ways progressivism and its legacy continue to surface all over contemporary America. Not long ago, historians debated the supposed end of progressivism as the nation emerged from the jarring experience of World War I and stumbled into the 1920s. But the bundle of ideas, motivations, and individuals that made up progressivism did not fade away without any legacy whatsoever, and this volume concludes with a tracing of just that legacy in a half century of state politics.

What is more, as students of California history and politics, we believe that this state demands far greater scholarly investigation (and attention) than it has traditionally received. California's present may or may not be the nation's future. Insistence on the state's supposedly prescient qualities would seem to support a greater level of historical inspection and introspection, which we of course hope this volume helps stimulate. But questions of the state's ability to forecast the nation's trajectory aside, this is an immensely important, inexplicably understudied region; and that alone strikes us as sufficient justification for the following eleven essays.

The progressive phenomenon continues to peek at us from the past, helping us clarify what we know and do not know about contemporary America. Not only does the turn-of-the-century Progressive Era mark a turning point in American political economy *writ large*—specifically, the transition from industrial capitalism to corporate capitalism—but that massive change is delineated by dozens of inventions still with us today. Political, social, legislative tools shaped generations ago—tools such as the initiative, referendum, and recall, workers' compensation, and nonpartisan political primaries—remain effective in the multifaceted arenas of American business and politics. Progressivism is alive and well four score years after its birth.

PROGRESSIVISM IN THE FAR WEST: CALIFORNIA HISTORY AND HISTORIOGRAPHY

The authors of the following essays hope to shake out some additional meaning from California progressivism, an important geographical subset of the complicated, turn-of-the-century progressive world. For one thing, the state's grab-bag progressive arenas and personnel are not nearly as well understood or investigated as they ought to be. What is more, California progressivism stands out in contemporary politics and political commentary as an important watershed, interpreted this way or that. Lou Cannon, senior *Washington Post* political reporter, noted only a few years ago that the national "Progressive movement reached its apogee in California, where Hiram Johnson was elected governor in 1910 after a bitter campaign against the Southern Pacific Railroad, then the West's dominant 'special interest.' "[4] We now know that there was more to the tale than that: both in the fight and in the victory. But, as Cannon continued, the state's progressives also did everything they were supposed to do. "The victorious Progressives kept their promises, and initiatives and referenda both weird and wonderful soon turned California into a laboratory for "direct democracy."[5] True or not, that sounds portentous, certainly important enough to sustain a closer look by the scholars here collected.

Such assertions about the import of western progressivism (and there are countless others) strongly suggest that scholars must once again focus on the era and the state. It has been twenty-five years since a major study of California's progressive legacy was produced (Spencer Olin's 1968 monograph, *California's Prodigal Sons*).[6] We take as our task in this book to air out a fuller understanding of the many-sided expressions of California progressivism. We self-consciously have set out to ask such questions as this: Is a progressive a progressive simply because he or she said so? Countless political opportunists, in California and elsewhere, knew a good thing when they saw it and began calling themselves progressives in polite company. The problem is not so much that they believed it; it is rather that historians have believed it. And that face-value acceptance is further complicated by our rare conviction that "we know what progressivism was,"—so that we immediately dress up the self-claimed progressive in appropriate political, social, cultural clothes—or, more likely, by our complete and utter uncertainty about what progressivism was. Such uncertainty is not necessarily a bad thing. It allows us to tear the paper and untie the string on a previously neat, and hence incomplete, package.

Forty years have passed since historian George E. Mowry gave us a fingernail sketch of the typical California progressive. In his still-important book, *The California Progressives,* Mowry dug deeply into the lives of that handful of men most important to the state's early-twentieth-century progressive movement.[7] His chapter titled "What Manner of Men: The Progressive Mind" offered a résumé of the state's representative progressive reformer, not so much a portrait of his psyche as a social and occupational description of the progressive Everyman.

The profile is a valuable one, and clearly many of the progressives most active in the state did fit the Mowry index.[8] Our progressive, then, would exhibit most of the following characteristics. He would be male. He would be a Republican, probably a lawyer or a businessman, his name on the letterhead of a bank or an insurance or title company. If not in business or law, he would almost certainly be a journalist. In his professional life, he would have chosen to steer clear of those giant industrial concerns so powerful in state politics and the regional economy. He lived and worked in the city. Middle age and mid-career status were important to his progressive orientation, as was recent arrival from the Midwest. Or perhaps our zealous reformer was a California native. He would likely be Protestant, even profoundly so; for, as Mowry gracefully writes, the "long religious hand of New England rested heavily upon California progressivism."[9] A progressive probably traced his ancestry through "old American stock," generations stretching back across the divide of the Civil War, nestling in Atlantic seaboard villages and small towns. Moral reform interested our California progressive, just as it likely did his forefathers. Community involvement and fraternity added to the progressive character; our man was an even bet to attend regular meetings of the Masons as well as the local chamber of commerce.

Toward the working class, the progressive displayed not so much an elite aloofness as a sort of noblesse oblige attitude. These political leaders, "fortunate sons of the upper middle class," as Mowry correctly generalized, were likely to be frightened of, or at least deeply concerned with, voices on the left, unable to distinguish individual chords from what seemed a disturbing, mysterious cacophony. California progressives could not readily differentiate the aims and goals of trade unionists from the platform of Socialist political hopefuls or even from the seemingly anarchic brutality exhibited by those who bombed the *Los Angeles Times* building in October 1910.[10] And many California progressives did not even try to draw distinctions between these groups and individuals, or to demarcate those boundaries of thought, word, and deed.

To the right, the progressive faced what must generically be called the Giant American Corporation, but which in California, Mowry tells us, could hardly be anything other than the Southern Pacific Railroad. Wariness of the corporate—especially railroad—exercise of power had been a watchword of state political reform for better than a generation, and California's progressives, marching beneath the anti-railroad standard shouldered by Hiram Johnson, merely took up where others, admittedly with often different goals, had left off.

In offering this portrait of a progressive squirming uncomfortably between the vague left and the ill-defined, corporate right, Mowry explicitly argues that the California progressive was a new political and economic type, fighting for existence *between* Big Labor and Big Capital
(though always friendlier to the latter). At the same time, Mowry suggests that his archetypal progressive scorned class-specific politics and
conflict as alien and undignified. "His church, his personal morality, and
his concept of law, he felt, were demeaned by the crude power struggle
between capital and labor."[11] Such sentiment prompted like-minded
progressives, "supreme individualists" all, to come together, joined by
"a group consciousness."[12] This group exhibited the classic symptoms
of what Richard Hofstadter (who had clearly read his Mowry) would
call status anxiety.[13] Ironies abound: progressives disdained "class politics" but were presumably forced to engage in them, if only out of motives of self-preservation. Such intentions even overwhelmed their individualist tendencies and forged a sort of progressive altruism, a weird
amalgam of self-defense and selfless reform.

PROGRESSIVISM REVISITED: A REEVALUATION
OF MOWRY AND THE OCTOPUS SCHOOL

The time is long overdue for a reevaluation of Mowry's characteriza-
tions. Apt though they may be for the lives of the fewer than fifty men
he inventoried, they leave us well short of any complete understanding
of California progressivism. Mowry's work continues to be read because it presents an illuminating description of the leadership of the California progressive movement. But we need to look further into the social bases of political reform, in order to say more about the progressive
constituency. After all, the state's progressives achieved real power only
through electoral success; we know very little about who voted for these
men and why.
    Mowry's "what manner of men" school—defining California pro-
gressives as a large handful of status- and class-anxious WASPs—no
longer provides a satisfying picture of the depth and breadth of the era's
political and social activists. It is a valuable collective biography, gathering in many of California's most important progressive leaders. But
there was far more to California progressivism than the clubmen of the
Lincoln-Roosevelt Republican League. The "Octopus school" of progressive understanding also needs to be derailed. It is an interpretation
alive and well, it seems, in popular understanding. California political
veteran Ed Salzman, for instance, noted very recently that, upon his elec-

tion as governor in 1910, Hiram Johnson "inherited a government essentially owned by the Southern Pacific Railroad."[14] Such a narrow view of government—not to mention such wholesale acceptance of the narrative offerings of progressive historians—can no longer withstand serious scrutiny. The progressive period in California was far more complicated—and more important, we argue—than an anachronistic duel between the Republican party and the Southern Pacific Railroad Corporation.

So where do we begin? We begin with Mowry himself, at least implicitly. The essays in our opening section, titled "Class Politics, Class Moralities," dissect the class dimensions of progressivism in the Far West through individual and group focus. This section begins with co-editor Tom Sitton's essay examining the life of John Randolph Haynes. In this essay, drawn from his recently published Haynes biography, Sitton presents an encapsulated look at one of the era's leading and busiest reformers, a man who best epitomizes the internal contradictions of a movement that could seemingly tilt right and left at the same time. In Sitton's portrait of Haynes, we not only learn about the personal complexities of a critical California figure but also are led to understand how the ideas behind social and political reform could bounce back and forth across public and private spheres, right and left politics. As Sitton points out, the irony may be not that the movement had so much complexity but that we scholars continue to expect consistency from an arbitrarily defined "movement" in the first place.

From a wealthy reformer in Southern California, we move to a northern counterpart. Anne Hyde of Colorado College, author of an award-winning book on the relationship between the western environment and understandings of national culture, continues her work in American environmental history by an examination of William Kent. As she notes early in her essay, Kent would at first blush seem to be the exact template of Mowry's progressive profile. But Kent is a far more complicated figure than this, unwilling to let historians pigeonhole him in a "what manner of men" compartment. As Hyde demonstrates in her essay, William Kent "out-progressed" the progressives one moment and seemingly turned his back on them the next. The evidence she presents that an important figure such as Kent does not easily fit any of our preconceived progressive notions alone makes Hyde's contribution important. Along the way, she helps us rethink one of the nation's most critical early conservation battles, the fight over the Hetch-Hetchy Valley.

Trained as a historian and the author of a dissertation on labor politics in Northern California, Mary Ann Mason of the School of

Social Welfare at the University of California, Berkeley, contributes an essay examining progressivism's shy embrace of labor. Professor Mason's study reveals the complex issues surrounding our too-easily arrived-at assumptions of progressive waffling between "Big Labor" and "Big Capital."

Continuing along the same road, coeditor William Deverell adds an essay on the Democratic party in California, which has for too long been unfairly left out of the progressive circle. Since many of the ideas of the eventually successful reformer wing of the Republican party originated in the strategic sessions of the Democrats, it makes sense to reanalyze the Democratic contribution to the state's Progressive Era. The simple, and critical, fact of California politics then and now—that it is easier to win from the Republican side than the Democratic—hardly makes study of the losers trivial. California's Democrats are its Whigs, hapless maybe, but not unimportant.

Gerald Woods, whose Ph.D. dissertation at UCLA stands as the finest study ever written about the Los Angeles Police Department, has taken progressive moral righteousness to task in his fine essay, "A Penchant for Probity." By holding a mirror to the progressives in San Francisco and Los Angeles, Woods has revealed the different character of the two cities as they approached the social problems that were so vexing to progressive reformers. In the process, he has reiterated the class, cultural, and ethnic narrowness of much of the progressive "vision thing."

Part Two of the book, "What Manner of Men? Women and the Progressive Impetus," addresses one of Mowry's greatest shortcomings, the issue of gender. The three essays in this section attempt to refocus attention on the contributions and complexities of women's Progressive-Era action. Historian Sherry Katz examines the world of California socialist women, who pushed for reforms across the divide that arbitrarily separated social and political spheres. Her deeply researched and engagingly written account brings to the fore this critically important group of dedicated reformers, who, among other endeavors, worked diligently toward women's suffrage. As a result of their work, California adopted suffrage years before the Nineteenth Amendment gave all women the right to vote. Like many of our other contributions, Katz's work stands as a further corrective to what was once a narrow vision of just who the progressives were.

In a similar vein, although her essay is more explicitly biographical, Judith Raftery takes as her task the job of resurrecting the important role played by several of California's most important clubwomen during the period under study. Following much the same approach as George Mowry, Professor Raftery offers us the life stories of three critically important California clubwomen—whose mere existence in the public political sphere is argument enough to dispense with the tendency to make California progressivism a single-sex organism. That these women played active and lasting roles as reformers demands that we take them seriously as representatives of that broader-conceived progressive world.

Mary Odem then takes us into a very different realm, the world of juvenile homes in early-twentieth-century Los Angeles. Her fascinating essay details the Los Angeles juvenile justice system and its "discovery" of women and young girls. Utilizing a wide array of sources and documents, Professor Odem offers us an entirely new vantage point from which to view the actors in this important arena, where distinctions were not always made between beneficent reform and social control. As the first city in the country to employ policewomen, Los Angeles is an ideal place for studying the changing world of municipal response to adolescence, particularly female adolescence.

The third section, entitled "Ethnic Dimensions, Ethnic Realities," furthers our search for the broadest dimensions of progressive thought and behavior. As with women, African-Americans and Mexican-Americans remain largely outside the arenas of our understandings of California progressivism. Part Three attempts to remedy that oversight with two superb essays. The author of a magesterial new book on the modern South, Douglas Flamming of the California Institute of Technology turns his attentions westward in his captivating essay on the historical roots of African-American political strength in Los Angeles. By examining the lives and leadership roles of key individuals and organizations, Flamming has given us one of a very few studies of an obviously important chapter in the long book of black political development in Southern California. And his concluding examination of the legacy of early-twentieth-century black political work raises intriguing questions about the origins of contemporary African-American urban activism and electoral success.

When read especially in the light of recent courtroom redistricting victories in Los Angeles County supervisorial districts, George Sanchez's compelling essay provides us with a much fuller view of Progressive-Era Mexican-American political development. As Professor Sanchez shows, our perceptions of the political maturation of the Mexican-American community must always be informed by appreciation of the complexities surrounding such concepts as nationalism, Americanization, and cross-border progressivism.

One of the most perceptive students of California politics, the distinguished historian Jackson Putnam, closes our anthology with a stimulating overview of state gubernatorial politics in the modern era. He posits certain key categories of progressive leadership and outlook—features that he traces forward in time from the triumphal Hiram Johnson 1910 victory. Professor Putnam's essay explicitly refutes the claim that progressivism faded away into nothingness sometime in the 1920s, battered by the reactionary retrenchment following World War I and kicked aside by the nation's furious attachment to the Roaring Twenties. On the contrary, Putnam finds progressive credentials pinned to the lapels of many a post-Johnson governor, men who have with varying degrees of success sought to portray themselves as heirs to the insurgents of 1910.

Progressivism, we understand all too well, is an embattled word, an embattled concept. Part of our purpose in the following collection of essays is to add to that strife by *again* arguing that "it was more than we used to think." But we are also motivated by the idea that, in all the wrestling over the word and its many meanings, we may have lost sight of many of the historical actors who somehow and somewhere fit into the Progressive Era and progressivism. We cannot rescue all of them from the hiding places of history, of course, nor can we clear up many of the critical questions regarding progressive reform and its mixed legacy of successes and failures.[15] But as a start, and as a self-conscious call for further work, we offer the following essays, the first such examination of California progressivism in several decades.

NOTES

Sources for epigraphs: Ambrose Bierce, *Devil's Dictionary* (New York: Doubleday, 1906); John Higham, "The Reorientation of American Culture in the 1890s," in John Weiss, ed., *The Origins of Modern Consciousness* (Detroit: Wayne State University Press, 1965), 40.

1. See Daniel T. Rodgers, "In Search of Progressivism," *Reviews in American History* 10 (December 1982): 113–32.

2. It is at least a bit ironic that Sklar nonetheless must use the term in his title. See Martin Sklar, "Periodization and Historiography: Studying American Political Development in the Progressive Era, 1890s–1916," *Studies in American Political Development* 5 (Fall 1991): 173–213. See also Sklar's stimulating collection of essays in *The United States as a Developing Country: Studies in U.S.*

History in the Progressive Era and the 1920s (Cambridge: Cambridge University Press, 1991). I have also learned much from Richard McCormick's book *The Party Period and Public Policy: American Politics from the Age of Jackson to the Progressive Era* (New York: Oxford University Press, 1986), especially chap. 7 and chap. 9.

3. As McCormick (in *The Party Period and Public Policy,* 268) notes, "We cannot avoid the concept of progressivism—or even a progressive movement—because, particularly after 1910, the terms were deeply embedded in the language of reformers and because they considered the words meaningful."

4. Lou Cannon, *Washington Post,* November 21, 1988, A2.

5. Ibid.

6. Spencer C. Olin, Jr., *California's Prodigal Sons: Hiram Johnson and the Progressives, 1911–1917* (Berkeley: University of California Press, 1968). Mansel Blackford's monograph *The Politics of Business in California, 1890–1920* (Columbus: Ohio State University Press, 1977) is a good study of the growth of far western corporate capitalism and corporate liberalism, but it is not a treatment of the state's progressive movement or actors.

7. George E. Mowry, *The California Progressives* (Berkeley: University of California Press, 1951).

8. Mowry's group biography is drawn from a sample of forty-seven men. Political history is now a different sort of animal than it was when Mowry wrote, and this sample hardly seems to "afford the historian an unrivaled opportunity . . . to inquire into the origins and the mentality of a grassroots movement" (Mowry, *The California Progressives,* 87).

9. "[The progressive's] mind was freighted with problems of morality, his talk shot through with biblical allusions" (Mowry, *The California Progressives,* 97; quote in text on 87).

10. This inability to differentiate platforms and political aims was not solely the fault of our representative progressive leader. West Coast labor had been marked by confusing platforms for years. As Michael Kazin has written of the end of the nineteenth century, "no clear ideological division existed between trade unionists and revolutionaries." See Michael Kazin, *Barons of Labor: The San Francisco Building Trades and Union Power in the Progressive Era* (Urbana: University of Illinois Press, 1987), 37.

11. Mowry, *The California Progressives,* 96.

12. Ibid.

13. See Richard Hofstadter, *The Age of Reform: From Bryan to FDR* (New York: Knopf, 1955), 145.

14. "Seeking Villains in a Sacramento Swamp," *Los Angeles Times,* January 21, 1990.

15. As it is, the authors of these essays must exhibit—or at least this book must exhibit—the progressive "nervous tick" that Daniel Rodgers ("In Search of Progressivism," 113) has referred to: the compilation of qualifiers, apologies, and untidy categories that go hand in hand with any scholarly investigation of "the thing" or "the time."

PART ONE

Class Politics, Class Moralities

John Randolph Haynes and the Left Wing of California Progressivism

Tom Sitton

The reinterpretation of the political nature of progressivism in the past two decades has enlightened our perception of how this movement developed in California. Past analyses of progressivism treated its leaders as like-minded "liberals" struggling to solve the problems of urbanization and industrialization and to modernize American institutions; as conservatives bent on controlling the lower classes, advancing their own entrepreneurial opportunities or professions, and ameliorating some defects in the socioeconomic system to undermine the arguments of radicals; as a displaced elite trying to reestablish its role in society; and so on. More recent conceptions of progressivism define it as a "dynamic general reform movement composed of many specific reform movements and shifting coalitions of self-interested groups uniting temporarily over different issues and behind different political leaders." This formula makes a little more sense of a complex phenomenon that on various occasions joined together altruists laboring to raise the downtrodden; conservatives advocating structural political changes to nullify the voting power of the lower classes; young people looking for vehicles of social advancement; opportunists, egotists, socialists, and reactionaries; and other groups with countervailing agendas.[1]

Among those comprising the "shifting coalitions" of progressivism was a left wing composed of individuals who occupied the ground between the Socialist Party of America and the more moderate reformers. Benjamin Parke DeWitt, an early participant and promoter of the movement and the Progressive party, portrayed this left wing as an integral

15

component of progressivism, a bridge between two political parties that differed mainly in the emphasis each placed on extending the power of government. "Radical Progressives and conservative Socialists, therefore, could almost meet on common ground," he wrote, optimistically believing that socialism "is an ideal which the [progressive] movement hopes someday to see realized." Historians such as Otis L. Graham, Jr., have found it difficult to define the boundary between the two, the point where "the progressive movement spilled over, on its Left edge, into socialism." Graham, Robert Crunden, and others include gradual socialists and even party members such as Upton Sinclair and Charles Edward Russell in the progressive fold, since they frequently worked with more moderate progressives, sharing common values and goals. In fact, right-wing Socialists who collaborated with organized labor for more palliative reforms aptly demonstrated their similarity to left-wing progressives, especially in campaigns to win municipal ownership of utilities and social welfare improvements. The occasional partnership of right-wing Socialists and left-wing progressives, most notably at the local level, pushed progressivism slightly to the left and often painted the Socialist party as a less radical entity.[2]

The left wing of California progressivism has received scant notice in the major works on the subject. Overshadowed by mainstream moderate leaders of the Lincoln-Roosevelt League, such as Hiram Johnson, Chester Rowell, and Meyer Lissner, a number of middle-class individuals with much more advanced views on social change were active in state and local progressive campaigns. Calling themselves Fabian or gradual socialists, they joined party members in advancing major reforms along the road to a cooperative commonwealth, while working with conservative peers for small incremental changes. Some of the more notable progressives, such as William Kent, Fremont Older, and Francis Heney, were not socialists but did favor more far-reaching economic changes than the moderates did. Others—for instance, self-avowed Christian socialists such as John Randolph Haynes and Caroline M. Severance—joined the Lincoln-Roosevelt League very late or not at all, but nonetheless contributed significantly to the progressive cause.[3]

Left-wing progressives in California were in the forefront of campaigns for more advanced social welfare objectives, such as protective legislation for workers (especially women), better health care, and public ownership, as well as the drives for women's suffrage, regulation of corporations, and direct legislation. They collaborated with Socialists and labor unions to increase economic opportunity for the lower classes and social services for the needy. The left wing forced progressive election platforms leftward, so much so that at times they almost mirrored those of the Socialists. (The result was evident in portions of San Francisco and Los Angeles County, where Socialist and progressive candidates received votes from the same constituency in consecutive elections.) At a time when Socialist party fortunes were on the rise in California municipal elections, left-wing progressives prodded their more moderate brethren to cooperate with Socialists in the quest for social reform goals.[4]

In many respects similar in their middle-class, professional backgrounds to right-wing Socialist leaders such as Job Harriman of Los Angeles and Reverend J. Stitt Wilson of Berkeley, some left-wing progressives could almost embrace the ideology of right-wing Socialists, sans the red card and Marxian notions of class revolt. As Kevin Starr has noted, these frequently wealthy social democrats became conduits allowing reform ideas to "flow from the far left to the reforming conservatives" unhindered by class barriers. With a strong commitment to fundamental change, left-wing progressives infused into their movement an altruistic zeal and a higher purpose, forcing it to embrace more far-reaching reform than it would otherwise. When reform enthusiasm waned during and after World War I as moderates tired or thought the job finished, it was the old left wing that inspired progressives to continue.[5]

The most active figure in the California progressive left wing was Dr. John Randolph Haynes. Born in rural Pennsylvania in 1853, and reared in coal-mining country, Haynes graduated from the University of Pennsylvania with Ph.D. and M.D. degrees and established a lucrative medical practice in a poor neighborhood of Philadelphia. He and his wife, Dora Fellows Haynes, amassed a small fortune there until John's chronic bronchitis and various ailments of his family members dictated their move in 1887 to the more salubrious climate of Southern California. In Los Angeles he became one of the city's busiest physicians and joined the social elite, which included many of his patients. He also continued to invest wisely in real estate and other financial ventures, thereby enhancing the fortune he later used to bankroll his social reform crusades.[6]

In his first decade in the City of Angels, Haynes rarely indulged in politics, although he claimed to be interested in major changes in America's socioeconomic structure. He had witnessed poverty and inequality in the coal-mining region during his boyhood and in the slums of Philadelphia while a young doctor, but was not quite sure how one person like himself could help bring about meaningful changes. The watershed of his activism occurred in early 1898, when his local Episcopal church sponsored a series of lectures by Reverend William Dwight Porter Bliss, a national spokesman for the Christian socialist movement. Bliss had just formed the Union Reform League (URL) and was touring the West Coast to enlist members. His social reform philosophy fused Christianity and secular socialism into a utopian commonwealth, which would be slowly created through the education of workers by middle-class Christian socialists. The latter also would work with their more conservative peers to transfer the nation's private means of production to public ownership and control. While striving for this metamorphosis of the economy in a gradual, nonrevolutionary manner, Bliss recommended a number of immediate reforms—including direct legislation, public ownership of utilities, women's suffrage, and abolition of child labor—to ameliorate some of the worst social injustices.[7]

John Haynes's response to the Bliss sermon was something akin to a religious awakening. The doctor suddenly acquired an agenda of immediate and long-range goals and an inspiration for activism. He joined the Union Reform League and soon became its president. While continuing his thriving medical practice, he found time to organize URL meetings and lectures, raise money, lobby local government, and arrange for the publication of URL literature. Although the URL gradually withered away after the departure of the charismatic Bliss from Los Angeles in 1899, Haynes helped to establish new organizations with similar goals—the Economic Club and the League of Christian Socialists—as substitutes. None survived more than a few years, but they did provide forums for local and national speakers to discuss reform issues and offer solutions to the problems of the day.[8]

While working with these organizations, Haynes met a legion of social reformers who would join him in further campaigns. The group included self-described Christian socialists, such as Caroline Severance, William Stuart, and William C. Petchner; single-taxers Abbot Kinney and Frank Finlayson; Socialist Party of America members Job Harriman, H. Gaylord Wilshire, and James T. Van Rensselaer; and moderates like Dana Bartlett and William Andrews Spalding. These reformers of different stripes worked together in a variety of organizations for individual goals and various degrees of progress along the path to social democracy. They created their own network of related groups, importing

noted speakers from the East to keep them abreast of the latest thought
and developments in social reform. In essence, this network resembled
a local version of James Kloppenberg's "transatlantic connection,"
whereby generations of U.S. and European philosophers and activists
formulated the political action program of social democrats in the early
twentieth century.[9]

Haynes's experience in turn-of-the-century social reform organizations also helped him define his specific reform goals. He would always
be committed to a distant and vague socialist utopia, to be attained gradually and democratically without violent overthrow of existing institutions. Along the way he would support many typical reforms of the Progressive Era: women's suffrage; an end to child labor; civil service;
structural and functional improvements to government; legal protection
for workers, women, children, and Native Americans; regulation of corporations; and the like. But his first and second priorities were direct legislation and public ownership of utilities. He would become California's
primary advocate of direct legislation—the initiative, referendum, and
closely related recall—with which he hoped the Socialist party, labor
unions, prohibitionists, women's groups, and others could combat the
corrupt plutocracy he believed to be dominating the state. With these
weapons, which had been endorsed for years by Populists and Socialists,
Haynes hoped that ordinary citizens could legalize needed reforms and
kick out the rascals beholden to greedy special interests. With public
ownership of utilities, especially municipal water and hydroelectrical
power systems, he hoped to demonstrate concrete examples of public
management of natural resources as prototypes for national operation
in the future.[10]

In the first decade of the twentieth century, Haynes worked diligently
for direct legislation and municipal ownership. He made numerous
speeches for the initiative and formed a Direct Legislation League consisting of many of his more conservative business and professional
friends to lend respectability to the idea (even though he and secretary
George Dunlop were the only league activists). In a 1902 election, with
the help of organized labor and Socialists, he directed the successful
campaign to incorporate the initiative, referendum, and recall (the first
municipal recall in the United States) into the Los Angeles city charter.
The measures gave local citizens more power in their political affairs,
although the immediate results were disappointing: the few early initiatives consisted of restricting the location of slaughterhouses and establishing prohibition; and the recall was used successfully to remove a

city councilman opposed by union labor, though his replacement was not much of an improvement. Despite the results, the opportunity for initiating social and political reform measures and deposing corrupt or inept officials before the end of their terms was at least now available.[11]

Haynes's advocacy of municipal ownership grew slowly after he embraced the concept as a member of the Union Reform League. In the early 1900s he convinced friends to petition the city council to take steps toward purchasing private utilities in the city. By late 1904 he began his public pleading for municipal ownership, and in the following year he and a few younger men founded the Voters' League, a voluntary group bound to this reform, as well as to direct legislation and other goals. Besides campaigning for the city's purchase of present utilities or its construction of new ones, the Voters' League supported Haynes's almost single-handed effort to force local traction companies to install safer fenders on streetcars. In this case, Haynes and his fellow reformers resorted to regulation simply because outright purchase of the utility was not feasible.[12]

Haynes also influenced a number of more conservative reformers in their quest for efficient and honest government. A nonpartisan organization consisting of several Voters' League members and allied businessmen and professionals was organized in 1906 to alter city politics. Though Haynes was far to the left of them, the leaders of the group accepted many of his own precepts—such as direct legislation, municipal ownership of at least some utilities and regulation of others, and removal of the two major national parties from purely local issues—and depended on his leadership in accomplishing some of those goals. In 1909 the municipal reformers chased out of office a mayor tied to underworld figures and selected George Alexander as the replacement. With a sympathetic city council majority elected later that year, the moderate progressives entrenched themselves in city hall. There they implemented some of the fashionable municipal reforms of the day, both to achieve efficiency and to keep themselves in control. Haynes found it expedient to cooperate with these city progressives, using his influence to convince the Alexander administration to expand municipal social services.[13]

Haynes joined some of the same Los Angeles reformers in the statewide progressive movement. Although much further to the left of the mostly young Republicans who formed the Lincoln-Roosevelt League in 1907, he is credited with inspiring its inception. In harmony with his desire to rid the state of the political influence of the Southern Pacific Railroad, the league consistently sought his advice, his financial support, and his membership. Sympathetic to the league's aims but skeptical of its success and wary of its one-dimensional platform, Haynes at first declined to join. He did work with some of its leaders in lobbying the state legislature for passage of a direct primary and other progressive laws.[14]

After Hiram Johnson and the league won the 1910 election, Haynes initially was distanced from the inner circle because of his close association with radicals. But he was a prominent figure in the successful 1911 campaign for state direct legislation. He personally had lobbied for these constitutional statutes at every state legislature session since 1903; he also had hired lawyers to protect direct legislation in local and state courts and had toured the state to promote the measures. During the Johnson years Haynes frequently aided the administration in the passage of labor laws and other social reform legislation, and at election time. Along with other left-wing progressives William Kent and Francis Heney, Haynes consistently cajoled Johnson and legislators to take action on social justice issues. Haynes's appointment by Johnson to the State Charities and Corrections Board in 1912 allowed the doctor to play an active role in the social welfare accomplishments of the progressive administration for a decade.[15]

At the same time that Haynes loomed as a towering figure in local and state progressive reform, he also toiled to a more limited extent for gradual socialism. Since his days in the Union Reform League, he had continued to correspond and meet with local socialists in reform societies and within the loose social democrat network. In this period he met noted Los Angeles Socialists such as Job Harriman, as well as out-of-towners Nelson O. Nelson of St. Louis and J. Stitt Wilson of Berkeley; and he became a friend and business partner of H. Gaylord Wilshire, publisher of the socialist *Wilshire's Monthly*. He was a frequent visitor to the home of Caroline Severance, a Christian socialist and noted suffragist, and served as the first president of the Severance Club, named in her honor. In 1902 he helped form a stock company that launched a Rochdale Plan cooperative store for the Los Angeles working class. Later that year he was courted as a mayoral candidate by the Union Labor party, a fusion of organized labor and the local Socialist Party of America chapter, testimony to his standing in the eyes of these two groups. He supported many local and national Socialist magazines and newspapers, donated funds to establish "Socialist libraries" in colleges across the nation, hosted gatherings for Jack London and others, and contributed to the local party. In 1906 he helped establish the short-lived state Public Ownership party, composed primarily of unionists and right-wing Socialists. His public stature in this area earned him the respect of fellow social democrats, the scorn of *Los Angeles Times* editors and other conservatives, and the suspicion of moderate reformers.[16]

The limit of Haynes's support for socialism surfaced in 1911, when Job Harriman ran for mayor of Los Angeles. Harriman's fusion of Socialists and labor unions won the primary that year and seemed to have a good chance to defeat the progressive incumbent, George Alexander. But many of the genteel "socialists"—prodded by the specter of class violence, as portrayed in the bombing of the *Los Angeles Times* building, and by their belief that the progressives appeared to be bringing about honest and efficient government—refused to back Harriman and his party. William H. Stuart, who was "never more certain of the eventual realization of the socialist ideal than I am at this moment," nevertheless congratulated another social democrat for backing the Alexander ticket, since the progressives would accomplish the same objectives in a gradual manner. Fabian socialist Caroline Severance also supported Alexander, though she was suspicious of the good government forces. John Haynes, who had been reappointed to the Board of Civil Service Commissioners by Alexander, decided to support the mayor, who cherished the doctor's advice. Although Haynes described his old friend Harriman as "an honest, courageous and able man," Haynes drew the line at endorsing the Socialist party and risking the possibility of an abrupt upheaval of the Los Angeles economy and social equilibrium and the loss of his own influence at city hall.[17]

But Haynes's borderline was a thin one. The following year found him working with Socialist leaders Harriman and Thomas W. Williams, progressives S. C. Graham and George Dunlop, and others in a People's Charter Conference formed to modify the city charter. Chief among the recommendations was the addition of a proportional representation system that would give the Socialists city council seats in proportion to the votes they received in an election. "Sooner or later the Socialists, through the oscillating pendulum of public opinion, are certain to come into power," Haynes reasoned. It would be "much better that they first have a taste of the sobering influence of responsibility such as is afforded by minority representation." His view was shared by other left-wing progressives such as John J. Hamilton, who wondered "why shouldn't the moderate reformers of today recognize their kinship to the advanced reformers and radicals whose turn is to come up next, instead of holding aloof from them?" The left-wing progressives failed to convince their more moderate counterparts to endorse this election system, but Haynes continued to recommend it in future charter revision sessions. He also continued to defend gradual socialism in publications and speeches, including one delivered to the World's Social Progress Congress in San Francisco in 1915.[18]

Haynes's hopes for the progress of local and state political developments and his association with California progressive leaders led him almost naturally into the national Progressive party. He was enamored with insurgent leaders Theodore Roosevelt, Robert La Follette, Hiram Johnson, and others who had battled corporations and reactionaries and stood, Haynes believed, for advanced social reform values. And the Progressive platform, which demanded equal suffrage, social and industrial justice for workers, a national health service, national transportation improvements, a graduated inheritance and income tax, and other features—appealed to Haynes as closer to the Socialist platform than that of the two major parties. He believed, very optimistically, in "the Socialist nature of the platform of the Progressive Party," and saw it as a blueprint for gradual, nonrevolutionary change. As Haynes the pragmatist advised one group in 1912: "If our watchword is to be ultimate principles with present defeat, then our votes should go to the Socialist Party; if, however, we seek practical tangible results now, we should vote for Roosevelt." With this view, Haynes was close to Benjamin Parke DeWitt, Amos Pinchot, and other left-wing Progressives, but far from the typical Bull Mooser, who expected much less from this party.[19]

The national Progressive party disintegrated during Woodrow Wilson's first term, and America's entry into World War I further dampened reform efforts throughout the nation. Winning the war became the nation's top priority; the Wilson administration and Congress became preoccupied with European affairs, national resources were directed to the war effort, and dissent was stifled.[20]

However, as Burt Noggle, Otis L. Graham, Jr., Eugene M. Tobin, and others have demonstrated, progressivism did not expire on the European battlefield. Although the popular mood of the nation in the decade after the War to End All Wars has been described as materialistic and intolerant, and 1920s presidents had little interest in social change, reform did linger on. It was most notable in the attempts of some former Bull Moosers to reorganize, in the efforts of a small group of feisty western senators to block retrenchment, in the determination of social welfare organizations to advance social reform measures, in the 1924 presidential bid of Robert La Follette, and in campaigns for public ownership of water and power facilities. Progressivism in the "Roaring Twenties" might not have been as successful as it was decades earlier, but it was not moribund.[21]

In fact, it was highly visible in California, where, as Jackson K. Putnam had observed, postwar progressivism, "while sharply challenged and perhaps oveshadowed by contrary forces, did not 'die' but lived on in a different and possibly less attractive form." Hiram Johnson, the movement's figurehead, moved on to the U.S. Senate, and many former insurgents abandoned reform; but progressives continued to occupy state offices, protect reform successes, and battle conservatives for more reform, while maintaining their fears of racial minorities and the far left. In this second thrust of California progressivism, the forces were kept together by the more left-wing leaders of the original insurgency such as John Haynes and Franklin Hichborn, by a few moderates such as Clement C. Young and Herbert C. Jones, and by younger activists— sometimes in coalitions with leftists and even conservatives.[22]

As many of the moderate insurgents retired from the political arena, John Haynes became a much more important figure in the later years of California progressivism. His enthusiasm for further reform would be mirrored by his drives for progressive and leftist objectives at the national and local levels. After the war he continued to support the educational arm of the American Socialist movement with generous donations to the League for Industrial Democracy. His home became an occasional overnight shelter for LID officials Harry W. Laidler and Norman Thomas on their trips to the West, and Haynes tried to establish a $100,000 trust fund for the LID in the 1920s. He also supported national and local Socialist publications and party functions, and again donated "$100 Socialist libraries" to American colleges. He continued his association with leftists of local and national importance in his network of social democrats who supported leftist goals. And during the war he began his close friendship with Socialist novelist Upton Sinclair, providing help and expertise for some of Sinclair's books, money for Sinclair's needy associates, and funds to republish *Cry for Justice*, Sinclair's anthology of social protest essays.[23]

But Haynes again drew the line of his support for socialism when he declined to contribute to Norman Thomas's 1932 and 1936 presidential campaigns as the Socialist party's nominee. "I think I realize as much as you do that civilization can only survive through a radical change in our capitalistic condition," he wrote to Thomas. But the doctor feared that a vote for Thomas was a half vote for Republican conservatives, and campaign money would be virtually wasted. The New Deal program of state capitalism did not go far enough for his taste, but it was better to support Franklin Roosevelt's limited progress than risk a return to the policies of the 1920s.[24]

Besides his left-wing political associations, Haynes supported many other political and social reform groups in the 1920s and 1930s. He was very active in the National Popular Government League, the American Association for Labor Legislation, and the American Indian Defense Association; and he contributed to the National Consumers League, national organizations devoted to outlawing child labor and legalizing birth control, and many others. In the early 1920s he became a benefactor and activist for Paul Kellogg, who published *Survey,* a journal for social welfare workers. By the mid-1920s Haynes even began describing himself as a sociologist (as well as a physician, though he had retired from medicine by this time). Because of his interest in social work, he served on several state, county, and city social welfare commissions. His activism in municipal social work placed him squarely in Otis L. Graham's category of old progressives who were more likely to support the New Deal, few though they were. Haynes's embrace of the New Deal included political cooperation in the 1930s with many Democrats in Congress and in the state legislature, continuing his nonpartisan method of political activism since early in the century.[25]

Locally, Haynes's service on social welfare and other city and county boards was only one of his many interests in furthering progressivism. Active in the Municipal League and other groups, he worked throughout the 1920s and 1930s to protect municipal direct legislation and civil service and to promote municipal ownership. A member of the Los Angeles Board of Water and Power Commissioners from 1921 until his death in 1937, he spearheaded the expansion of the city's water and power system in an official capacity, as well as from behind the scenes. Throughout the period he was deeply involved in local politics, working with "bosses," Socialists, labor leaders, and others to protect progressive gains of earlier years and give other groups more access to city decision making. In his many battles with local conservatives, led by *Los Angeles Times* editors and corporate executives, he emerged as the most important local progressive leader of that era.[26]

The same depth and vigor of his postwar activism in local and national reformist politics can be seen in his devotion to California progressivism. Before the war he was one of many who contributed to the success of the insurgents. During the European conflict, as some former progressive leaders left the scene, Haynes became a major adviser to Governor William D. Stephens, successor to Hiram Johnson. From that time until 1922, the doctor had tremendous influence in the governor's appointments to public offices and official positions on various issues. Although Haynes tried to push the very moderate Stephens to the left, he failed, especially in his efforts to mitigate Stephens's policy toward labor radicals. Nonetheless, the doctor helped to secure Stephens's election as governor in 1918, and Stephens responded by appointing Haynes to several state commissions, two labor arbitration committees, and the University of California Board of Regents.[27]

While advising the state's chief executive, Haynes also kept more than one eye on the legislature. In 1919 he began paying part of the lobbying expenses of state labor leader Paul Scharrenberg. After that year, Haynes subsidized the lobbying of progressive journalist Franklin Hichborn at nearly every session until the doctor's death. Hichborn kept tabs on state lawmakers and alerted the doctor to impending legislation. With these warnings Haynes could halt or help to stop many anti-progressive bills with pleas to governors, sympathetic legislators, and interest groups. His most visible work along these lines was a six-year crusade to prevent alteration of the state's initiative law; his money, activism, and friends saved this measure, as well as many others he favored.[28]

Haynes also tried to advance new progressive objectives, such as the 1922 state Water and Power Act. He joined Rudolph Spreckels of San Francisco in sponsoring this initiative for regulation of water and hydroelectric power resources in California. The two spent considerable sums of their own money—but much less than the private power companies trying to crush the initiative. In this case money talked: the initiative was defeated handily in three elections.[29]

Haynes again worked with Spreckels in the 1924 state campaign for Robert La Follette's presidential bid. Along with Francis Heney, William Kent, Fremont Older, and other variously left-wing progressives, many of whom had joined Spreckels and Haynes in supporting Woodrow Wilson's reelection in 1916, the group backed the old Wisconsin senator with a national coalition of labor, Socialists, and other groups. La Follette ran as a Progressive; but he was deprived of a ballot spot for that party in California and had to be listed as the Socialist candidate that year. This designation spurred the conservative press to shower further abuse on Spreckels, Haynes, and other La Follette leaders, but it did little to impede their campaigning. Although La Follette lost in the Coolidge landslide, he far outdistanced his Democratic rival in California.[30]

The Water and Power Act and La Follette campaigns were fought without benefit of the type of closely knit organization that had characterized the Lincoln-Roosevelt League of 1910. One casualty of the departure of some of the moderate state progressives during the war was the unity within the insurgent ranks. After the war Haynes and other left-wing reformers tried on several occasions to reunite progressives split by personal animosities and political differences. In 1920 Haynes organized a meeting in Sacramento to bring together the old leaders and renew the insurgent spirit. A year later he advanced his idea of creating another state Progressive party along the lines of a national party advocated by Amos Pinchot and other former Bull Moosers. William Kent also tried his hand by hosting a meeting at his home in Kentfield in 1923 for similar objectives. Without the backing of Hiram Johnson and other moderates, however, the meetings failed to achieve their purposes. While progressives did continue to work together at times, the old unity was noticeably absent in the new era.[31]

What harmony there was would be sorely needed in 1923, a low point for progressive fortunes. Governor Stephens had been defeated in the 1922 election and was succeeded by Friend Richardson, an apostate progressive turned reactionary in the eyes of Dr. Haynes. Richardson quickly began dismantling state humanitarian commissions created by the progressives, and encouraged lawmakers to emasculate the initiative and other reform laws and remove progressives from office. The governor was backed in this endeavor by the Better America Federation (BAF), a Red Scare–era band of superpatriots who carried on an assault against radicals, organized labor, civil liberties, and progressivism in general. The BAF published anti-labor literature, encouraged students to spy on disloyal teachers, and diligently campaigned to elect legislators in agreement with its "American Plan."[32]

Dr. Haynes was a prominent leader in countering both Richardson and the BAF. Resigning from his position on the State Board of Charities and Corrections before Richardson could fire him, Haynes rallied progressive leaders to block the governor's "economy" budget and most extreme appointments. Throughout the next four years Haynes was one of Richardson's chief adversaries, though the governor won many of the battles. Against the BAF Haynes did much better. After a number of BAF-endorsed legislators were elected, Haynes fought the BAF in speeches, publications, and initiative campaigns, attracting affected in-

terest groups in his crusades. In the midst of this activity he helped to
create the Progressive Voters League as a temporary defense strategy.
Supplying much of its operational expenses, Haynes joined the league
officers in establishing an organized opposition to Richardson and running candidates for state offices against BAF supporters. Successful in
the 1924 election, the league remained intact to contest Richardson in
1926 and won.[33]

The progressives returned to power in the administration of Governor Clement C. Young, and Dr. Haynes's influence rose once again. One
of the increasingly fewer old progressives still actively advocating reform, Haynes continued to be a major progressive strategist and benefactor. Governor Young appointed him to state commissions charged
with recommending revisions to the state constitution and taxation
system and relieving Depression-Era unemployment. Haynes offered advice on appointments and policy positions (which the governor frequently followed), while also lobbying the state legislature to restore
programs cut by Richardson, to protect progressive laws, and to propose
new ones.[34]

With Young's reelection defeat in the 1930 primary, Haynes and the
remaining progressives were barred from the governor's office. The doctor did, however, continue to work with like-minded legislators to
thwart the retrenchment actions of new governors and conservative lawmakers. The 1932 and 1934 elections brought waves of New Deal
Democrats to Sacramento, and Haynes found it expedient and easy to
work with them for common goals. By this time progressivism had
disappeared, replaced by New Deal liberalism as the dominant reform force.[35]

In spite of his personal limitations and the political obstacles he faced,
Dr. Haynes made significant contributions to California and local reform as a leading social democrat of the state. He was instrumental in
promoting social reform among wealthy capitalists with whom he associated in business spheres, and he gave generous financial and personal aid to progressives and the left. Particularly in the areas of direct
legislation and public ownership, his leadership and activism were
determining factors in the success of these measures, both locally
and statewide.

A quarter of a century ago, Spencer Olin concluded that California
progressivism was "an impressive effort to improve the living conditions

and to increase the wages of urban and rural workers, as well as to assimilate immigrants into American society."[36] Far short of the hopes and expectations of left-wing progressives, it did accomplish some degree of success in improving the social welfare of the state's citizens, as well as modifying its political system. As the historiography of California progressivism increasingly casts it in a more conservative and class-interest mold, we should remember that the movement did have a left wing of atypical progressives, such as John Randolph Haynes, who played a significant role in the limited achievements of progressivism in the Golden State.

NOTES

This essay is based on the author's *John Randolph Haynes: California Progressive* (Stanford, Calif.: Stanford University Press, 1992).

1. John Whiteclay Chambers II, *The Tyranny of Reform: America in the Progressive Era, 1900–1917* (New York: St. Martin's Press, 1980), 105–14, quote on 108. For the historiographical background of progressivism, see Robert H. Wiebe, "The Progressive Years, 1900–1917," in William H. Cartwright and Richard L. Watson, Jr., eds., *The Reinterpretation of American History and Culture* (Washington, D.C.: National Council for the Social Studies, 1973), 425–42; and Daniel T. Rodgers, "In Search of Progressivism," in Stanley I. Kutler and Stanley N. Katz, eds., *The Promise of American History: Progress and Prospects* (Baltimore: Johns Hopkins University Press, 1982), 113–32.

2. Benjamin Parke DeWitt, *The Progressive Movement: A Non-partisan, Comprehensive Discussion of Current Tendencies in American Politics* (New York: Macmillan, 1915), 89–100, quotes on 98, 99; Otis L. Graham, Jr., *An Encore for Reform: The Old Progressives and the New Deal* (New York: Oxford University Press, 1967), 129–50, quote on 130; Robert M. Crunden, *Ministers of Reform: The Progressives' Achievements in American Civilization, 1889–1920* (New York: Basic Books, 1982), 13, 35, 46–51, 108–11, 160–74; William L. O'Neill, *The Progressive Years: America Comes of Age* (New York: Dodd, Mead, 1975), 66–67; John A. Thompson, *Reformers and War: American Progressive Publicists and the First World War* (Cambridge: Cambridge University Press, 1987), 33–36.

3. George Mowry, *The California Progressives* (Berkeley: University of California Press, 1951), 100, 200–10, 219–21; Spencer C. Olin, Jr., *California's Prodigal Sons: Hiram Johnson and the Progressives, 1911–1917* (Berkeley: University of California Press, 1968), 219–22. See also Robert E. Hennings, *James D. Phelan and the Wilson Progressives of California* (New York: Garland, 1985), 87.

4. Royce D. Delmatier, Clarence F. McIntosh, and Earl G. Waters, eds., *The Rumble of California Politics, 1848–1970* (New York: Wiley, 1970), 179;

Thomas R. Clark, "Labor and Progressivism 'South of the Slot': The Voting Behavior of the San Francisco Working Class, 1912–1916," *California History* 66 (September 1987): 201; Ira Brown Cross, "Socialism in California Municipalities," *National Municipal Review* 1 (October 1912): 611–19.

5. Kevin Starr, *Inventing the Dream: California through the Progressive Era* (New York: Oxford University Press, 1985), 218. David A. Shannon, in *The Socialist Party of America: A History* (New York: Macmillan, 1955), 40–41, says of Harriman that except for his "occasional genuflection toward the cooperative commonwealth, it was difficult to distinguish him from progressives of either of the two major parties." As mayor of Berkeley, Wilson was constantly at odds with the left wing of his party. See Wilson to Caroline M. Severance, August 26, 1911, et al., box 24, Caroline M. Severance Papers, Huntington Library, San Marino, California.

6. Tom Sitton, "California's Practical Idealist: John Randolph Haynes," *California History* 67 (March 1988): 3–4.

7. Richard B. Dressner, "William Dwight Porter Bliss's Christian Socialism," *Church History* 47 (March 1978): 66–82; Peter J. Frederick, *Knights of the Golden Rule: The Intellectual as Christian Social Reformer in the 1890s* (Lexington: University Press of Kentucky, 1976), 84–98; James Dombrowski, *The Early Days of Christian Socialism in America* (New York: Columbia University Press, 1936), 96–107; *Los Angeles Evening Express,* January 10, 1898.

8. *Los Angeles Times,* January 21, February 10, 1898; *Los Angeles Evening Express,* October 27, 1900, February 27, 1901; Howard H. Quint, *The Forging of American Socialism: Origins of the Modern Movement,* 2nd ed. (New York: Bobbs-Merrill, 1964), 257–64.

9. Quint, *Forging of American Socialism,* 259; James T. Kloppenberg, *Uncertain Victory: Social Democracy and Progressivism in European and American Thought, 1870–1920* (New York: Oxford University Press, 1986); Joan M. Jenson, "After Slavery: Caroline Severance in Los Angeles," *Southern California Quarterly* 48 (June 1966): 175–86.

10. John R. Haynes to Frederick H. Rindge, October 10, 1902, Haynes to National American Woman Suffrage Association, June 13, 1905, box 50, John Randolph Haynes Papers, Special Collections, University Research Library, University of California, Los Angeles.

11. Haynes, "Introduction of the Initiative" speech, "Recall" Scrapbook, Haynes address to Second Annual Social and Political Conference (1901), "Public Ownership" Scrapbook, and direct legislation files in boxes 35–40, Haynes Papers; Eltweed Pomeroy, "How Los Angeles Got Direct Legislation," *Wilshire's Monthly* 5 (April 1903): 12–15; Grace H. Stimson, *Rise of the Labor Movement in Los Angeles* (Berkeley: University of California Press, 1955), 282–86.

12. John R. Haynes, "Plea for Municipal Ownership," *Graphic* 21 (December 3, 1904): 15, and "The Electric Juggernaut," *Pacific Outlook* 3 (September 21, 1907): 10; Tom Sitton, "The Los Angeles Fender Fight in the Early 1900s," *Southern California Quarterly* 72 (Summer 1990): 139–56.

13. Martin Schiesl, "Progressive Reform in Los Angeles under Mayor Alexander, 1909–1913," *California Historical Quarterly* 54 (Spring 1975): 37–56;

Albert Howard Clodius, "The Quest for Good Government in Los Angeles, 1890–1910" (Ph.D. diss., Claremont Graduate School, 1953); "Triumph of Democracy," *Pacific Outlook* 7 (December 18, 1909): 2–3.

14. Alice M. Rose, "Rise of the California Insurgency" (Ph.D. diss., Stanford University, 1942), especially 399–400; Mowry, *California Progressives*, 57–83; Haynes to Meyer Lissner, February 8, 1908, box 17, and Lissner to Haynes, December 21 and 28, 1908, box 1, Meyer Lissner Papers, Special Collections, Stanford University; Franklin Hichborn, *Story of the Session of the California Legislature of 1909* (San Francisco: James H. Barry Co., 1909), 68–112.

15. Meyer Lissner to Hiram Johnson, December 14, 1912, Part 2, box 20, Hiram W. Johnson Papers, Bancroft Library, University of California, Berkeley; Haynes to Johnson, May 19, 1915, et al., box 87, Haynes Papers; V. O. Key and Winston W. Crouch, *The Initiative and Referendum in California* (Berkeley: University of California Press, 1939), 434–44.

16. *Los Angeles Socialist*, July 2, 1904; *Common Sense*, December 16, 1905; John R. Haynes–H. Gaylord Wilshire correspondence and business files, Haynes Foundation addenda, Haynes Papers; *Fresno Evening Democrat*, February 22, 1906; *Los Angeles Times*, November 14, 1907, March 3, 1908.

17. William H. Stuart to Caroline Severance, November 11, 1911, box 23, Severance Papers; Severance to Dora Haynes, "1911," Autograph Book, Haynes Papers; *Los Angeles Times*, November 2, 1911.

18. *Los Angeles Express*, March 18, 1913; Haynes to Meyer Lissner, February 24, 1913, box 168, Haynes Papers; John J. Hamilton to Lissner, September 27, 1912, box 17, Lissner Papers; Haynes, "Democracy and Social Progress," in William M. Bell, ed., *Addresses, World's Social Progress Congress* (Dayton, Ohio: Otterbein Press, 1915), 336–50. Proportional representation had yet to be established in any U.S. municipality at that time.

19. Haynes address to Women's Progressive League, May 4, 1912, box 228, Haynes Papers; Kirk H. Porter and Donald Bruce Johnson, *National Party Platforms, 1840–1964* (Urbana: University of Illinois Press, 1966), 175–82. I have capitalized *Progressive* in this sentence to denote the political party.

20. On the World War I homefront, see David M. Kennedy, *Over Here: The First World War and American Society* (New York: Oxford University Press, 1980).

21. Burt Noggle, "Configuration of the Twenties," in Cartwright and Watson, *Reinterpretation of American History*, 469–71; Otis L. Graham, Jr., *The Great Campaigns: Reform and War in America, 1900–1928* (Englewood Cliffs, N.J.: Prentice-Hall, 1971), 114–19; Eugene M. Tobin, *Organize or Perish: America's Independent Progressives, 1913–1933* (Westport, Conn.: Greenwood Press, 1986), especially 3–8.

22. Jackson K. Putnam, "The Persistence of Progressivism in the 1920s: The Case of California," *Pacific Historical Review* 35 (November 1966): 395–411, quote on 395.

23. In Haynes Papers: copy of Kate Crane Gartz to Milbank Johnson, October 12, 1920, box 6; Paul Blanshard to Haynes, September 21, October 15, 1928, box 92; Harry Laidler to Haynes, May 31, 1927, box 93; League for Industrial Democracy files, boxes 92 and 93; Upton Sinclair–Haynes cor-

respondence in Haynes Foundation addenda. See also Starr, *Inventing the Dream*, 218.

24. In Haynes Papers: Haynes to Judson King, September 26, 1932, Haynes Foundation addenda; Haynes to Norman Thomas, June 23, 1936, box 63; Haynes to Thomas Amlie, August 26, 1935, box 3.

25. *Saturday Night*, February 6, 1926, 1–2; Haynes to Meyer Lissner, May 21, 1919, box 7, Lissner Papers; Haynes to Paul Kellogg, December 1, 1925, et al., Haynes Foundation addenda, Haynes Papers; Charles J. Lang, ed., *Who's Who in Los Angeles County, 1927–1928* (Los Angeles: Charles J. Lang, 1927), 37; Graham, *Encore for Reform*, 109–10.

26. Sitton, "California's Practical Idealist," 10–17.

27. Haynes to William Stephens, March 17, 1919, et al., box 19 and Haynes Foundation addenda, Haynes Papers; Jackson K. Putnam, *Modern California Politics*, 2nd ed. (San Francisco: Boyd and Fraser, 1984), 4–10.

28. In Haynes Papers: Haynes to Franklin Hichborn, January 12, 1921, box 19; Haynes to Paul Scharrenberg, May 12, 1919, Haynes to William Stephens, April 9, 1919, and Haynes to members of Direct Legislation League, November 14, 1916, box 36. See also John Randolph Haynes, "California Sticks to the Initiative and Referendum," *National Municipal Review* 12 (March 1923): 116–18; Franklin Hichborn, "Sources of Opposition to Direct Legislation in California," *Transactions of the Commonwealth Club of California* 35 (March 3, 1931): 512–39.

29. Haynes to Rudolph Spreckels, July 28, 1921, et al., box 159, Franklin Hichborn Papers, Special Collections, University Research Library, UCLA; Haynes to Clement C. Young, January 13, 1923, box 178, Haynes Papers; Franklin Hichborn, "California Politics, 1891–1939," 5 vols. (Unpublished typescript, 1939), 3: 1958–2053, 2118–2264.

30. Copy of Rudolph Spreckels to Haynes, August 1, 1924, box 39, Herbert C. Jones Papers, Special Collections, Stanford University; Haynes speech, "How I Shall Vote on Nov. 4, 1924, and Why," typescript, Haynes Foundation addenda, Haynes Papers; Hichborn, "California Politics," 3: 2176–2208; John L. Shover, "The California Progressives and the 1924 Election," *California Historical Quarterly* 51 (Spring 1972): 17–21; Thomas G. Paterson, "California Progressives and Foreign Policy," *California Historical Society Quarterly* 47 (December 1968): 336.

31. Haynes to Hiram Johnson, September 23, 1922, box 42, Haynes to Johnson, June 29, 1921, box 88, Haynes Papers; Haynes to Chester Rowell, September 16, 1920, box 1, Chester Rowell Papers, Bancroft Library; Elizabeth T. Kent, "William Kent, Independent: A Biography," typescript, 1950, 401–3, Bancroft Library.

32. Haynes to B. R. Baumgardt, July 16, 1928, and Haynes to Dr. Harry Harrower, April 13, 1921, box 6, Haynes Papers; Katherine P. Edson to Mrs. Medill McCormick, August 19, 1920, box 1, Katherine Philips Edson Papers, Special Collections, University Research Library, UCLA; Edwin Layton, "The Better America Federation: A Case Study of Superpatriotism," *Pacific Historical Review* 30 (May 1961): 137–47.

33. Will C. Wood to Haynes, July 23, 1920, and BAF files in boxes 5 and 6, Progressive Voters League files in box 166, Haynes Papers; Russell M. Posner, "The Progressive Voters League, 1923–26," *California Historical Society Quarterly* 36 (September 1957): 251–56.

34. Items in Haynes Papers: Haynes to C. C. Young, November 23, 1928, et al., box 43 and Haynes Foundation addenda; Haynes correspondence to legislators, boxes 19, 20, 39.

35. Haynes to Hichborn, February 12, 1937, Frank Waters to Haynes, June 3, 1935, Haynes correspondence with Waters, Culbert Olson, and Dewey Anderson, boxes 20 and 40, and Haynes-Rolph correspondence, Haynes Foundation addenda, Haynes Papers.

36. Olin, *California's Prodigal Sons*, 181.

William Kent

The Puzzle
of Progressive Conservationists

Anne F. Hyde

This essay began as a reinvestigation of the meaning of the early conservation movement and its relationship to California progressivism.
When I discovered William Kent, I thought I had found the perfect vehicle. I planned to tell the story of a California progressive known primarily for his work in conservation. Kent certainly fit that bill. He came
from one of the early families of Marin County, and his family home still
stands in Kentfield. Kent entered national office as a congressman in the
progressive landslide of 1910 that brought Hiram Johnson to the governorship of California. He corresponded with leading progressive
thinkers like Lincoln Steffens and Jane Addams. As a conservationist
Kent is remembered for his donation of Muir Woods, a glorious stand
of virgin redwoods in Marin County, and for his sponsorship of the bill
that created the National Park Service in 1916.

However, as I started looking more carefully at William Kent's career, it became clear that the labels "progressive" or "conservationist"
fit him loosely at best. Though he called himself a progressive, Kent ran
for national office as an independent because he refused to toe the line
of any one political group, particularly the Lincoln-Roosevelt Republican League in California or Theodore Roosevelt's Bull Moose party.
Kent's conservationist credentials seem equally problematic. By 1913,
John Muir, for whom Kent named Muir Woods, refused even to say
Kent's name because of Kent's support of the Hetch-Hetchy Valley reservoir plan. Opposition to Hetch-Hetchy is often used as a litmus test for
early conservationists, and Kent failed it.

Because of his failure to pass this test, Kent no longer seemed the ideal figure I had envisioned. Ultimately, however, I concluded that the puzzle was not William Kent but, rather, historians' definitions of conservation and progressivism. Those terms meant something quite different in 1910 than they mean to us. Kent called himself both things, and he believed he had a cohesive political ideology. And even though Kent would be booed by the Sierra Club today, his ideas about conservation made sense in the context of the early twentieth century.

George Mowry introduced his path-breaking study of progressivism in California by describing the state as an advanced microcosm of what was happening in the rest of the nation. In a strikingly urbanized state, political machines and powerful editors ran the large cities. Overseeing this morass of municipal corruption, in Mowry's view, a single gigantic trust, the Southern Pacific railroad, controlled the state's economic and political life. According to Mowry, homegrown businessmen, professionals, and writers banded together to battle this obvious evil. Progressivism grew out of the fight to rid the state of the grip of the Southern Pacific—the octopus with a thousand arms—and other kinds of reform were ignored. In California at least, progressivism addressed a single issue, and its practitioners were satisfied once they had solved the problem of the Southern Pacific.[1]

William Kent and his version of progressivism, however, add considerable complexity to Mowry's portrait. Though Kent fits Mowry's general profile of who and what California progressives were—white, native, Protestant, well educated, professional, financially comfortable[2]—his thought and his action took him far beyond Mowry's realm of progressive politics.

Even though he was the son of a Chicago meat-packing magnate, William Kent spent much of his boyhood in rural Marin County, California. His father had retired early after a successful career in meat packing and land speculation.[3] However, after graduating from Yale in 1887, William Kent moved to Chicago to take on his father's business. Chicago proved to be a shock after his Marin County childhood. Trained to believe in the reality and fairness of laissez-faire capitalism, social Darwinism, and the rights of private property, Kent discovered that the system which had given him great wealth had produced waste, poverty, corruption, and misery.[4]

The variety of his father's business interests gave Kent a quick introduction to the possibilities and grave problems of American business.

Real estate, insurance futures, ranching, construction, banking, and mining provided him with insight into the resources and enterprises of different regions of the nation. Life in Chicago, however, with its urban poverty, blatant political corruption, and dishonest businessmen, illustrated for Kent the costs of the American enterprise system.[5]

By 1894 William Kent had seen enough. When Florence Kelley of Hull House accused Kent of being a typical slumlord, he reacted by donating his slum property to Hull House, tearing down the tenements, and building one of the first public playgrounds in the United States. His efforts for Hull House brought him into contact with the leading reformers of the day and convinced him of the absolute corruption of Chicago politics. He ran for alderman in 1895 and formed the Municipal Voters League in 1896, an organization that used publicity to remove corrupt politicians from office. Kent and the League successfully drove out many of the worst offenders and provided a model for other cities.[6]

Kent soon realized, however, that the fundamental problem was not corrupt politicians but the ties between government and business that had created a stranglehold over utilities and transit systems. These systems provided basic human needs in a modern city, and Kent believed that they were being handled in a way that generated big profits for the few, but expensive and inefficient service for the many. As a result, he came to be a firm believer in strict regulation, if not outright public ownership, of vital services and industries.[7]

The issues of public ownership and the efficient use of resources became the focus of Kent's career. In this respect Kent begins to stray from Mowry's depiction of California progressives. He showed little interest in the usual progressive concerns of election reform and worried instead about basic economic questions of use and distribution of resources. As early as 1896 he insisted that, despite the seeming abundance in the nation, "we are victims of a system of distribution unjust and inadequate" and that "want and misery, already at our doors, make riot inevitable and revolution more than probable, unless the verdict of the people is for fairness and efficiency."[8] Such concerns began to push Kent toward more radical solutions to the problems of poverty and unequal opportunity, but first they led him to conservation and, indirectly, to California.

Growing disenchanted with business and politics in Chicago, Kent began to look for new opportunities. After his father's death in 1903, he delegated most of the business operations of A. E. Kent and Son to trusted managers. Kent spent most of his time on politics and had a role in a variety of organizations, including the Playground and Recreational Association of America, literary clubs, good government leagues, and the arts and crafts movement. However, his primary concern was establishing municipal ownership of the Chicago transit system, a battle that he found increasingly frustrating.[9] His family home in Kentfield, California, where his mother still lived, looked more and more attractive to Kent as a place to raise his growing family, and a place to rethink his career.

In 1907 Kent left Chicago and moved back to California. Though he announced his intention to retire from politics, he was far too ambitious and active to do that. Even before he moved west, Kent managed to get his fingers into the local political pie. He happened to be in Kentfield, just outside of San Francisco, in 1906, when the earthquake and fire ravaged the city. Kent immediately swung into action, organizing camps for the refugees who had fled to Marin County.[10] He wrote to former mayor James D. Phelan, offering to help in the reconstruction of the city, explaining that "although a resident of Chicago, I have many interests in California. . . . Therefore, I have a personal interest in San Francisco's future." Having explained his qualifications, Kent went on to tell Phelan how to rebuild the city in the safest and most efficient way, using broad avenues. He noted, "Van Ness Avenue is all very well to bisect the city, but there should be many more such fire trails."[11] Phelan chose not to heed this bit of unsolicited advice, but he and Kent continued to correspond.

Kent chose an auspicious moment to return to California. The geological earthquake of 1906 preceded the political earthquake of the San Francisco graft trials that resulted in the complete shake-up of municipal politics. Kent could not resist getting involved. He became friendly with the leading attorneys in the graft case, Francis Heney and Hiram Johnson, both of whom would figure importantly in California's political future. In 1908 Kent served on the commission to investigate the causes of graft in San Francisco.[12] He was also active in the new Lincoln-Roosevelt Republican League, dedicated to freeing state politics from the grip of the Southern Pacific railroad.

Kent also became committed to conservation issues. He had always been interested in outdoor activity and was rumored to be one of the best shots in the nation. For Kent, like many other wealthy Americans, escape to the wilderness provided mental and physical health. However, in Kent's view, conservation was far more than preserving bits of wilderness suitable for wealthy hunters and aesthetes. Kent saw conservation of natural resources as a key issue for progressivism, particularly his increasingly radical version. Conservation meant more than Gifford Pinchot's scientific efficiency; it meant a redistribution of power and resources from private industry to the public.

Kent's views were quite extreme in comparison to those of most progressive politicians. Much like Henry George, he believed that private land ownership stood at the root of American economic problems. Speaking rather apocalyptically, he described the situation created by the American penchant for giving away the public domain. "Our forests have been wastefully cut. Our anthracite fields are in private hands. . . . Our vast resources of petroleum have been rounded up and cornered," Kent noted, with the result that "there are days of want ahead of us . . . unless we stop the heedless squandering."[13] Though he recognized that few Americans were ready to give up private ownership, Kent believed that the federal government had the power and the duty to control all aspects of the remaining public domain and to prevent private enterprise from grabbing what was left.[14]

Given Kent's radical beliefs about private ownership and public control, his approach to conservation seems inconsistent at first glance. He could be categorized as a "Muir" preservationist in some instances, a pragmatic "Pinchot" conservationist in others, and a friend of development in some cases.[15] However, his stance had logic. Kent believed first that resources existed to be used by humans, but he also believed that use should be made in the most efficient possible manner. Some resources served people best by being preserved for aesthetic reasons, while others should be utilized. As he explained to a friend in 1918, the key to successful conservation was "to take it up coherently, to find out what land is good for what purpose."[16]

Kent developed his earliest ideas about conservation in Marin County. His first efforts at conservation were in the realm of creating parks, something he was familiar with from his experiences with playgrounds in Chicago. As early as 1903, he began lobbying for a national park in the region around Mt. Tamalpais in Marin County. In a speech advocating such a park, Kent made a rather sophisticated argument. Conservation, he argued, had value on many levels. Preserving the natural grandeur of Mt. Tamalpais had aesthetic attractions as well as economic ones. He explained that "Marin County would be the showplace of the State" because of the beauty of the proposed park; he also pointed out that the hordes of eager tourists from San Francisco and beyond would produce a booming economy.[17]

Neither the federal nor the state government showed much interest in Kent's Tamalpais park scheme; so, after moving to Kentfield in 1907, he took matters into his own hands. Disgusted that a water company intended to cut down a large stand of redwoods on the south slope of Mt. Tamalpais in order to build a reservoir, Kent bought the land himself. Searching for a way to donate the land to the public, he discovered the 1906 Antiquities Act, which allowed private citizens to give land that had historic or scenic value to the government.[18]

The donation of the spectacular grove of redwoods in 1908, which Kent proposed be named Muir Woods after the noted naturalist and writer John Muir, brought Kent national attention. President Theodore Roosevelt wrote Kent, "All Americans who prize the national beauties of the country and wish to see them preserved undamaged and especially those who realize the literally unique value of the groves of giant trees, must feel that you have conferred a great and lasting benefit upon the entire country."[19] John Muir waxed equally enthusiastic, saying that "saving these woods from the axe and saw, from money changers and water changers is in many ways the most notable service to God and man I have heard of since my forest wanderings began, a much needed lesson to saint and sinner alike."[20] After the donation of Muir Woods, Kent became a regular correspondent with Muir; with Gifford Pinchot, Roosevelt's influential chief forester; with Roosevelt himself; and with other significant leaders in the conservation movement.

Kent's efforts to protect the redwoods that became Muir Woods and to create a national park around Mt. Tamalpais also led him into the more practical aspects of conservation. From his experiences in Chicago, Kent believed that the public should own and operate its own water source in Marin County. From his contact with Gifford Pinchot and other forestry experts who were advocating wise use of lands, Kent learned that cutting down trees in a watershed for lumber or for suburban development was short-sighted. Forming a public water district in Marin County would prevent private companies from charging usurious rates and from destroying the watershed itself. Kent worked for years to get the water companies' lands into public ownership and to organize public control of reservoirs, waterlines, and pumping stations.

In Kent's view, conservation—as represented by the Marin Water District and the Muir Woods—would enable him to achieve his conception of progressive reform. He believed that conservation served the highest aesthetic needs of humans and simultaneously fostered productive efficiency and social justice. It required the kind of positive government action that Kent viewed as serving democratic ends: turning power and resources over to the people. Conservation also provided him with a new political platform on which to rebuild his career in California.

Kent had long been a supporter of President Theodore Roosevelt's conservation policies, particularly those that advocated the establishment of public control over natural resources and the creation of national forests and parks. He avidly supported Gifford Pinchot and his wise-use policies developed for the new Forest Service. These activities meshed with Kent's ideas about active government and its role in improving the lives of common Americans. Like most progressive Republicans, Kent assumed that William Howard Taft, Roosevelt's chosen successor, would continue these policies. He corresponded actively with Taft during the 1908 campaign and, according to Elizabeth Kent, "greeted his election with enthusiasm."[21]

Taft, however, did not live up to Kent's expectations. He had far more traditional notions than Kent, Roosevelt, or most progressives about the role of the executive and about the efficacy of private development. Particularly in the areas of conservation and public ownership of natural resources, Taft began to undo Roosevelt's policies. Taft's appointment of the conservative westerner Richard Ballinger as secretary of the interior and his battles with Gifford Pinchot signaled to Kent that something was seriously amiss.[22]

In a barrage of letters in early 1909, Kent began questioning Taft about his conservation policies. He asked the president directly, "Are you satisfied that the land and power grabbers are being held level?" He pushed his point further by saying that it was crucial to "keep monopoly control of the water power" out of the hands "of promoters and exploiters."[23] Taft's lack of response to such queries and Ballinger's granting of oil leases and water power sites to private companies drove Kent to despair. He wrote to a friend in September of 1909 that he had been having "a lively time with a large person in Washington and gaining less and less appreciation of his mental and spiritual make-up as the days pass by." Kent complained specifically that Taft's "inability to see a point where Conservation and public interests are at stake is certainly remarkable."[24] By this time, Kent had decided that Taft and Ballinger were enemies of both progressivism and conservation.

The issue that pushed Kent irrevocably into an anti-Taft position, however, was a local one. In 1909, just as the president was coming under fire from many of his progressive supporters, Kent discovered that Taft and Ballinger had approved a plan to divert water from Lake Tahoe to run a series of privately owned hydroelectric plants and to provide water for irrigation in the Truckee-Carson reclamation project.

Everything about the project alarmed a progressive and conservationist like Kent. The power plants were owned by the Stone and Webster Engineering Corporation, one of the largest public utilities corporations in the nation. Stone and Webster received the rights to the water flowing from Lake Tahoe in return for guaranteeing the Bureau of Reclamation a certain amount of water each year to reclaim the land in the arid, alkaline Carson Valley of Nevada. In order to provide reliable amounts of water for the reclamation project and produce electricity, the contract allowed the power company to bore a hole through the Sierra Nevada, dropping the level of the lake more than fifty feet if necessary.[25]

Even more horrifying, from a progressive's point of view, the Stone and Webster Company would be granted these rights in perpetuity. Ominously, the company began to buy out every small power company in northern Nevada and California, clearly intending to create a monopoly. William Kent did not need to be told that such a contract was dangerous. Not only could the beaches of Lake Tahoe be destroyed (Kent owned a vacation home there), but a private company would reap unlimited profits from public resources.[26]

Kent flew into action. He rallied Tahoe property owners in opposition to the proposed contract and hired engineers to document the effects of the water diversion and tunnel on Lake Tahoe. He wrote letters to his influential friends, alerting them to Ballinger's actions. As he explained to Charles D. Norton, the secretary of the treasury, the danger was clear. Ballinger, Kent warned, "has either given away or intends to give away the whole watershed of the Tahoe Basin to the Truckee River Power Company, practically without any restriction of any kind, and in perpetuity."[27] His efforts resulted in a terrific political battle. Taft and Ballinger were left with little congressional support for the project, and eventually they dropped the contract.

The fight over the Tahoe-Truckee project again put Kent in the national spotlight. Both Theodore Roosevelt and Gifford Pinchot came to Kent's aid. His attack on Ballinger and his efforts on behalf of the state brought Kent to the attention of local progressive politicians. Finally, Kent's disgust with the Taft administration and his fear that it would give up all gains in conservation prompted him to run for Congress in 1910.

Kent chose a good year to reenter politics, particularly in California. Though he was a member of the Lincoln-Roosevelt League, Kent made it clear that he was not interested in the Southern Pacific or in the nitty-gritty of state politics. However, he recognized the political realities of his situation. Early in 1910, he consulted Chester Rowell, the Fresno editor and founder of the Lincoln-Roosevelt League, about the possibility of running for Congress. Rowell did not respond eagerly to Kent's queries. Kent's district already had a Republican congressman, Duncan McKinlay, who, as Rowell put it, was "not the worst Congressman from California, nor yet the best."[28]

Kent's desire to run for office presented a ticklish problem. Since McKinlay was not part of the Southern Pacific machine, the League had little to gain from ousting him from office. Kent would certainly be a more active congressman, but his ideas were far to the left of most California progressives. But Kent threatened to run as a Democrat if the league would not sponsor him, and having someone as well connected as Kent bolting from the league would prove to be an embarrassment. Finally, in April, Rowell gave his approval to Kent, saying "it would be a great thing for California to have one genuine insurgent in Congress . . . and if you can see your way at all clear, go to it."[29] Kent did.

He went at it, however, on his own terms. "I would not be a dredger Congressman, or a farm Congressman, or a fresh egg Congressman, or a dairy Congressman," he said to the voters of his district, where dredging and dairies flourished. Instead, he explained, "I would like to be an American Congressman, recognizing the union and the nation."[30]

Kent also made it clear that conservation would be the center of his national approach to progressivism. His first campaign statement described the nation as "sort of a grab bag in which it is certain that the most powerful will not only grab the most, but will get the last grab." Because of this situation, Kent stated, "conservation of our natural resources . . . is the most necessary, insistent and immediate policy for our nation to enforce."[31] This, of course, was a direct attack on Taft and Ballinger's policies of opening up public resources to private exploitation. By extension, his emphasis on conserving national resources and on public ownership put Kent in direct opposition to his opponent, Duncan McKinlay, a devoted Taft supporter whom Kent called privately "the President's poodle." Taft's sagging support among Republicans made this approach a sound one.

By this time, Kent had a national reputation as a conservationist and a progressive; and he used that reputation to great advantage in the campaign. Progressives like Lincoln Steffens and Jane Addams provided endorsements, and progressive periodicals like *Collier's* and *LaFollette's*

Weekly described Kent as "a Republican of the Abraham Lincoln type . . . a man of right convictions, political intelligence, and moral courage."[32] Most significant, Gifford Pinchot, leader of Roosevelt's conservation efforts, toured the state with Kent. At meetings all over Kent's largely rural district, Pinchot spoke on the importance of conservation, its connection to progressive reform, and its practical value to Americans. He pointed out William Kent's important role in "foiling the selfish interests of power companies in the Tahoe-Truckee controversy."[33]

Kent's emphasis on conservation—on conservation that protected hard-working Americans from greedy land grabbers—worked well. The approach was a gamble because western Americans in general distrusted conservationists, who usually wanted to put control of public land— often the majority of land in western states—in the hands of the federal government. And the federal government often prevented land and resources from being developed quickly, anathema to western boosters.[34] William Kent, however, convinced his constituents that conservation meant using resources for the long-term benefit of the people, not simply locking them up. Kent won both the primary against Duncan McKinlay and the general election using conservation, broadly defined, as his major issue and without mentioning the Southern Pacific railroad. This approach put Kent far outside the mainstream in California progressivism, and would soon do the same in the national arena as well.

When Kent arrived in Washington in January of 1911 to begin work as a Republican congressman from California, it was clear that he did not intend to toe the Republican line or to limit his interests to California issues.[35] Kent wanted national influence and independent ideas, a somewhat grandiose set of goals for a freshman representative from California.

Rather understandably, Kent found his first term in office frustrating. Though he stood up in Congress and made sweeping statements about the state of the nation and the dire need for progressive reform, he achieved little. His lack of seniority, his impatience with the dull routine of writing and lobbying for legislation, and his naiveté about how Congress worked limited his effectiveness. Shocked by the realities of influence and partisan politics at the national level, Kent wrote with disgust to Hiram Johnson about the "tendency on the part of some of our progressive friends to wallow over into the Taft sty."[36]

Despite his evident frustration at not being able to change the course of the Taft administration, Kent did have an impact in the area of conservation. He took on Taft and Secretary of the Interior Ballinger for one last round of the Tahoe-Truckee controversy when they tried to re-negotiate the contract in 1911. Kent quickly warned California governor Hiram Johnson of Ballinger's plans, and he bullied the president into calling for a White House conference on the issue. The conference and a threatening resolution from the California legislature made the potential damage to Lake Tahoe and the nature of the contract with the private power company clear. Because of the hue and cry that Kent raised in California, and because of the damaging reports made by the engineers hired by Kent, he won the battle. Ballinger canceled the contract.[37]

The defeat of the Tahoe-Truckee contract represented Kent's only success in his first term in office. He learned several lessons from this experience. First, he would eschew partisan politics. His views could not be contained by the platforms of the Republicans or the Democrats, or even by the goals of the insurgent progressives of either party. Second, Kent realized, he had to specialize. Congress was too big and complex for him to be an expert on all issues. He chose conservation and the public domain as his field of expertise. These turned out to be wise decisions. Political independence gave him the freedom to develop a coherent outlook and to avoid taking uncomfortable stands in election years. Kent's already considerable reputation as a progressive conservationist gave him significant influence on those issues.

Kent cut himself loose from the national Progressive party and from the Lincoln-Roosevelt League of California in 1912. Disgusted with the Republicans because of Taft, frustrated with the Progressives because of their waffling over choosing a candidate, and sympathetic with Democrat Woodrow Wilson's ideas, Kent found independence a logical step.[38] Even without the financial or political support of the progressive Republicans in California, Kent easily won his congressional election.

By this time, Kent had become widely recognized as an independent thinker. The progressive pundit Mark Sullivan of *Collier's* magazine called him "one of the commanding figures in Congress" and commented approvingly that "when Kent answers a roll call, everyone knows that vote was dictated by no other consideration whatever except the excellent muscle inside of Kent's skull."[39] Not all progressives found such independence a positive quality. California progressives described Kent as "erratic" because of his reluctance to stick to the party platform and were frankly relieved when he ran without their endorsement.[40]

Independence gave William Kent a great deal of influence in Congress, and he now came into his own politically, particularly on conservation issues. Because he had supported Woodrow Wilson so strongly and because he had connections with so many progressive organizations and politicians, Kent became an important adviser for Wilson, especially in conservation matters. He also wielded considerable power from his position on the Committee on Public Lands, which increased his impact on the conservation policies of the Wilson administration.[41]

As always, Kent saw conservation of natural resources as a vital part of progressivism. In the interests of efficiency and fairness, some land should be preserved, some should be reserved for small farmers, some should be reserved for large operations, and some specific sites should be managed by the government. Kent supported traditional conservation with the creation of national parks and wildlife reserves. In fact, Kent introduced the bill to create the National Park Service in 1916 because supporters thought he was the best known and liked of the conservationists in Congress.[42] Kent, however, had a much broader view of what conservation meant.

Many of the bills he proposed simply limited the ways that private enterprise could use the public domain. For example, he worked on legislation to limit ownership of oil- and coal-producing lands to long-term leases with careful controls over their use.[43] Other bills seemed to support big business. Kent introduced a bill to rationalize the use of public grazing lands. Recognizing that much land was too dry for traditional homesteading, he advocated a leasing plan for large cattle and sheep farmers. This plan enraged small farmers and western developers, who demanded that the grasslands be given or sold to private owners in small plots.[44] Kent lost out on this particular battle when the Stock-Raising Homestead Act of 1916 was passed. As Kent had predicted, homesteading on the arid grasslands proved to be a disaster, and thousands of farm families lost their fortunes and their lives in the next decades. He recalled rather bitterly that "demagogues, harping on free range and settlers, threw away the national assets, rendered impossible the existence of small stockmen, and condemned the animal population to hazardous starvation existence."[45] His advice about the rational use of the grasslands became law during the New Deal with the Taylor Grazing Act of 1934.

The issue that Kent regarded as most important was water power. The power created by water rushing through dams provided cheap and safe electricity, a resource that power and oil companies coveted. Large corporations had gained control of most of the nation's other energy resources, and conservationists like Kent were determined that water power should not meet the same fate.

When Kent first came to Congress in 1910, hydroelectric power was a relatively new resource. Many of the best sites for dams and hydro-electric facilities were located in the public domain, and Kent intended to keep it that way. He warned President Wilson in 1913 that water power was the biggest issue facing his new administration. He lectured Congress on the vital importance of federal control of waterways and rivers, cautioning that "the water power of the country, indestructible, perennial, must be held for the public welfare or else there can be nothing ahead of us but a revolution."[46]

The debate over federal control of water sources and water power continued for years with Kent at its center. Ideally, he wanted the government to develop water power and to avoid private interests entirely. However, he realized that the costs involved meant that the government would not be able to develop the power in many sites for decades. This fact made some kind of private enterprise necessary. Kent explained to his colleagues that the choice was simple: "Either the Federal Government, as a corporate entity, should utilize this water power, or if it grants authority to an agent to utilize it, it should limit and control that agent."[47] Few western members of Congress shared these views because they resented any form of federal control, particularly in situations where they felt their state or region's development was being hampered.

Railing against several bills that, in his view, provided insufficient protection against private monopolies, Kent introduced several bills of his own, which Congress rejected as being too restrictive. Kent didn't want to "lock up" water power, as westerners and power interests accused him, but he did believe in strict limitations. Fortunately, President Wilson agreed with Kent that "it is better to let water power run to waste than to settle the question in the wrong way."[48] The struggle continued throughout World War I until the Federal Water Power Act of 1920 was passed, containing most of the provisions that Kent demanded.[49]

Kent's ideas about the significance of water power are compatible with his notions about conservation. They also help to illuminate his stand in the Hetch-Hetchy controversy, which divided conservationists all over the nation in the first years of the twentieth century and remains a sore point today. Kent's rationale for approving the Hetch-Hetchy reservoir explains the seeming inconsistencies about progressive conservationism and puts the evolution of conservation in a proper context.

The debate over Hetch-Hetchy put the conservation movement on the national stage and, in doing so, forced the movement to splinter because of differing definitions of what conservation actually meant. "Conser-

vationist" came to mean Gifford Pinchot utilitarians, and "preservationist" defined John Muir protectionists—a split that has continued into
the present. Historians have presented the controversy as a battle between pure nature lovers and short-sighted, greedy business interests
who hoodwinked the city of San Francisco and the United States Congress into approving the grant in 1913.[50] However, the story, when
placed in the context of progressive reform and conservation at the turn
of the century, is much more complex than the morality play described
by historians using the advantages of hindsight.

Like many episodes in California history, the Hetch-Hetchy controversy began as a search for water. San Francisco had few local sources
of pure water. As early as the 1870s, city officials began to search for
alternatives to the water sold by the Spring Valley Water Company,
which was expensive and inadequate. By the 1890s, three separate reports cited the Hetch-Hetchy Valley and its Tuolumne River as a potential source of water for the city.[51]

The engineering reports mentioned other sites in the Sierra Nevada,
but the Hetch-Hetchy Valley seemed most attractive. As Marsden Manson, who later became the city engineer, explained in 1899, the valley
had "absolute purity; abundance, far beyond possible demands for all
purposes; the largest and most numerous sites for storage; freedom from
complicating 'water rights'; and . . . hydro-electric power possibilities."[52] It sounded perfect. The only problem was that Hetch-Hetchy
was part of Yosemite National Park, created in 1890.

This difficulty did not faze Mayor James Phelan of San Francisco,
who had long wanted to rid the city of the Spring Valley monopoly.
After the Spring Valley Water Company refused to sell out to the city,
Phelan began to look into the legal question of using national park lands
as a municipal water source. The national parks were never intended to
be inviolate wilderness areas. The legislation creating the parks permitted limited building, grazing, lumbering, and even farming. With this
precedent, Phelan pressured Congress to pass a bill that allowed rights
of way through the national parks for "domestic, public, or other beneficial uses."[53]

With such legislation in place, the city applied for the right to turn
Hetch-Hetchy into a reservoir in 1901. Secretary of the Interior Ethan
Hitchcock turned down the application, saying that he did not want to
set a precedent of violating a national park. A few years later, city officials tried again. This time they believed their chances were better. The
great earthquake and resulting fires of 1906 created national sympathy
for San Francisco and its water needs. In addition, both President

Roosevelt and Gifford Pinchot strongly believed in the progressive concept of multiple uses of national resources.[54]

San Francisco officials, however, had not counted on the strength of
the conservation movement. Led by John Muir and Robert Underwood
Johnson, the fight against the Hetch-Hetchy reservoir became headline
news. Muir, a naturalist and writer of national standing, and Johnson,
editor of the influential *Century* magazine, had worked together for
years to create Yosemite National Park, and they were not about to
let it go down the drains of San Franciscans. They organized an opposition effort including many of the wilderness clubs and outdoor preservation societies that had sprung up among elite Americans in the
late nineteenth century. With this impressive array of resources, they
felt confident that they could prevent San Francisco's grant from being
approved.[55]

Despite their efforts, Secretary of the Interior James Garfield approved the application in 1908. However, because the land was within
a national park, Congress had to pass legislation giving final approval.
During the lengthy hearings before the House and Senate Committees
on Public Lands and the arguments before Congress, the decision on
whether to dam the Hetch-Hetchy became a debate over moral values
and American ideals.

Most historians present the battle as between right-thinking, nature-
loving Americans and naive politicians fooled by double-talking engineers in the pay of power companies and the city of San Francisco. They
describe the valiant efforts made by Muir in California and Johnson in
Washington, D.C., and the testimony of leaders of civic groups, college
and university presidents, and important intellectuals before congressional committees in protest of Yosemite's desecration. Anyone who opposed Muir's views on preserving the Hetch-Hetchy had to be greedy,
insensitive, or irresponsible. For many historians, Hetch-Hetchy became
the ultimate litmus test of environmental morality.[56]

However, a look at the debate over the Hetch-Hetchy plan in the context of progressivism reveals that the situation was more complex. Even
though Johnson, Muir, and their supporters mounted an impressive
show, their efforts were doomed from the start.[57] For most people, including many conservationists, the issue was clear. Conservation was intended to serve human needs, and San Francisco needed water. Therefore, as President Roosevelt's personal secretary put it, "the Hetch-
Hetchy Valley will have to be given them. No other action could even
be thought of."[58] It would be immoral to deny a thirsty city.

The issue of building the reservoir divided even the most staunch conservation groups. The Sierra Club, founded by John Muir in 1892, found itself so divided on the issue that a significant minority of the club's members resigned.[59] In fact, the engineer and principal lobbyist for Hetch-Hetchy, Marsden Manson, was a member of the Sierra Club, and he saw no conflict in his position.[60] In a similar vein, Caspar Whitney, the editor of *Outdoor America*, wrote to Robert Underwood Johnson, expressing his regrets at not being able to oppose Hetch-Hetchy. He explained that using the water in Yosemite to quench the thirst of San Francisco represented the highest use of natural resources and that "the plea for its preservation is only one of sentiment."[61] And, in the context of the progressive notion of improving the lives of Americans through active government and efficient use of resources, sentiment had little import.

William Kent's stand on Hetch-Hetchy illustrates the intersection between conservation and progressivism, as well as the danger of imposing late-twentieth century environmental ethics on another era. When Kent entered office in 1911, the Hetch-Hetchy battle had been dragging on for years. Muir and Underwood assumed that someone who had donated Muir Woods, who knew Muir personally, who was an avid outdoorsman and an active member of the Sierra Club, and who had made conservation central to his political career would oppose making a reservoir in a national park.[62] They could not have been more wrong.

William Kent certainly believed in preserving land for recreation and sheer aesthetic value. For Kent, however, conservation meant finding the most efficient and the most democratic use of resources. In the case of Hetch-Hetchy, providing a municipally owned water and power source for San Francisco while at the same time creating a lake in the dry Sierra foothills represented, in Kent's words, "the highest sort of conservation."[63]

Kent noted the arguments of those who opposed the reservoir. He decided, finally, that because the project affected only a tiny corner of Yosemite and that because a reservoir could also provide recreation and aesthetic enjoyment, their arguments were simply selfish. Kent went as far as to call the opposition to Hetch-Hetchy the work of "misinformed nature lovers" and to describe John Muir as "a man entirely without social sense."[64]

Because he believed he was upholding the ideal of conservation, by 1913 Kent was one of the key supporters of the Hetch-Hetchy Dam. He helped draft the Raker Bill, which permitted San Francisco to build the reservoir, making sure that the language of the bill specifically forbade the city from selling power to a private company. Kent's position on the House Committee on Public Lands helped him guide the bill through the legislative process. In addition, Kent's Washington home became a headquarters for supporters of the Raker Bill.[65]

Kent resented "the criticism that we who stand for this bill are opposed to conservation." He explained that "as a nature lover and a conservationist I certainly believe that this bill is the highest and best type of conservation."[66] Kent believed that both conservation and progressivism aimed to improve human lives by allowing every American to reap the benefits that progress had brought. Hetch-Hetchy presented a perfect example of progressive action. This opportunity, of course, could only be obtained at the cost of destroying a chunk of spectacular wilderness and by invading a national park. In Kent's view, this was a necessary compromise, and "conservation demands that I do my duty and try to help rather than hinder such a worthy project."[67]

Many Americans seemed to agree with Kent's assessment. The fact that well-known conservationists such as William Kent, Theodore Roosevelt, and Gifford Pinchot supported the bill made it difficult to create opposition. Samuel Bowles, the influential editor, reflected a common response when he turned down Robert Underwood Johnson's plea to oppose the Hetch-Hetchy. Bowles wrote that "we were naturally earnest supporters of the effort to preserve the Yosemite." But, he confessed, he was "much impressed by the arguments in support of the bill . . . and by the fact that such strong conservationists as Congressman William Kent . . . have favored the San Francisco bill."[68] Bowles's response was typical, and consistent, for someone struggling to support both conservation and progressive ideals. Finally, after long and bitter debate, Congress passed the Hetch-Hetchy Bill. President Wilson signed it into law on December 19, 1913.

Wilson, Kent, and others who considered themselves conservationists believed they had done the right thing. Certainly, preserving a beautiful piece of Yosemite National Park was important, but providing water and power to millions of people represented a more practical sort of progress. Few Americans in 1913 saw the need to preserve wilderness for its own sake. Even those who advocated preservation justified their stand by saying that humans needed wilderness. The notion of the rights of nature, put forth by John Muir and a few others, would not be discussed on a wide basis for several decades. For Kent, and for most conservationists in the early twentieth century, conservation was intended to improve the human condition—sometimes by preserving land and sometimes by using it.[69]

William Kent's stand on Hetch-Hetchy is consistent with the rest of his career. His interests in protecting water power sites from private development, in using the public domain rationally, and in creating more national parks and a national park service all represent facets of the human-centered conservation that characterized the late nineteenth and early twentieth centuries. In fact, Kent's views on Hetch-Hetchy were not very different from the views of those who opposed building the dam. It was simply a matter of choosing how to use the land to improve the lives of Americans: should it be preserved as wilderness to reinvigorate tired urbanites, or should it be turned into a lake to provide them with water, electricity, and recreation? Throughout his career, William Kent would make these choices again and again.

Though he had made considerable contributions to the progressive agenda in conservation, Kent left Congress in 1917. He retired because of his frustration with campaign politics and with the minute concerns of his congressional district. He hoped to be appointed to the Federal Trade Commission, where he could work on a more rational system of distribution and regulation of national resources. President Wilson, however, appointed him to the Tariff Commission instead, a job he accepted but despised because of its wartime limitations.[70]

Disgusted with the conservatism bred by World War I, and the narrow concerns of the wartime Congress, Kent told his friends that retiring from Congress had been the worst mistake of his life. As his wife wrote to a friend, "Will has been turned down so many times lately in his efforts to do things with this administration that he's lost faith in his ability to accomplish things here."[71] Kent decided to run for Senate as a Republican in the 1920 election. He timed this decision poorly, given the postwar political climate. Kent's stands on nationalizing resources and his support of free speech during the war put off conservative Californians. The Republican party had a hard time supporting a candidate who had been an independent and a close friend of Democrat Woodrow Wilson. Kent lost the primary and retired from elective politics.[72]

Kent continued to be active in California conservation issues after his retirement. His choice of issues reflected his broad and flexible definition of conservation. Water power, public control of resources, protection of beautiful pieces of land, and the creation of state and national parks all occupied his time.

Almost immediately upon returning to Kentfield, Kent served as the chairman of the campaign committee to get a California Water and Power Act passed. The act would authorize state-controlled dams and power plants that would make the state self-sufficient in providing itself with water and electric power—a progressive and conservationist's dream. Private water and power companies found this proposal threatening and warned voters that they would be saddled "with a crushing burden of debt."[73] California voters rejected the bill by an enormous margin. Bitterly disappointed, Kent wrote to a friend that people must be suffering from "temporary dementia."[74]

Kent had more success in other areas. He had long been interested in preserving California's coastal redwoods. In 1908 he had created Muir Woods, in 1913 he had introduced a resolution to create Redwood National Park, and in 1918 he became a founding member of the Save-the-Redwoods League. Kent's efforts in this organization demonstrate his conception of how conservation should work. He did not want to preserve all the redwoods, only small stands that seemed especially attractive and that could be made accessible to the public. The other trees should be managed scientifically, grown and harvested like any other crop. The Save-the-Redwoods League convinced lumber companies and wealthy philanthropists to donate pieces of land with the goal of creating a long strip of publicly managed woods along the new Redwood Highway. Kent gave large sums to the cause, urged his influential friends to do the same, and worked hard to establish public campgrounds and roads in the region.[75]

Even though his health began to fail after a series of strokes in the late 1920s, Kent continued his efforts to make sure that American resources were used to benefit people in the most efficient manner. Making the region around Mt. Tamalpais a national park and preventing the Pacific Gas and Electric Company from getting its hands on the power produced by Hetch-Hetchy continued to be important issues for Kent. He failed on both fronts; but a few hours before he died, on March 13, 1928, he managed to donate another large chunk of land to be attached to Muir Woods.[76]

Kent's version of conservation, based on human needs, allowed for a wide variety of stands, which do not always seem consistent with late-twentieth-century ideas about what conservation should be. But his career tells us a lot about what conservation meant at the turn of the century and about the context in which it developed. Conservation evolved out of the progressive notion of improving human lives; and, according to the progressives, such improvement came with education, efficiency, and wise use. In this context, William Kent's views on land and other resources make sense and reveal him as a progressive and a conservationist.

NOTES

1. George E. Mowry, *The California Progressives* (Berkeley: University of California Press, 1951), 1–22.
2. Ibid., 87–104.
3. Robert L. Woodbury, "William Kent: Progressive Gadfly, 1864–1928" (Ph.D. diss, Yale University, 1967), 1–22; Elizabeth Thacher Kent, "Biography of William Kent," typescript, 1949, 1, and "William Kent, Independent: A Biography," typescript, 1950, 13–14, both in Bancroft Library, University of California, Berkeley; William Kent, *Reminiscences of Outdoor Life* (San Francisco: A. M. Robertson, 1929), 3.
4. Woodbury, "William Kent," 20–32; Elizabeth Kent, "Biography," 2.
5. Woodbury, "William Kent," 23–36; Elizabeth Kent, "Biography," 2–6.
6. Elizabeth Kent, "Biography," 2–3; Woodbury, "William Kent," 61–63, 75–84.
7. Woodbury, "William Kent," 97–105.
8. William Kent, "Practical Politics," September 13, 1896, in *Speeches of William Kent*, Bancroft Library.
9. Woodbury, "William Kent," 105, 119–20; Mowry, *California Progressives*, 121.
10. Kent to Elizabeth Kent, April 27, 1906, William Kent Papers, Beinecke Library, Yale University; Elizabeth Kent, "William Kent, Independent," 103–4.
11. William Kent to Phelan, April 26, 1906, box 65, James D. Phelan Papers, Bancroft Library.
12. Woodbury, "William Kent," 167–68; Elizabeth Kent, "William Kent, Independent," 168; Mowry, *California Progressives*, 34–37; Denman Report, Kent Papers. See Walter Bean, *Boss Ruef's San Francisco: The Story of the Union Labor Party, Big Business, and the Graft Prosecution* (Berkeley: University of California Press, 1952), for a description of the graft trials.
13. William Kent, "Federal Control," July 23, 1914, and "Need and Waste and the Problem of the Unemployed," May 21, 1910, in *Speeches of William Kent*, Bancroft Library.
14. Woodbury, "William Kent," 252–54.
15. For a discussion of the differences between Muir and Pinchot, see Roderick Nash, *Wilderness and the American Mind*, 3rd ed. (New Haven, Conn.: Yale University Press, 1982) 134–38.
16. William Kent to Anne Martin, December 13, 1918, box 3, Anne Martin Papers, Bancroft Library.
17. William Kent, "Tamalpais as a National Park: An Address by William Kent," 1903, n.p., 1–2, Bancroft Library.

18. Elizabeth Kent, "Biography," 3; Elizabeth Kent, "William Kent, Independent," 180.

19. Theodore Roosevelt to William Kent, January 22, 1908, Roger Kent Papers, Bancroft Library.

20. Quoted in Elizabeth Kent, "William Kent, Independent," 183.

21. Elizabeth Kent, "William Kent, Independent," 188.

22. Elmo Richardson, *The Politics of Conservation: Crusades and Controversies, 1897–1913* (Berkeley: University of California Press, 1962), 121; Woodbury, "William Kent," 169–70. Of the vast literature on the Ballinger-Pinchot affair, Richardson's *Politics of Conservation* seems to me to be the most complete.

23. William Kent to Taft, June 22, 1909, William Howard Taft Papers, Library of Congress (microfilm edition).

24. William Kent to William Washburn, September 13, 1909, William Kent Papers.

25. George Wharton James, *The Lake of the Sky: Lake Tahoe* (Boston: L. C. Page & Co., 1915), 354; Douglas H. Strong, *Tahoe: An Environmental History* (Lincoln: University of Nebraska Press, 1984), 99–102; Donald J. Pisani, "Conflict over Conservation: The Reclamation Service and the Tahoe Contract," *Western Historical Quarterly* 10 (April 1979): 170–75.

26. Pisani, "Conflict over Conservation," 178–79; Elizabeth Kent, "William Kent, Independent," 319–20; Woodbury, "William Kent," 171.

27. Pisani, "Conflict over Conservation," 179–80; William Kent to Charles D. Norton, August 18, 1909, William Kent Papers.

28. Chester Rowell to William Kent, January 12, 1910, Chester Rowell Papers, Bancroft Library.

29. Woodbury, "William Kent," 176–77; Mowry, *California Progressives*, 120; Rowell to William Kent, April 20, 1910, Rowell Papers.

30. San Francisco *Bulletin*, August 18, 1910.

31. William Kent and Gifford Pinchot, "Speeches delivered at the Cluny Opera House, Sacramento, July 20, 1910," Bancroft Library; Speech at Tamalpais Center, May 21, 1910, Kent Papers.

32. Woodbury, "William Kent," 186–90; Lincoln Steffens to Fremont Older, May 20, 1910, box 2, Fremont Older Papers, Bancroft Library; "William Kent for Congress from California," *LaFollette's Weekly Magazine* 2 (May 28, 1910): 4.

33. Richardson, *Politics of Conservation*, 125–26; Elizabeth Kent, "William Kent, Independent," 213; Kent and Pinchot, "Speeches."

34. See E. Louise Peffer, *The Closing of the Public Domain* (Stanford, Calif.: Stanford University Press, 1951), for western attitudes toward public lands.

35. Woodbury, "William Kent," 202–3.

36. Ibid., 211–12; William Kent to Hiram Johnson, August 25, 1911, Part II, box 18, Hiram Johnson Papers, Bancroft Library.

37. William Kent to Chester Rowell, January 16, 1911, Rowell Papers; William Kent to Hiram Johnson, January 16, 1911, Part II, box 18, Johnson Papers; Pisani, "Conflict over Conservation," 183–84; Richardson, *Politics of Conservation*, 110–11.

38. Mowry, *California Progressives*, 161–65, 189–90.

39. Mark Sullivan, "Comment on Congress," *Collier's* 49 (August 31, 1912): 12.

40. Chester Rowell to Hiram Johnson, November 21, 1913, Rowell Papers.

41. Woodbury, "William Kent," 223–24; William Kent to Phelan, November 11, 1912, box 65, Phelan Papers; Elizabeth Kent, "William Kent, Independent," 189.

42. John Ise, *Our National Park Policy: A Critical History* (Baltimore: Johns Hopkins University Press, 1961), 190; Donald C. Swain, *Wilderness Defender: Horace Albright and Conservation* (Chicago: University of Chicago Press, 1970), 56–59.

43. Arthur S. Link, *Wilson: The New Freedom* (Princeton, N.J.: Princeton University Press, 1956), 126–27; Elizabeth Kent, "William Kent, Independent," 265–66; Woodbury, "William Kent," 259–61.

44. Woodbury, "William Kent," 270–78; Link, *Wilson*, 128.

45. William Kent, *Reminiscences*, 100.

46. Woodbury, "William Kent," 265–66; William Kent, "Federal Control of Water Power," House of Representatives, July 23, 1914, in *Speeches of William Kent*.

47. Woodbury, "William Kent," 265–66; William Kent, "Federal Control."

48. Wilson to Kent (1914), quoted in Elizabeth Kent, "William Kent, Independent," 266.

49. Link, *Wilson*, 131–32.

50. For the standard interpretation see Nash, *Wilderness and the American Mind;* Holway R. Jones, *John Muir and the Sierra Club: The Battle for Yosemite* (San Francisco: Sierra Club, 1965); Ise, *Our National Park Policy;* Samuel Hays, *Conservation and the Gospel of Efficiency: The Progressive Conservation Movement* (Cambridge, Mass.: Harvard University Press, 1959).

51. Jones, *John Muir*, 83–88.

52. Quoted in Jones, *John Muir*, 88.

53. George D. Duraind, "Plan of the Life Story of James D. Phelan, Mayor of San Francisco and Senator from California," unpublished typescript, 4 vols., 2: 41, Phelan Papers; Michael L. Smith, *Pacific Visions: California Scientists and the Environment, 1850–1915* (New Haven, Conn.: Yale University Press, 1987), 174; Jones, *John Muir*, 89–90.

54. Nash, *Wilderness and the American Mind*, 161; Richardson, *Politics of Conservation*, 44.

55. Jones, *John Muir*, 94–95; John Muir to Robert Underwood Johnson, September 2, 1907, box 4, Robert Underwood Johnson Papers, Bancroft Library.

56. For descriptions of the Hetch-Hetchy fight in these terms, see Jones, *John Muir;* Nash, *Wilderness and the American Mind;* and Ise, *Our National Park Policy.*

57. Michael Smith, *Pacific Visions*, 179–81, makes an interesting argument about the "genderizing" of the issue from the very start. Muir and his supporters were described as "hysterical," as using "verbal lingerie and frills," while Pinchot and Kent were viewed as solid, practical men of science.

58. Gifford Pinchot to Johnson, April 23, 1908, box 5, Johnson Papers; William Loeb (TR's secretary) to Johnson, April 22, 1908, box 3, Johnson Papers.

59. Michael P. Cohen, *The History of the Sierra Club, 1892–1970* (San Francisco: Sierra Club, 1988), 24–26; Nash, *Wilderness and the American Mind*, 171.

60. Smith, *Pacific Visions*, 175–76; Kendrick A. Clements, "Engineers and Conservationists in the Progressive Era," *California History* 58 (Winter 1980): 297–99.

61. Whitney to Johnson, November 12, 1909, box 6, Johnson Papers.

62. Nash, *Wilderness and the American Mind*, 172–73; Woodbury, "William Kent," 258.

63. William Kent to Sydney Anderson, July 13, 1913, William Kent Papers.

64. William Kent to Sydney Anderson, July 2, 1913, William Kent Papers.

65. Nash, *Wilderness and the American Mind*, 174–75; Woodbury, "William Kent," 259–60; Elizabeth Kent, "William Kent, Independent," 325–26.

66. William Kent, Senate Hearings, September 24, 1913, quoted in San Francisco *Examiner*, December 2, 1913.

67. *Congressional Record* 50 (August 31, 1913): 3963.

68. Samuel Bowles to Johnson, November 1, 1913, box 1, Johnson Papers.

69. See Susan R. Schrepfer, *The Fight to Save the Redwoods: A History of Environmental Reform, 1917–1978* (Madison: University of Wisconsin Press, 1983); and Samuel Hays, *Beauty, Health and Permanence: Environmental Politics in the United States, 1955–1985* (New York: Cambridge University Press, 1987), for a discussion of the changing conceptions of the role of the environment.

70. Woodbury, "William Kent," 285–86.

71. Ibid.; Elizabeth Kent to Anne Martin, December 17, 1919, box 3, Martin Papers.

72. Woodbury, "William Kent," 316–25.

73. "Kent Urges Water Power Measure Support," San Francisco *Examiner*, October 19, 1924; "The Most Dangerous Proposition," San Francisco *Chronicle*, October 31, 1924.

74. William Kent to Peter Crosby, September 28, 1922, box 18, Rowell Papers.

75. Schrepfer, *Fight to Save the Redwoods*, 12–20; Samuel Blythe, "The Last Stand of the Giants," *Saturday Evening Post* 192 (December 6, 1919): 153; Madison Grant, "Saving the Redwoods," *National Geographic* 37 (June 1920): 527; William Kent to Newton Drury, September 8, 1921, March 28, 1923, box 1, Save-the-Redwoods League Papers, Bancroft Library.

76. Elizabeth Kent, "William Kent, Independent," 416–17.

Neither Friends nor Foes

Organized Labor and
the California Progressives

Mary Ann Mason

A generation ago, the elusive relationship between the progressives and labor in California was the subject of a lively scholarly debate. Almost without exception, historians separated into two camps: those who studied progressive leaders, particularly Hiram Johnson, through their behavior and what others said about them, and those who studied the voters who supported progressive politicians, especially Hiram Johnson, through voting statistics. Not surprisingly, given the disparity in focus and methodology of these two groups, their findings were almost in complete opposition to one another. The first group in the main asserted that labor and the progressives were on uneasy if not hostile terms, while the second group concluded that labor formed the progressives' most enthusiastic and dependable block of support.

The leader of the first camp was undeniably George Mowry, who in his ground-breaking work, *The California Progressives*, developed a model of the progressive mentality in California.[1] That model has served as the focus of the debate and was widely used as a model for national progressivism as well. Investigating a variety of state leaders, with a special focus on Hiram Johnson, Mowry described the progressives as predominantly urban, native-born, high-status Protestants from the established, independent middle classes. He asserted that they had no love for labor. They nostalgically defended an individualistic ethic and feared that capital and labor, in the form of trusts and unions, would introduce class conflict and overthrow traditional morality.

Mowry also maintained that union labor was not cordial to progressivism. In the 1910 primary, Johnson's weakest vote was in San Francisco and its surrounding counties, the stronghold of union labor. Mowry admitted that the progressives passed some labor legislation, but he claimed that by 1914 their desultory interest in social and industrial justice had died, and thus no further significant labor legislation was enacted. Although his work is provocative, Mowry failed to explain why, if Johnson and most of the other progressives were cool to labor and if labor reciprocated these feelings, this period represents the most fruitful era for labor legislation in California's history. Over one hundred pieces of labor legislation were passed between 1911 and 1915—including such milestones as the Workmen's Compensation Act, the eight-hour day for women, an Industrial Safety Commission, and the establishment of a free employment office.

Reexamining the question along the guidelines set by Mowry, others, notably Spencer Olin, have found the relationship of labor and the progressives to be more harmonious, but they generally accept Mowry's basic assumptions regarding the progressive mentality.[2] Still other studies, however, focusing almost entirely on voter statistics rather than progressive leaders, point out that the labor vote, in fact, became the primary source of Hiram Johnson's strength after 1910. These studies more or less completely reverse Mowry's analysis and speculate, on the basis of their statistics, that organized labor became the self-conscious core of progressive strength after 1910.

In one of the most interesting of these statistical efforts, Michael Rogin analyzed the change in the voting pattern between 1910 and 1916. He found that initially Johnson's strongest support was in Southern California, particularly the rural communities, but that by 1916 the San Francisco area had been transformed from Johnson's weak spot to his area of greatest strength. The most dramatic shift within this general trend occurred among San Francisco's workers. Why? Because once in power, the progressives passed an incredible amount of labor legislation in the 1911 session, thus nurturing the gratitude of the working classes while somewhat alienating the rural elements. In spite of this change in the power base, the language of the progressives, Rogin concludes, remained " 'classless,' oriented toward moral virtue and fearful of conflict." He suggests that this alliance between labor and reformers, at least in California, indicates that workers may also have been fearful of class conflict and rallied to an ideology that later became the base for the New Deal middle class–labor coalition.[3]

This nicely drawn controversy about the role of labor was largely sub-verted by the next generation of historians, who became preoccupied with determining whether progressives could, in fact, be considered a coherent movement in sociological and ideological terms. As Daniel Rodgers observed in his 1982 review essay, "Only by discarding the mis-taken assumption of a coherent reform movement could one see the pro-gressives' world for what it really was: an era of shifting, ideologically fluid, issue-focused coalitions, all competing for the reshaping of Amer-ican society."[4]

Undaunted by what seemed to be the total deconstruction of progres-sivism, recent scholars have once again taken up the old questions in essentially the old terms. Retreating to the Mowry-Olin tradition of de-picting the progressives as middle-class reformers committed to abolish-ing class conflict, Michael Kazin looked at the relationship between pro-gressives and labor from the point of view of the San Francisco Building Trades. Kazin took the high ideological road, proclaiming that these union members were not simply American Federation of Labor–style business unionists but, rather, had faith in a larger, although not clearly articulated, class consciousness. Kazin asserted that these unionists failed to act on their radical beliefs mainly because they had been in-fluenced by progressive officeholders and their concept of a "classless so-ciety." "By embracing the [James] Rolphs and [Hiram] Johnsons, labor blurred the political lines and diluted the program that made it an al-ternative force to be reckoned with. But when the reform wave receded and organized business turned hostile, labor activists found themselves isolated. Having jettisoned the class combativeness of old, they could not convincingly revive it."[5]

Thomas Clark, on the other hand, following directly in the Rogin tra-dition of examining working-class voting statistics, tested Rogin's the-ory on San Francisco working-class neighborhoods. While maintaining a cautious reserve about attempting to classify a "progressive" world-view, Clark examined working-class votes for all candidates who ran as progressives between 1912 and 1916; he also examined over one hun-dred propositions that came before San Francisco voters during these years. With this larger focus, Clark found distinctly different patterns from those found by Rogin, and he contradicted Kazin's hypothesis as well. He did not find, as they did, that labor was particularly supportive of progressive candidates and issues; rather, he found that, "as a group Progressives fared no better among working-class voters than any other party: and to the extent that one can speak of "progressive" propositions, working-class voters—like everyone else—were most likely to vote according to what appeared to be in their best interest."[6]

Although Kazin and Clark are, I believe, moving in the right direction by turning the old controversy on its head and viewing it from the point of view of labor rather than that of the progressives, they fall short of seeing organized labor as a dynamic entity that successfully initiated and pushed through its own agenda. They have assumed that labor simply responded to progressive actions; and they fail to recognize adequately the complicated maneuvering engineered by organized labor, bargaining with the strength of its solid San Francisco voting bloc. In many instances, labor did not respond to progressives; progressives responded to labor.

The relationship between the progressives and labor can perhaps best be illuminated by a careful examination of organized labor—its organization, its tactics, and its attitude toward progressive legislators in general and Hiram Johnson in particular. In some important ways, these are two different stories, since Hiram Johnson enjoyed a special relationship with organized labor not shared by other progressives. By 1911 California labor had one of the strongest and most effective state federations in the country; its membership of 45,000 represented 267 unions. The core of the state federation's strength was San Francisco, whose Labor Council founded the state organization in 1901, when that city held a national reputation as the most unionized city in America. Indeed, throughout the Progressive Era the federation was dominated by San Francisco unions, both in numbers and in leadership.[7] The southern part of California had not begun to achieve the level of industrialization or unionization that prevailed in the Bay Area, and, in fact, Los Angeles was the focus of a massive "open-shop" campaign during most of the Progressive Era.

From the California state federation's beginnings, its leadership was moderate and nonideological. Walter Macarthur, Andrew Furuseth, and Paul Scharrenberg—all from the San Francisco–based Sailors Union of the Pacific, the largest union in California—dominated the organization during its first years. The main tenets of this organization were that of business unionism: get the best deal for labor that you can within the system, and at election time "elect your friends and defeat your enemies." This philosophy did not require hostility to groups of a more radical persuasion. The state federation had a friendly working relationship with the Socialists, who had become something of a minor force in the Bay Area by 1911. And before the 1920s, the federation leadership was sympathetic to the Industrial Workers of the World as well. The federation strongly supported a pardon for Blackie Ford and Herman Suhr in the 1911 Wheatland murder episode, took a major supportive role in the 1910 trial of the McNamara brothers (indicted for bombing the *Los Angeles Times* building), and later was among the few early defenders of Tom Mooney and Warren Billings in the 1916 Preparedness Day bombing incident.[8]

By 1910, when Johnson was first elected governor, the state federation had focused its efforts on legislation in Sacramento and had developed a well-oiled lobbying machine headed by Paul Scharrenberg. He and an assistant set up headquarters in Sacramento and coordinated the activities of the labor lobbyists from the San Francisco Labor Council, the State Building Trades Council, and the Joint Legislative Board of the Railroad Brotherhoods of California. This group pooled its resources for the mandated purpose of investigating proposed legislation, formulating bills, furnishing legislators with information on the bills they should push, and compiling the voting records of the legislators on labor bills. By 1911, there were enough labor lobbyists in Sacramento to have a labor representative at every meeting of the committees of both houses.[9]

In 1912 Scharrenberg more formally united the four lobbying groups in a legislative conference whose chief function became the joint publication and circulation of pamphlets containing information on political candidates' attitudes toward labor issues. To ascertain these attitudes, the lobbyists sent out a questionnaire in 1912, but it proved unsatisfactory. Therefore, by 1913 Scharrenberg had begun a systematic publication of the legislators' voting record. This method was highly distrusted by legislators, who looked on it as blacklisting. Even the San Francisco Labor Council was divided over the use of this tactic, and dissidents within the council complained that the end result was a one-man record, referring to the compiler of the statistics, Scharrenberg.[10] Whatever the ethical merit of this technique, the resulting vote tallies—which were first published in complete form after the 1913 session and thereafter following the end of each session—provide an interesting study of exactly who did vote for labor legislation.[11]

Next to the 1911 session, the 1913 legislative session was considered by labor to be the most favorable in its history. The 1913 labor voting record shows that in a Republican-dominated legislature there was no

62 Mary Ann Mason

TABLE 1
VOTING RECORD OF THE 1913 LEGISLATURE
ON TWENTY-EIGHT BILLS FAVORED BY LABOR

	No. Who Voted for Half or More of the Bills	No. Who Voted against Half or More of the Bills
Senate		
Republicans	14	16
Democrats	5	5
Assembly		
Republicans	34	21
Democrats	14	10
Socialists	1	

significant partisan bloc (see table 1). There was a slight Republican edge, but this cannot be counted as a progressive advantage, since progressives were found in both parties.

In 1915 a proliferation of amalgamated party designations appeared, with an ecumenical tendency to combine old party labels—indicating a trend away from traditional single-party divisions and a new categorization along progressive and non-progressive lines. Since the primary election system allowed cross-filing in any party, this nomenclature was designed to win votes from all sides. For instance, this addition led to a listing where a legislator might be represented by as many as four titles (e.g., Progressive, Republican, Democratic, Prohibitionist). The listing could be awkward, but for the purposes of deciding who considered himself progressive, it is most useful, because self-identified progressives embraced nonpartisanship and rejected single-party dictates.

The 1915 session was also a triumph for labor. Only with the 1917 legislature did labor's good fortunes decline. An examination of the voting behavior of those bearing progressive nametags in the 1915 and 1917 legislatures shows a significant majority (averaging around 75 percent) favoring labor legislation (see table 2). By contrast, the balance for the non-progressives is almost reversed, with a relatively small percent (averaging 30 percent) voting for labor legislation in the 1915 legislature, although there is a more even distribution in that of 1917 (42 percent).

At first glance these statistics appear to bear out the hypothesis that progressives were increasingly currying the favor of the labor bloc. This seems especially true in the Senate, where the percentage rises markedly, from 71 percent in 1915 to 89 percent in 1917. It is more difficult to analyze the situation in the Assembly, since the total number of those who

TABLE 2
NUMBERS OF PROGRESSIVES AND
NON-PROGRESSIVES (AS INDICATED BY THEIR
TITLES) VOTING FOR HALF OR MORE OF THE
BILLS FAVORED BY LABOR

	1915	1917
Senate		
Progressives	10 (71%)[a]	16 (89%)
Non-progressives	7 (29%)	8 (42%)
Assembly		
Progressives	22 (61%)	10 (82%)
Non-progressives	18 (32%)	33 (41%)

[a]Numbers in parentheses indicate percentage of total progressives or non-progressives.

called themselves progressives declined drastically (from 34 percent of the full Assembly to 12 percent).

A close examination of the voting record, however, indicates that it is not the political bloc of progressivism but the regional representation from San Francisco that is contributing the consistent support to labor legislation. An analysis of the legislatures of 1913, 1915, and 1917 reveals that the San Francisco delegation provided an almost solid battering ram for labor legislation: of the twenty legislators (ten in each house) who supported the most labor bills, more than half were from San Francisco, providing a major percentage of the total support (38 percent in the Senate, 24 percent in the Assembly). (See table 3.)

Even more significantly, when the San Francisco progressive votes are separated out from the total progressive vote on labor legislation, it becomes clear that, with one exception (the Senate in 1917), the progressive majority has been supplied by the San Francisco bloc. Without this bloc the progressives would have done no better than the non-progressives on labor legislation (see table 4). Such voting data indicate that, as far as labor legislation is concerned, the ideological category is far less important than the regional one. Organized labor recognized that fact. As chief lobbyist Scharrenberg observed after the 1913 session: "We repeat without fear of contradiction our assertion of two years ago that from labor's point of view, there were genuine progressives and real reactionaries among the three dominant political parties. In fact, party lines were almost entirely eliminated in passing or defeating 'labor bills.' "[12]

TABLE 3
VOTING RECORD OF SAN FRANCISCO
LEGISLATORS ON BILLS FAVORED BY LABOR

	1913	1915	1917
Senate: San Francisco Senators			
No. in top ten statewide supporters	5	5	4
No. who voted for half or more of the bills	6	7	6
No. who voted against half or more of the bills	0	0	1
% of total "yes" votes	32%	41%	42%
Assembly: San Francisco Assemblymen			
No. in top ten statewide supporters	7	4	7
No. who voted for half or more of the bills	11	9	10
No. who voted against half or more of the bills	1	3	3
% of total "yes" votes	22%	25%	26%

TABLE 4
VOTING RECORD OF SAN FRANCISCO LEGISLATORS
WITH "PROGRESSIVE" IN THEIR TITLES

	No. Who Voted for Half or More of the Bills, 1915	No. Who Voted for Half or More of the Bills, 1917
Senate	5 (50%)[a]	4 (25%)
Assembly	6 (22%)	4 (40%)

[a]Numbers in parentheses indicate percent of entire progressive vote.

The combined labor lobby worked diligently to elect legislators who would support labor. At election time, beginning in 1913, the labor leadership distributed among union members the carefully compiled labor record of each legislator and solicited a statement on labor from each candidate.[13] In the legislature, however, the main tactic was to bargain: labor leaders offered legislators the vote of the San Francisco bloc on their "pet bills" in exchange for their support of measures that interested labor. As Scharrenberg recalled: "I learned you could always get a bright young man if you knew or learned to know what his pet bill was. Then you would go to him and say: 'I understand that you have such and such a bill.' And he would say, 'Oh yes.' 'Well I'm interested in that bill. Maybe I can help you on it.' Before the meeting was over I'd have him all lashed up by a promise that I'd get the San Francisco boys to vote for his bill and he'd vote for mine."[14]

At that time San Francisco had thirteen or fourteen assemblymen and seven senators. Since the city was the stronghold of unionism in the state, if not the country, organized labor had close control over this group, both through the efficient use of the published *Labor Record* and by persistent personal pressure. This policy was clearly in line with the state federation's stated policy of "reward your friends and defeat your enemies."

George Mowry in *The California Progressives* agrees that labor controlled the San Francisco delegation and cites progressive columnist Chester Rowell's description of the situation: "On labor issues they would vote the way Paul Scharrenberg, San Francisco labor leader, directed: on moral questions [temperance] they would listen to the Royal Arch, the liquor leaders' association, but on all remaining items they were at the service of the administration."[15]

Although the record indicates that progressives in general did support labor legislation, the friendship of the progressive leader, Hiram Johnson, was immeasurably important to labor from 1911 through 1915. Most analysts have tended to confuse the relationship of Johnson to labor with the more complicated issue of labor and the progressive movement.

What was organized labor's attitude toward Johnson? Was the overwhelming Johnson labor vote in 1914 a direct response to his legislative programs, particularly the all-important Workmen's Compensation Act—perhaps the most important piece of state legislation passed during the progressive years? To a certain extent, the answer is "yes," but the situation is clearly a complicated one. As a San Francisco lawyer, Hiram Johnson had served as the attorney for the Teamsters' Union and had made many friends among union leaders in San Francisco. According to Scharrenberg, the secretary of the Teamsters' Union tried to round up the traditionally Democratic labor support for Johnson in 1910. Scharrenberg claims: "I swung in line and so did all the leaders but the rank and file in the labor districts, they were Democrats, and they couldn't just switch over because some new guy appeared on the horizon had said, 'Here, vote for me.' "[16]

Moreover, Johnson's 1910 gubernatorial campaign was not aimed directly at the labor vote—taking the form, as it did, of a holy crusade against the Southern Pacific Railroad. The more specific proposals of his inaugural address, however, did include many items that were close to labor's heart. He mentioned not only an employer's liability law (later called the Workmen's Compensation Act) but also the initiative, referendum, and recall—issues that were not generally recognized labor concerns but had long been promoted by labor. Labor's support for these democratic proposals was prompted by the belief that with these measures organizations such as unions, that could turn out votes, could compete against large amounts of corporate money on the legislative scene.

Once the Workmen's Compensation Act was passed in 1911, the rank-and-file members followed their leaders in rushing into an ardent, if a bit one-sided, love affair with Johnson. Labor's gains were so spectacular in the first session of the Johnson administration, with the passage of thirty-nine out of a possible forty-nine bills, that the state federation greatly praised the governor and declared: "The thirty-ninth session laid the foundation for the regeneration of the state government in the interest of the people at large."[17]

In 1913 a law was passed which rendered the Workmen's Compensation Act compulsory, rather than voluntary, and set up a State Compensation Insurance Fund with an appropriation of $100,000 to pay for claims. The state federation expressed its special thanks to Johnson: "Throughout the fight the governor lent his special assistance to the measure."[18]

Although the state federation's lobbying activities and close control of the San Francisco bloc were undoubtedly the chief factors in the successful passage of legislation, the governor's influence and his veto power were key elements as well. The importance of the veto is illustrated by the history of the fight to repeal a law that made it a misdemeanor to entice a seaman to desert his vessel. This law, which had strong labor support, had been passed by both the 1907 and 1909 sessions of the legislature but was vetoed by a governor who was no friend of labor. Part of the reason that so much labor legislation was passed in the 1911 session is that many of these previously thwarted bills were allowed clear sailing by the newly elected Johnson.[19]

From labor's point of view, there was also a negative side to Johnson—as can be seen in his response to perhaps the single but crucial piece of labor legislation of which he did not approve: the anti-injunction bill. Organized labor's greatest disappointment in 1911 was the defeat of that proposal. This measure stipulated that no court could issue a labor injunction except under extraordinary circumstances. This bill also prohibited employers and their workers from entering into an agreement stipulating that workers would not join a labor union. The measure recognized peaceful picketing as well as primary and secondary boycotts, and forbade yellow-dog contracts and the blacklist (the props of the open shop). The bill passed the Senate after a stormy twenty-hour session, and in spite of the opposition from open-shop Los Angeles, whose five progressive senators all voted against it. Business forces throughout the state were furious about Senate passage of the bill, and the conservative press could not think of strong enough epithets to fling at Johnson. Although the Assembly was generally more favorable to labor legislation, the measure was subjected to a long series of hostile parliamentary maneuvers and unexpectedly was not voted out of Judiciary Committee.

Apparently this defeat was engineered in the governor's office. Many years later Scharrenberg recalled the maneuverings that were kept from the public and from the rank and file of the labor movement at the time.

> Hiram went along with the labor programs, but he couldn't go for that one. He didn't make a public utterance, but he told me, "That's going too far," he said, "I can't see that." Well, but for policy's sake it wasn't very good to say that in the open, so between him and Al McCabe, who was his private secretary and manipulator, they lined up enough votes in the assembly, which was supposed to be ours, to kill the bill. That's how it really happened. It was killed from the office of the governor, not from anywhere else. We had the votes in there to put it over after we got it through the senate.[20]

This incident illustrates first that Johnson, if he wished, could muster forces to block labor-supported legislation, and, second, that although he was sympathetic to the state federation's programs and worked closely with its leaders, there were definite limits to his concern. The defeat of this bill also indicates that the leaders of the state federation were so concerned about maintaining Johnson's good graces that they did not reveal important information to their membership.

Los Angeles at this time was the site of a bitter and ultimately successful open-shop campaign, and its legislative delegation strongly supported business interests. The anti-injunction law seemed directly aimed at breaking that city's open-shop movement by giving legal sanction to strike activity. For all his sympathy with the labor movement, Johnson simply could not afford to alienate this important part of his constituency. After all, Los Angeles business interests had strongly supported him in 1910 when San Francisco labor did not. Ironically, in the first session after Johnson had left Sacramento to become a U.S. senator, the anti-injunction bill passed both houses, only to be pocket-vetoed by William Stephens, the new governor. Johnson had made sure that he did not have to perform such a public act.[21]

TABLE 5

VOTING RECORD OF SAN FRANCISCO
LEGISLATORS ON BILLS FAVORED BY LABOR, 1919

	No. Who Voted for Half or More of the Bills	No. Who Voted against Half or More of the Bills
Senate	7	1
Assembly	13	0

By 1917 the state federation declared that the "Progressive era of the Golden State has come to an end." Johnson, now a U.S. senator, had been replaced by the unsympathetic Stephens. The most serious reason for the reversal, however, was the newly energized open-shop movement. Spawned in Sacramento in 1915, this movement was called the Chamber of Commerce Law and Order Committee. By 1916 the committee had achieved significant support in San Francisco, Oakland, Los Angeles, Stockton, and smaller towns. The anti-union movement fed on the fear of radicals engendered by such incidents as the 1916 Preparedness Day bombing in San Francisco (which led to the imprisonment of Tom Mooney and Warren Billings). The committee amassed a million-dollar slush fund, which it used to promote various legislative policies, including the passage of a compulsory arbitration bill (opposed by labor), an anti-boycott proposal (also opposed by labor), and the destruction of the anti-injunction measure. The San Francisco bloc held firm, and the legislature defeated part of the Law and Order Committee's program; Governor Stephens's pocket veto meant that "the legislative program of the union busters" (to use Scharrenberg's words) did not receive "a clean knockout."[22]

By 1919 World War I and prohibition had eclipsed the interest of the legislature in labor issues, and the state federation itself, beginning to feel the pinch of the postwar union slump, was no longer as powerful a force as it had been. The San Francisco delegation remained pro-labor (see table 5), but little additional support was available. Labor's legislative salad days were definitely over.

With this analysis from the point of view of organized labor, progressivism takes on a new face. The image of the middle-class reformer benevolently helping the laboring classes gives way to the picture of a dynamic, organized labor lobby bargaining with a progressive-dominated legislature for important bills. From labor's perspective, the term *pro-*

gressive was redefined to mean all those who were friends of labor. The progressive and the labor programs were not, of course, completely at odds with each other. In fact, many of the major progressive reforms—such as the initiative, referendum, and recall—were eagerly sought after by organized labor as well. Although these reforms are not normally considered part of labor's demands, labor leaders, thinking in very practical terms, simply believed that such measures would strengthen their political clout. The Alien Land Act of 1913, designed to prevent Japanese competition, and the Commission on Immigration and Housing, empowered to supervise immigration to the state, also won labor support, probably for less than noble reasons. Labor in San Francisco was a major proponent of Asian exclusion. The Commission of Immigration and Housing, established in 1911, is a good example of the working relationship between labor and the progressives in nonlabor issues. Johnson's appointment of Scharrenberg to the committee was clearly designed to assuage labor, which had repeatedly managed to stall the bill, fearing that its purpose was to attract more immigrants to the state. In fact, the main concern of the commission's creator, the progressive politician Simon Lubin, was that the opening of the Panama Canal would introduce a flood of immigrants to California who previously would have gone to the eastern seaports. Since this threat did not materialize, Scharrenberg was then able to help turn the commission's attention toward an improvement of migrant workers' conditions.[23]

Organized labor, then, generally gained from progressive programs, but not because there was any strong progressive commitment to labor. Whatever the philosophical base of progressivism, whatever it was that united some people into a self-conscious reform movement, it was not a particular concern for workers. Nor is there evidence, on the other hand, that labor was attracted by the "classless rhetoric" of the progressives, any more than it was drawn by the IWW's or the Socialists' classless appeal. Both in their behavior and in their public utterances, labor leaders adopted the pragmatic business union maxim: support your friends and defeat your enemies. Friends of labor during this period included some progressives but by no means all. Hiram Johnson was a proven friend whose importance to labor should not be underestimated. More useful than either the progressives or Johnson, however, and the group most responsible for labor's gains in this period, was the bloc of San Francisco legislators.[24]

This analysis tells us more about the real workings of organized labor than it does about the elusive "progressives." For, in fact, from labor's point of view, the progressives were not the leaders; they were only the not entirely dependable supporters of labor's agenda. Thomas Clark's findings regarding labor's half-hearted support of progressive candidates and progressive issues in San Francisco support this observation. On the other hand, Kazin's portrayal of labor as seduced by the progressives with their claim of a society without class conflict is not very convincing, since organized labor actively orchestrated its own legislative victories, effectively bargaining for votes with the strength of its solid San Francisco bloc. With the exception of Hiram Johnson, labor regarded progressives as neither friends nor foes, but, rather, as potential votes to be secured.

NOTES

1. George Mowry, *The California Progressives* (Berkeley: University of California Press, 1951). See also, for example, Richard Hofstadter, *The Age of Reform: From Bryan to FDR* (New York: Knopf, 1955); and Henry May, *The End of American Innocence* (New York: Knopf, 1959).

2. Spencer C. Olin, Jr., *California's Prodigal Sons: Hiram Johnson and the Progressives, 1911–1917* (Berkeley: University of California Press, 1968).

3. Michael Rogin, "Progressivism and the California Electorate," *Journal of American History* 55 (September 1968): 297–314, quote on 314. See also Alexander Saxton, "San Francisco Labor and the Populist and Progressive Insurgencies," *Pacific Historical Review* 34 (November 1965): 421–38; and John L. Shover, "The Progressives and the Working Class Vote in California," *Labor History* 10 (Fall 1969): 584–602.

4. Daniel T. Rodgers, "In Search of Progressivism," *Reviews in American History* 10 (December 1982): 113–32, quote on 114. Among the leading debunkers of the progressive "myth" are John D. Buenker, *Urban Liberalism and Progressive Reform* (New York: Scribner's, 1973), who refuses to use the term *progressive*, except to describe the historical period chronologically; and Peter G. Filene, "An Obituary for the Progressive Movement," *American Quarterly* 22 (1970): 20–34, the title of which speaks for itself.

5. Michael Kazin, *Barons of Labor: The San Francisco Building Trades and Union Power in the Progressive Era* (Urbana: University of Illinois Press, 1987), 286.

6. Thomas Clark, "Labor and Progressivism South of the Slot," *California History* 71 (September 1987): 197–207, quote on 206.

7. Paul Scharrenberg, "History of the State Federation of Labor" (unpublished manuscript), Scharrenberg Collection, Bancroft Library, University of California, Berkeley; Robert Knight, *Industrial Relations in the San Francisco Bay Area* (Berkeley: University of California Press, 1960).

8. Scharrenberg, "History of the State Federation," passim; Richard Frost, *The Mooney Case* (Stanford, Calif.: Stanford University Press, 1968); Mary Ann Burki, "Paul Scharrenberg: White Shirt Sailor" (Ph.D. diss., University of Rochester, 1971).

9. California State Federation of Labor, *Proceedings* (Sacramento: California State Federation of Labor, 1911), 87:93.

10. San Francisco *Daily News*, July 3, 1915.

11. California State Federation of Labor, *Labor Record of Senators and Assemblymen* (Sacramento: California State Federation of Labor, 1913), hereafter cited as *Labor Record*.

12. *Labor Record*, 1913, 4.

13. *Labor Record*, 1913, 1915, 1917, 1919.

14. Paul Scharrenberg, "Reminiscences," 1955, taped interview, Bancroft Library, University of California, Berkeley.

15. Quoted in Mowry, *California Progressives*, 135.

16. Scharrenberg, "Reminiscences," 55.

17. *Labor Record*, 1913, 6–7.

18. Ibid., 7.

19. Philip Taft, *Labor Politics American Style* (Cambridge, Mass.: Harvard University Press, 1968), 45.

20. Scharrenberg, "Reminiscences," 54.

21. Knight, *Industrial Relations*, 319.

22. *Coast Seamen's Journal*, May 16, 1917; *Labor Record*, 1917, 4.

23. Scharrenberg, "Reminiscences," 67; see California Commission of Immigration and Housing, *Report* (Sacramento: California Commission, 1915–1917).

24. It is clear that more attention must be paid to the state and local labor organizations and their influence on politics. For the Progressive Era some of the useful works outside California are Irwin Yellowitz, *Labor and the Progressive Movement in New York State, 1887–1916* (Ithaca, N.Y.: Cornell University Press, 1965); J. Joseph Huthmacher, "Urban Liberalism and the Age of Reform," *Mississippi Valley Historical Review* 44 (September 1962): 231–41; Henry Beford, *Socialism and Workers in Massachusetts, 1886–1912* (Amherst: University of Massachusetts Press, 1966); and Frederick M. Heath, "The Progressive Movement in Connecticut" *Labor History* 12 (Winter 1971): 52–68. See also Gary M. Fink, *Labor's Search for Political Order: The Political Behavior of the Missouri Labor Movement, 1890–1940* (Columbia: University of Missouri Press, 1973); Barbara L. Musselman, "The Quest for Collective Improvement: Cincinnati Workers, 1893–1928" (Ph.D. diss., University of Cincinnati, 1975); James Weinstein, *The Decline of Socialism in America, 1912–1925* (New York: Monthly Reviews, 1967). These studies all indicate that the role of organized labor was a far more dynamic agent in progressive legislation than previously considered.

The Neglected Twin

California Democrats and the
Progressive Bandwagon

William Deverell

The chief difference between the Democratic and Republican
parties is that in the Republican party the reactionaries are
in the majority, whereas in the Democratic party they are in
the minority.

Woodrow Wilson, c. 1912

You must remember that in those days, and for some years
afterwards, the Republican nomination was equivalent to
election in this state, just the way a Democratic nomination
is equivalent to election in the South.

William Jarvis Carr, on the Progressive Era
in California

Pundits, journalists, politicians, and scholars dearly enjoy writing off the
modern Democratic party. Somehow the crazy 1968 Chicago convention marks an end to the party's once-strong Rooseveltian unity. And
there is much truth to the epitaphs of recent Democratic death, although
Bill Clinton may be the one to change all this. Be that as it may, recent
internal battles over nonissues and the ever present factionalization
between insurgents and old-school adherents have handicapped the
party's once obvious ability to win general elections. As many scholars
and commentators have pointed out, the Democratic party has simply
lost punch in the last several decades. Thomas Byrne Edsall and Mary
Edsall, in their recent book *Chain Reaction,* describe that decline
succinctly:

Under siege, the national Democratic party has, to a large degree, lost its creative strength. Alienated from the general electorate by racial polarization and by a values barrier, and deeply enmeshed in a network of special interests, the national party has faltered repeatedly over the past twenty-five years in its efforts to develop strategies and policies successful in winning back majority support.[1]

When we look back on the chronological brackets that embrace most of this book, roughly 1900 through 1920, the story seems strikingly similar. Lost somewhere between an end-of-the-century romance with William Jennings Bryan and eventual presidential success in the person of Woodrow Wilson, Democrats and their party seemed even in the early twentieth century to exhibit much of the now-familiar malaise. As Robert Wesser has recently written, "in many states . . . the Democracy seemingly did little to commend itself to the electorate." Democrats were viewed as "essentially obstructionist in their tactics, provincial in their outlook, and wrongheaded on the issues."[2]

Lost then, lost now: whether between Bryan (who of course never captured the presidency) and Wilson or between the Great Society and what has come after, the Democratic party has suffered odd periods of virtual unconsciousness. It seems light-years ago that, following Lyndon Johnson's 1964 presidential victory, people seriously considered that it was the Republican party that had died.

Thanks to the pioneering work of J. J. Huthmacher and others, we know of course that Progressive-Era Democrats not only existed but did subscribe to (if not construct) much of the progressive reform agenda.[3] There were important ties connecting urban bossism to strains of progressive reform, and many in-the-trenches social progressives of the first two decades of this century were the Democratic forebears of those New Dealers later sent into the cities by Franklin Roosevelt's federal programs.

Let us turn to California. This national story of apparent party decline and enervation is no less true on the Pacific Coast, again in reference to both the present and the past. California, in fact, as much of this book suggests, is an apt geographical subset of national political features. Both nationally and in California, the Democrats, unable to mount an effective challenge to Republican power, remain unfocused, seemingly unable to weave coalitions into blocs, hampered by liabilities that could be turned to strength. The party seems constitutionally unable to lessen the divisive effects of those glaring boundaries (especially visible, it seems, in California): ethnicity, class, race, geography. Socioeconomic and cultural cleavages have taken on the appearance of dangerous chasms, so deep and so frightening that even like-minded individuals and groups refuse to help one another navigate *party* terrain, much less the uneven ground of party-versus-party battles. Whether Bill Clinton's victory in November 1992 stitches up these Democratic party wounds is uncertain. The problems have already proved immense (though not, I would argue, insurmountable); moreover, as was evidenced in at least some displays of vociferous support for California's Jerry Brown, there is a Democratic constituency out there that seems willing to stir up party trouble, Clinton victory or no Clinton victory.

In the meantime, California runs hot and cold about exporting to Washington the next domino in the long line of conservative political pieces bred in the Far West. Coming of age simultaneous to the political apprenticeship of a young Richard Nixon and growing into maturity with Ronald Reagan's gubernatorial and presidential terms, the conservative California mind-set now looks (albeit skeptically) to the state's sitting governor as a leading candidate for 1996 Republican presidential anointment. Or perhaps Republican businessman Richard Riordan, newly elected mayor of Los Angeles, will catch the eye of his party's kingmakers. One is forced to ask: Where are the Democrats?

And what of California Democrats eighty and ninety years ago? What of far western urban liberalism as practiced by Democrats during the Progressive Era? The pattern seems set: at first glance, Democrats out west seem to have been wiped off the map by the Lincoln-Roosevelt Republican insurgents. We know some names, of course, of the era's Democratic politicians. They filter down to us from the hazy and overwhelmingly Republican progressive past: James Phelan, Stephen White, Franklin Lane. Who were they?

James D. Phelan fits well into that lace-curtain world of San Francisco Irish machine politician, where politics, public service, and noblesse oblige intermingled. Elected to three consecutive terms as mayor of San Francisco, Phelan served the city in the decade before the great earthquake and epitomized the politician in that first turn-of-the-century wave of reformers. As World War I broke out, Phelan went to the United States Senate, the first California Democrat to serve in that august body since Stephen White in the century before. Phelan even fits the Mowry progressive profile in many ways—except that his Democratic loyalty stands out as an exception to the state Republican ascendancy.

Were it not for the curse of alcoholism, Stephen White might have risen to even higher political station than the Senate. His political career was a West Coast comet, snuffed out by his tragic death in his forties. White exists in the progressive framework established by Mowry at least as well as Phelan does. Leading the charge in the 1890s Los Angeles harbor fight, White squared off against the Southern Pacific Railroad and won. Accordingly, then, in a sort of "the enemy of my enemy is my friend" equation, White became (in death) a hero to Republican progressives, who wished to commemorate the harbor fight as an instance of selfless urban trust-busting. Because these progressives (and the historians they always stabled nearby) made so much out of the "St. George and the dragon" drama of Hiram Johnson and the Southern Pacific, White provided an appealing 1890s anticipation of 1910.[4] Lincoln-Roosevelt Republicans could easily excuse White's party affiliation simply because, first, he was dead, and second, he fought the Octopus. The latter made him an important icon; the former rendered him harmless.

Franklin Lane left California—and for all intents and purposes left California politics—to become first a member of the Interstate Commerce Commission at Theodore Roosevelt's request and, later, Woodrow Wilson's secretary of the interior. In the latter position, he did offer a peculiarly effective way for California progressive politicians to get the ear of the president, especially during the upheavals of the Mexican Revolution, when many a Southern California progressive holding ranch property south of the border had real reason to be skittish.

As testimony to the close connection between progressive Republicans and Democrats, Lane even considered swapping his Democratic credentials for Republican ones in early 1909, believing (in a striking parallel to the Woodrow Wilson view above) that there "does not seem to be any line of demarcation between a Democrat and a Republican these days."[5]

The fact that Lane and others held on to their party memberships allows us to find Democrats in the middle of a staunchly Republican period. Lane (an understudied figure in California history) did not switch parties. Something, including a misplaced and naive belief that the Lincoln-Roosevelters of the Republican party "could be rather easily beaten," kept him on the Democratic side of the fence. Perhaps during the Progressive Era that fence—made up of traditions, party loyalty, and some differences in platform—became less a dividing line than it had been previously, either in the state or in the nation. Lane, for one, thought that a party switch would not "in itself be an act of suicide."[6]

Lane, White, Phelan (and there are of course others): we *can* find Democrats from the era, important political actors. Nevertheless, for more than a century, the first rule for prospective officeholders in California has been to run as a Republican. If a political hopeful wishes to win an election, particularly as governor, history insists that he or she first declare Republican party fealty. The Democratic party did not elect a governor in this state from the end of the nineteenth century until well into the New Deal triumphalism of Franklin Roosevelt's second term! And Democrats did not do much better before the 1890s.

Of course this ineffectual record raises questions about the Democrats' relationship to progressivism, questions the following essay may shed some light upon.

One note: Historians are fond of dating the progressives' arrival in California politics at 1910, when Lincoln-Roosevelt darling Hiram Johnson was elected governor, a not unreasonable benchmark. Where were the Democrat voters? Regression analysis of voting returns indicates that those Democrats who voted the party ticket in 1906 (for candidate Theodore Bell) did the same in 1910 (again for Bell). Republican voters in 1906 voted the same four years later. Not only was party loyalty high, but neither party convinced voters to cast crossover votes.[7] Did Democrats play no role in the before, during, and after periods of California progressivism?

We *can* learn from studying California Democrats, much in the same way we can learn of nineteenth-century America by studying the hapless, yet never unimportant, Whigs. And much important work has been done on the California Democrats.[8] To be sure, examination of the other side of the two-party coin, the neglected twin of this essay's title, can tell us much about California politics during the dramatic years of progressive insurgency.

"GINGER UP!" CALIFORNIA DEMOCRATS IN THE EARLY 1900s

In 1908, the state Democratic party in California tried to beat some life into its loyal adherents by urging them to "Ginger Up!" The State Central Committee issued a slogan that was to inspire activity on the part of lapsed party members:

> Ginger Up!
> Boost, don't roost;
> Don't croak like a fool crow;
> Be full of "Go;"
> Help poke the slowboys;

> Make a noise;
> Show you are alive;
> Ginger Up!⁹

State party officials believed that they could coax voters into the fold. Certainly, the activities of Los Angeles reformers under the direction of Republicans like Meyer Lissner and Russ Avery must have prodded the Democrats into some action. Some believed that they could get the state to go Democratic, a bit wishfully perhaps. But there was at least a chance. What was needed "more than anything else," wrote one prominent party executive, was "active, continuous organization."[10]

And what of Democratic leaders? Who was out there? We have met Phelan, who (like the party itself) stepped away from politics into what his biographer calls "political eclipse" in 1902 and remained in eclipse for the better party of a decade.[11] Franklin Lane left the state in 1905 at Theodore Roosevelt's request. Theodore Bell ran a smart campaign for governor in 1906, adopting a viable anti–Southern Pacific platform that anticipated Hiram Johnson's successful massage of that effective single-issue approach four years later, but Bell's problem (both in 1906 and in 1910) was with party rather than message. Bell's campaign garnered fewer votes—in the tens of thousands fewer—than previous, equally unsuccessful, Democratic gubernatorial gambles.

Of course, there was always the mercurial attorney Francis J. Heney. But Heney was hot-headed by all accounts—there was that story of his shooting a man in Arizona—and, no less important, Heney himself had taken a slug in the head during the San Francisco graft trials. What is more, Heney had shown little of the hesitation that apparently kept Lane from switching political sides. In fact, as Lincoln-Roosevelt advisers and staffers freely admitted, Heney played a critical role in advising Hiram Johnson, his former prosecutorial apprentice, both before and especially after the 1910 election. "You must help him," muckraking gadfly Lincoln Steffens (whose first name was not, but might as well have been, the inspiration for half the Lincoln-Roosevelt label) wrote Heney of Johnson not long after the November victory. "Roosevelt and I both suggested some books to him, and I wish you would stimulate him to read. But best of all talk to him. He feels beautifully towards you."[12]

Down south in Los Angeles, the Democrats had Charles Dwight Willard, a strange, sickly, and phenomenally ambitious man who had essentially tied his kite to the Lincoln-Roosevelters in the years before Johnson's victory. Tubercular and a likely candidate for opium or cocaine addiction, Willard nonetheless kept himself together long enough to become the city's "Citizen Fix-It," and an annoying thorn in the side of the traditional Republican power structure as epitomized by the dynamic duo of Harrison Gray Otis and Harry Chandler of the *Los Angeles Times*.[13] But Willard, who earned the respect of progressive leaders like Meyer Lissner (he said of Willard that he "wore long distance glasses and to him the world looked better every day"), was no politician.[14] Health and temperament kept him in the smoke-filled rooms of the Chamber of Commerce and various reform organizations instead of the hustle bustle of electoral politics.

So who else was there? For one, there was attorney Thomas E. Gibbon, a staunch and lifelong Democrat and a man not at all unimportant in the politics of the city, the state, even the nation. Based primarily on Gibbon's recently discovered personal and business papers, this essay will attempt to reconstitute the life and times of an influential Democrat who wandered around in mostly Republican circles. In doing so, I hope to urge the reader to ponder anew the California progressive profile that George Mowry gave us forty years ago, a profile handicapped by lack of attention to just who was putting those several dozen progressives Mowry surveyed into office.

This essay is hardly meant to address that problem wholesale. In fact, it replicates one of Mowry's most troubling tendencies, a focus on progressive elites standing in for a focus on progressivism. The two need not be the same. Nor is this essay meant to be some sort of corrective cover for the sum of Mowry's work on California progressivism. In fact, I have self-consciously gone in the other direction, narrowing Mowry's subset approach to a single point, a single life. Although we do need more studies of the broad social bases of reform and political activism, we also need to examine Mowry's conclusions on his own methodological terms—through biographical sample and example. In short, by looking at one Californian, I hope to raise questions about Mowry's assumptions regarding the elite progressive ethos.

The following discussion necessarily leaves certain of Mowry's conclusions unchallenged. For instance, because this essay is concerned with the professional life of precisely one of those "fortunate sons" that Mowry writes of, it does not explicitly address what is perhaps the most glaring inadequacy of Mowry's profile: gender. To etch women out of the world of California progressivism is obviously invalid. The actions of women's suffrage activists, settlement house and temperance workers, and others (activities ably addressed by colleagues elsewhere in this volume) clearly added to the Progressive-Era reform ethos that historians like Mowry have chronicled in their work.[15]

This essay does challenge many of Mowry's other conclusions. And it does so by placing the life and times of a single political actor and reformer against the Mowry template. It would of course be unreasonable to expect that every identifiable progressive leader from turn-of-the-century California would exhibit each characteristic that Mowry identified; he attempted to define a movement of like-minded individuals, not a collection of reformer clones. But the personal and professional attributes of Thomas Gibbon often prove so at odds with the Mowry profile that they raise puzzling questions about who and what constituted California progressivism.

WHAT MAKES A PROGRESSIVE PROGRESSIVE?

Thomas Gibbon arrived in Los Angeles a sick man. Like many thousands of others in the late nineteenth century, Gibbon traveled west in search of health, arriving in Southern California in 1888. He came from Arkansas, a small-town attorney who had risen through the party ranks of the post–Civil War Democratic Redemption. At twenty-five, he sat in the Arkansas legislature: the "boy member." At twenty-eight, he alighted from the train in Los Angeles, a near invalid, his health shattered by what surely must have been tuberculosis.

In the arid, mild climate of the Los Angeles Basin, Gibbon slowly regained his health and was "able to take up all of the occupations and ambitions of life."[16] He had the advantage of timing as well as pluck. Los Angeles in the late 1880s experienced a short, passionate romance with real estate mania. That, coupled as it was with the arrival of thousands and thousands of new settlers, made the entire region a promising arena for an industrious lawyer.

His health restored, Gibbon went right to work, and he picked his clients well. Within a few short years of opening his law practice in Los Angeles, Gibbon was legal counsel for an extraordinarily ambitious collection of empire builders—among them, a set of railroad men gambling on the growth of Southern California and on their own ability to trump the Santa Fe and the Southern Pacific companies. Neither aim was particularly promising. Though there were certainly encouraging signs on the horizon, the future prosperity of the city was not at all obvious or inevitable in 1890. And the power of the two giant railroad corporations made it unlikely that any upstart competitor would make much headway.

Nonetheless, as Gibbon and his partners correctly surmised, the people of Los Angeles cared about transportation. This concern extended beyond a desire to bring in new settlers and tourists. Transportation also meant marketing: shipping Southern California's agricultural bounty eastward as well as collecting eastern goods in return. "Think of it!" Gibbon remembered. "Here we were two to three thousand miles from the parts of the country from which almost everything that we didn't produce here came. Here we were producing things for markets lying two or three thousand miles away from us. It seemed to me . . . there was nothing so important to this community as the matter of transportation."[17] And to Thomas Gibbon, that importance took the form of two specific items: a decent Los Angeles harbor and a competing transcontinental railway. These developments would invite competition; competition would force down shipping and freight rates. "Some men have ambitions to be U.S. Senators," Gibbon recalled in 1911. "My ambition has been for twenty years, and is now to help put my city in the position where it will enjoy the broadest possible commercial advantages, and this can only be done by giving it the best possible transportation rates for handling its business."[18]

Gibbon allied himself with a consortium of investors trying to accomplish these goals. Headed by wealthy St. Louis railroad builder Richard C. Kerens, this group formed the Los Angeles Terminal Railway Company in 1891. Gibbon, named vice president and legal counsel, drew up the incorporation papers. Additional investors included Senator Stephen B. Elkins of West Virginia, former Los Angeles mayor W. H. Workman, and other prominent local businessmen.

The aim of the company was simple. With viable harbor facilities on the Pacific, any competing transcontinental railroad would have the added advantage of an open mouth to the sea. The Panama Canal, though many years off, nonetheless offered the tantalizing promise of increased Pacific trade. If Los Angeles could somehow dig out a usable harbor—one to eclipse San Diego's wharf and effectively compete with San Francisco's superb bay—trade revenue in the basin would grow phenomenally. And if that harbor could in some way be coupled to a big railroad line, there loomed the very real possibility that investors might get a lock on traditional trade markets. What is more, the allure of monopolizing a transportation nexus provoked other Southern California entrepreneurial visions: rapid urban growth, aggressive land subdivision, acre upon acre of valuable citrus groves. Banal civic necessity—harbor improvements and a few more miles of railroad track—never existed apart from sugar plum dreams of unfathomable wealth.

Of course, that same sort of revelation had occurred to the immensely powerful men behind the major railroad corporations already entrenched in the day-to-day routines of the state's political and economic life. If Gibbon and his associates were to realize much gain from their ambitious projects, they would necessarily do so at the expense of their larger competitors. And in the case of the Los Angeles harbor, that competitor would clearly, unavoidably, be the Southern Pacific Railroad. The resulting 1890s clash of titan and would-be titan produced many things, among them drama, fortunes, and a legacy of muddled scholarship.

Before leaping into the harbor story, we ought to return briefly to George Mowry and the ways in which his work has been interpreted over the years. Mowry opened his book with a discussion of "the Southern Pacific's California." According to Mowry, the gargantuan railroad corporation controlled most aspects of California politics through strong-arm and blunt tactics. Therefore, opposition to the company—especially by those progressives Mowry chronicles later in the book (men always quick to display their anti–Southern Pacific credentials)—becomes, by definition, civic virtue. Battling the corporate straw man—or even suggesting that such a battle should be fought—is synonymous with selfless, hence "progressive," behavior.

This equation, an important underpinning to the "Octopus school" of California historiography, raises many questions of intentions and motives. For one, what constitutes aggressive opposition to the railroad company? Pullman strikers in the 1890s seized railroad yards, commandeered locomotives, beat up nonstrikers, brought rail traffic in the state to a standstill for better than a month. Clearly, that sort of collective action represented a powerful assault on the full cultural expression of the railroad company: materiel, employees, schedules, authority, political muscle. And when those same strikers extended a hopeful hand to the state's emergent populist movement (complete with its naive hope for railroad nationalization), collective anti-railroad action could conceivably be said to have challenged the mere existence of the corporation itself. But none of this has been interpreted as progressivism, nascent or otherwise.[19]

The harbor fight became public news just as the worker-initiated Pullman boycott began, in the summer of 1894. By that time, the opponents in the harbor controversy had taken to their respective corners.

One camp championed Santa Monica as the place for Southern California harbor improvements. The other side shouted for San Pedro. Besides opposing each other, both sides fought for federal recognition. Even the mighty Southern Pacific, purse strings straining from thirty years of California railroading, could not come up with the necessary wherewithal to manufacture a harbor where none but a poor substitute existed. That required federal money. After maneuvering into the enviable position of owning most of the seacoast along Santa Monica—or certainly enough to run a well-protected railroad—the Southern Pacific argued that that place should receive the government largesse in creating a harbor. Gibbon and associates countered, insisting that San Pedro enjoyed all the natural advantages of being a harbor waiting to happen. Not coincidentally, the Terminal Railroad and its sister land company controlled a sizable portion of San Pedro harbor and wharf facilities.

In most traditional accounts of the harbor fight, the proponents of San Pedro take on the armaments of reform as knights out to slay the Southern Pacific dragon. This is the story they told of themselves, this is the story that contemporaries recounted, and this is essentially the interpretation that many historians have repeated. Opposition to the Southern Pacific provides enough progressive character to make the pro–San Pedro contingent stride to the forefront of Southern California political reform.

But, as I have argued elsewhere, there are significant problems with this argument. For one, it begs the question of what opposition to the Southern Pacific means. If the most powerful opponents of the railroad company earn their progressive stripes simply by arguing that the new Los Angeles harbor should be placed where they will profit most from its location, is that a "progressive" aim? Yes, they planned to beat the Southern Pacific—and beat it they did, at least temporarily—but they triumphed by playing the Southern Pacific's game. The harbor fight is a story of political competition between elites for the helping hand of the federal government. It is a story of drama, intrigue, and deal-making. But it is not a story of the emergence of progressivism in swaddling clothes. Some of the same characters may have played roles in the harbor fight and the building of early-twentieth-century progressive coalitions. But active, too, in the harbor fight were men such as Harrison Gray Otis, at best an unusual candidate for inclusion into the progressive fold.[20]

It is simply too easy to bathe the San Pedro contingent of the harbor fight in the warm light of selfless civic virtue. Beating the Southern Pacific may or may not have been in the best interests of the city of

Los Angeles. But it surely was in the best interests of men like Thomas Gibbon. As he himself declared, "I have always felt that as soon as it became evident to the world that the San Pedro harbor would be fully improved by the Government, that place would open up the best opportunity for making large profits on investments, with quick returns, than has ever been done in this country."[21] Gibbon's rise to prominence in city politics and public life, then, makes him look like a progressive in the old mold, by having all the right enemies. But that interpretation is far too vague to be an accurate portrayal of progressive credentials. And what of Thomas Gibbon's friends? By the close of the century, Thomas Gibbon had associated himself with the elite of Los Angeles business and political figures. A respected attorney, he had plenty of legal business to attend to. On the side, he was an aggressive speculator in all types of mining and land ventures. He dabbled in the newspaper business: after masterminding the purchase of the formerly Republican *Los Angeles Herald* during the height of the harbor fight, Gibbon gradually withdrew from the newspaper world until early in this century, when he would again be affiliated with the *Herald*. In city politics, he was seen as a reformer, and he served on the Board of Police Commissioners as well as the Harbor Commission.

Gibbon threw himself into his work with prodigious energy, and nearly killed himself doing so. Despite his reform activities, his efforts at century's end were primarily motivated by an overarching enthusiasm to get rich. Again, Gibbon chose his friends well. And by the early years of this century, he had become extremely well off.[22]

The cornerstone of that treasure hunt was the competing transcontinental railway. Parlaying their success in the harbor fight into political and fund-raising capital, the backers of the tiny Terminal Railway redoubled their efforts to push across the Southern California desert into Utah and north to Salt Lake City.

Gibbon tried hard in the last decade of the nineteenth century to be a railroad man. His closest friends were railroad tycoons, and he clearly wished the Salt Lake line to bring him to their financial standing. With the coming of the twentieth century, though, Gibbon's ideals changed, and he placed many of his financial marbles into the real estate bag. In this respect, he was only mimicking his best friend, Harry Chandler of the *Los Angeles Times*.

Harry Chandler did not make modern Los Angeles. But it would be difficult to think of a single individual who had a greater effect on the city's look, shape, and feel in the first half of the twentieth century.

A shrewder businessman probably did not exist. Chandler may have shared most of the reactionary political outlook of his father-in-law, but where Harrison Gray Otis was bombastic and showy, Harry Chandler was sophisticated and deftly ambitious. No one in Los Angeles, with the possible exceptions of quirky leftist physician John Randolph Haynes and Title Insurance and Trust tycoon O. F. Brant, knew better how to construct a real estate deal than Harry Chandler.[23]

Through a friendship spanning several decades, Gibbon affixed many a financial dream to Harry Chandler's coattails. Some of their schemes were far-fetched, illustrative of the sheer wide-open nature of California investments at the time. Others proved visionary: putting together the Suburban Homes Company, which masterminded the watering and subdividing of the San Fernando Valley; manufacturing a consortium to buy and develop the Tejon Ranch in Kern County; and gathering up into one massive package nearly a million acres of land, stretching south from Imperial County into Mexico, that became the C & M Ranch.[24]

How are we to explain Gibbon's passion for real estate deals, his energetic coddling of infant companies and infant stock offerings, with his supposed progressive character? After all, his financial derrings-do—from vice president of the Bull Frog Mining Company and the Fire Pulp Plaster Company to several San Fernando Valley enterprises—hardly distinguish him from Harry Chandler. Harry Chandler was not a progressive. Harrison Gray Otis was not a progressive. Was Thomas Gibbon?

If we look to the Mowry profile again, we are left to check certain boxes "yes" and leave others unchecked. On the "progressive" side of the ledger, Gibbon shares these traits with Mowry's representative sample: he was a lawyer, he was a businessman, he evinced a certain wariness of big labor and big capital. He clearly valued expertise, that most progressive of beliefs. For instance, he brought in expert planners to help redesign the harbor and provide a municipal rail connection from the ocean to the city, in hopes that Los Angeles could provide a model for other municipalities across the nation.[25] He believed in municipal oversight, if not outright ownership, of utilities. But "non-progressive" characteristics leap out as well: Gibbon was a Democrat, a southerner no less, who clearly shared many an entrepreneurial vision with Southern California's most recognizable political reactionaries. Gibbon's on-again, off-again rating against the Mowry scale suggests two interpretations. The first is that Gibbon was simply not progressive enough, and the Mowry portrait holds in the main. Or Gibbon was enough a progressive to merit both a rethinking of the character of the movement and George Mowry's membership checklist.

We are left to explain Gibbon's political allegiance by looking largely at his own actions and behavior. And here the record gets even more muddled. For one thing, Gibbon recognized as well as anyone, and better than many historians, that in the first decade of this century the reform wings of the two major parties grew to look very much alike.[26] If we are to accept the argument that the Lincoln-Roosevelt League, which groomed Hiram Johnson for the statehouse in 1910, embodied the progressive ethos in state politics, then Gibbon's attitude toward that organization would seem to mark him as deeply sympathetic to the movement. In June of 1910, as the Johnson machine began to run at full steam under the able direction of Gibbon's close friend Meyer Lissner, Gibbon wrote that political matters "appear to be in very good shape in this state. With the assistance of the independent element known as the Lincoln-Roosevelt party, there seems to be little doubt that the Southern Pacific machine will be pretty thoroughly wrecked at the coming election—How far this will be done by Democratic victory, it is now impossible to say." If Johnson were to win the Republican primary, which Gibbon expected, he would win the governor's chair. And his election would prove "a fatal blow to the machine, and that would be a great consolation for the loss of the Democratic candidate."[27] Once that outcome was assured, Gibbon immediately congratulated Lissner "on the splendid victory which your generalship gave your party, and on having completed your work of destroying the Southern Pacific machine in your party and the state government."[28]

Gibbon's friendship with Lissner and his stance toward the Lincoln-Roosevelt crowd incited a good deal of opposition from apparently more traditional Democratic circles. In the editorial pages of the *Herald*, the Democratic County Central Committee, just prior to the 1910 election, approached Gibbon for a commitment to back Democratic candidates. Members of the committee apparently felt that Gibbon curried too much favor with the Republican-backed good government and Lincoln-Roosevelt forces. If he agreed to push for the Democratic party's candidates, the committee desired "to know whether such support will be merely formal or whether it will be real and active." The mouthpiece for the County Central Committee, the *Los Angeles County Democrat*, took Gibbon to task for toadying to Lissner and prominent newspaperman E. T. Earl and for not strongly supporting Democratic gubernatorial nominee Theodore Bell; the paper also alleged impropriety on the part of Gibbon in the improvements of the San Pedro waterfront.[29]

Gibbon responded to such charges with characteristic affrontery, every inch the offended southern gentleman. Declaring that such attacks were insulting and impertinent, Gibbon defended his decisions on the high ground of principle. "During that portion of the last ten years when I was connected with the Railroad Company I took no active part in Democratic politics because I believed it bad taste for men who are officials or employees of public service corporations to attempt to take a prominent part in the politics of the country, and I merely contented myself with voting the Democratic ticket."[30]

The Democratic County Central Committee backed down, albeit briefly. Just after making private amends to Gibbon, the committee apparently placed a headline in the *Los Angeles County Democrat*, declaring that "Gibbon's Duplicity Has Found Him Out." The story went on to argue that Gibbon was merely a lackey for Lissner and the Lincoln-Roosevelt League, that he was a Lincoln-Roosevelt supporter in Democratic guise. Los Angeles Democrats ought no longer "stand by, muzzled, and permit such men as T. E. Gibbon to prostitute [the *Herald*] for Mr. [E. T.] Earle [*sic*], Meyer Lissner or the Times office."[31]

Again the *Times* connection. Only in this instance the reference is to something other than the clubby camaraderie and mutual investment schemes connecting Gibbon and Harry Chandler. The suggestion, in the same sentence, that Gibbon would be a toady to both Lissner, the leading architect of progressive reforms in the city, if not the state, *and* the reactionary *Los Angeles Times* only emphasizes the complexity of political and other alliances in the city.

Take the relationship between Gibbon, the *Herald,* and the *Times,* for instance, the intricacies of which have only recently come to light in the Gibbon papers. More than displaying Gibbon as an ambitious "wannabe," they detail a thick connection among the members of the city's ruling elite, the group that Mike Davis has recently refered to as "a McKinleyite version of the *Cosa Nostra.*"[32]

As noted above, Gibbon had masterminded purchase of the *Herald* in the mid-1890s by a consortium of pro–San Pedro Democrats. His affiliation with the paper did not last, and he leaped from the sinking ship before century's end. But he returned to the paper in the early years of this century, just as the progressive movement was beginning to crystallize. After buying a half-interest in the *Herald* in the summer of 1907, he wrote to fellow Democrat Franklin Lane that he and his associates were "endeavoring to make a straight-out Democratic journal of that paper."[33]

Like a good progressive, Gibbon apparently wanted to keep the paper free from corporate, especially Southern Pacific, taint. "I don't know that you know it," he wrote to Marie Lobdell, who helped him purchase the paper, "but the journalistic graveyard of California is full of deceased newspapers, whose epitaph might be "Died from too close connection with the Southern Pacific Company." With admirable presience, Gibbon fully expected to meet public expectations regarding opposition to the railroad corporation during the Progressive Era. "Within the next two years," he wrote, "every newspaper in the State of California which desires to enjoy any part of the public confidence and respect must be prepared to take extreme grounds against the Southern Pacific Company on certain public issues which are in my judgment as certain to arise as time continues."[34]

But the story was hardly that simple. There were other principals in the deal, ones whose presence muddies the waters. Most obvious is the presence of Harrison Gray Otis and Harry Chandler. Otis, after all, owned the paper. In negotiating for the purchase of the *Herald* in the spring of 1907, Gibbon had recognized that—given his affiliation with Otis and, especially, Chandler—he might have trouble running an ostensibly rival newspaper. "One of the difficulties which the undersigned in their efforts to establish the independent character of the paper will particularly labor under for a while will arise from the somewhat intimate business and personal relations which have heretofore existed between them and your journal."[35]

Surmounting those affiliations in the attempt to establish "independence" seems not to have been one of Gibbon's major concerns in his capacity as editor. And those ties that bound Gibbon to Otis and Chandler cast suspicion on the *Herald*'s supposedly Democratic credentials. Gibbon seems simply to have been General Otis's pet. For instance, in the winter of 1907, he wrote to Otis about issues of labor and capital in the city. Both labor and capital had the right to organize to protect their interests, Gibbon believed, but neither had the right to use force. "To apply these principles to a possible situation which may develop in Los Angeles, I will say that I personally, and the paper whose editorial policy I control, will resist to the bitter end and the last ditch any effort upon the part of organized labor to interfere by force, fraud, or chicane with the very satisfactory industrial conditions as they exist in this city today." But in true progressive confusion, Gibbon equated force with strikes. Were labor to attempt to organize through the use of strikes, "I and the paper whose editorial policy I control would oppose such action to the utmost of our power." Fealty was assured: "This you may depend upon." The fact that Gibbon appended an apologetic note to General Otis regarding the *Herald*'s financial indebtedness merely ices the conflict-of-interest cake.[36]

By the summer of 1908, both Otis and Chandler were providing the new owners of the paper with significant financial assistance to keep the paper alive. But the going was still rough. Gibbon informed his close friend Harry Chandler that he had three choices: he could sell the paper, he could return it to General Otis, or he could keep it going with additional help from Otis and Chandler. If the paper could be kept alive with added help from the *Times* ownership, secrecy was of course crucial: "it would just ruin us to have the public know they were interested."[37]

Gibbon again and again denied that Otis was at all involved in the *Herald*. "As far as the Otis control is concerned, you can tell everybody that neither General Otis nor any one else connected with the Times has one cent of interest in the Herald or any business connection whatever with it in any way."[38] In the spring of 1908, he assured powerful politician Marion Cannon of the paper's independence: "I desire to assure you upon my word of honor that neither General Otis or any other person connected with the Times or interested in that paper has one cent interest in the Los Angeles Herald." Such insistence rings hollow, given Gibbon's note to Harry Chandler only two weeks earlier granting Chandler the authority to vote Gibbon and the *Herald*'s proxy at an Associated Press meeting.[39]

Furthermore, Otis attempted to get Gibbon to fire certain employees—"strange freaks"—in the paper's editorial offices. "They should be discharged, and I have a right to say so." Not long after, still trying to cashier Socialist editor Frank Wolfe, Otis wrote to Gibbon that "the time is ripe for both Wolfe and Baillie to go. In fact, the time and the persons are over-ripe." What is more, Otis thought that the paper was losing money—a great deal of money—because it "has been circulating among a class of people many of whom do not mean to pay their newspaper bills." And the general's editorial input into the paper was often hardly subtle; he urged Gibbon in the midst of the McNamara case to make particular points editorially.[40]

Gibbon felt that the paper's Democratic slant, particularly its support of progressive causes and candidates, was critical for the paper's success. Although he insisted that the paper occupied this niche on the political spectrum, it is clear that finances and attempts to placate Otis (by making the paper into the Democratic yin to the *Times*'s reactionary yang, hence widening the market) played a prominent role as well. It would be "absolutely suicidal" to pull the paper away from the forces of good government; the paper would lose all that it had gained in circulation since Gibbon had taken over, a fact Otis would surely realize since "you have paid the bills."[41]

Frank Wolfe later testified before the United States Commission on Industrial Relations about this shrewd cornering of the market by Otis and his minions: "We took the side of progress on progressive measures with our paper; that is to say, one of the general's papers took the side of progress and the other took the side of the reactionaries. . . . We played the people . . . for suckers. . . . We played both ends against the middle."[42] Despite such subterfuge, the local Socialist community thought of Gibbon and the paper as a friendly voice.

Otis lost patience as the paper lost money. At one point, he took the paper back from Gibbon. Gibbon responded by pulling together the necessary funds to purchase the paper again. Interestingly, Gibbon relied on the influence of rival newspaperman E. T. Earl (an archenemy of Otis) to gather up $130,000 in the spring of 1911. Investors included Lyman Stewart, president of Union Oil, and A. J. Wallace, Hiram Johnson's junior partner on the 1910 progressive ticket. Though utilizing Earl for his contacts within the Los Angeles elite, Gibbon assured Otis that the paper would not fall into Earl's hands.[43]

Was Thomas Gibbon merely an anomaly? His friends and business partners included those whom the progressives hated most (recall Hiram Johnson's vicious denunciation of Harrison Gray Otis); yet he could often sound and act very much like the leading members of the progressive wing of the Republican party, though always holding to his Democratic loyalties. Clearly, he supported the aims of the Lincoln-Roosevelt League, albeit from outside of party ranks. "We should not fail once in a while by some editorial utterance which can be made appropriate to some local or state occurrence to show our sympathy for the Lincoln-Roosevelt movement. This of course is outside of our own party, but there is no reason why we should not encourage its war on the Republican party against the Southern Pacific machine and every reason why we should."[44]

There are other linkages, Gibbon acting as linchpin. For one, when the leading progressive figure in Los Angeles mulled over ideas for a nominating speech for Theodore Roosevelt in 1912, he turned to Thomas Gibbon for suggestions. Gibbon suggested to Meyer Lissner that he ought to "begin by endeavoring to sketch briefly but strongly the necessity which had arisen in the progress of our Government for certain reforms. . . . I would then dwell somewhat at length upon the fact that Mr. Roosevelt had been the leader in crystallizing this general recognition of the necessity of the reform, into aggressive action and translating it into what has become known as the 'progressive movement.' "[45]

There is no doubt that Gibbon had it in him to sound exactly like the classic "Mowry progressive." In a letter to newly elected senator John D. Works, Gibbon correctly surmised the role of Los Angeles progressives in helping spark an entire program of western political reform. The East had no clear conception of democratic reforms, "those instrumentalities designed to bring government nearer to the people." Through the "applied science of government," progressives could surmount the obstacles of party politics. "I can see no difference between a progressive Republican and a progressive Democrat on the one hand, and a reactionary Republican and a reactionary Democrat on the other, and I cannot tell you how I would welcome the day which sees all the progressives of both parties lined up under the same party banner, and it makes no difference to me what the party name on that banner shall be."[46]

A few years earlier, just as the San Francisco graft trials concluded and the state progressive movement began to coalesce within the ranks of disgruntled Republicans, Gibbon had written to Fremont Older: "I sincerely hope that now that you have saved the situation in San Francisco, you and your friends will be able to a little later clear the deck so as to admit of giving some more direct and active attention to the great criminal, the Southern Pacific Company."[47]

Of course, the infamous *Times* explosion in the early-morning hours of October 1, 1910, polarized camps in Los Angeles as well as across the nation, not just "radicals" and "conservatives" but Democrats and Republicans as well. Well before the celebrated trial, before the humiliation and disappointment of the brothers' confessions and Clarence Darrow's bribery trials, lines had been drawn. The bombing was simply too dramatic and volatile. Jolted out of their beds by the massive explosion that obliterated the *Times* building and killed a score of the paper's employees, Los Angeles citizens wasted little time in carving out propaganda campaigns atop the ruins.

The cause of the explosion was by no means clear throughout that winter of 1910. The *Times*, and Harrison Gray Otis in particular, leaped immediately to the sabotage theory, linking unionism and terrorism in its patched-together edition, which hit the streets as firemen and thousands of onlookers gazed at the wreck of the *Times* building in downtown Los Angeles.[48] Organized labor, of course, counterattacked, suggesting that the explosion had been caused not by dynamite but by the *Times*'s own dangerously faulty gas heating system. Some even claimed that Otis himself had engineered the blast in a Machiavellian plot to discredit organized labor and take the offensive against labor's goal of the closed shop.

Gibbon followed Otis's lead in analyzing the "crime of the century." A scant three weeks after the explosion, Gibbon responded to a critic of the *Herald*'s stance on the controversy—namely, that the blast was evidence of class warfare. "After investigating the matter pretty thoroughly," Gibbon wrote, he and the paper that he edited "came to the conclusion that the *Times* was wrecked and twenty people killed by a horrible crime whose perpetrators were inhuman monsters."[49] As evidence for this conclusion, Gibbon insisted that he had heard dynamite explosions before and that descriptions of the blast that shook the *Times* building sounded like dynamite to him.

Even as its exact cause remained a mystery, the *Times* explosion helped further polarize city politics. It has long been a chestnut of Los Angeles history that Job Harriman's 1911 mayoral campaign terrified the progressives, who were worried not only about the electoral threat of the left but about the specter of violence as well. Gibbon wrote of the political struggle in a letter to a friend in northern California, noting that the city was in the midst of a "very hard fight with the nominal socialist party, which is in reality, the party of militant labor unionism. Our opponents are provided with the sinews of war . . . and we are really making a fight against the whole national force arrayed in defense of the McNamaras. This is going to give us a good big job to attend to, and leave no time for anything else until after the election."[50]

Gibbon acted as an errand boy for the city's conservative elite, those most frightened by the prospect of Harriman's winning the mayor's seat. Probably at the request of Harry Chandler or Harrison Gray Otis, Gibbon rode forth in the fall of 1911 to challenge Harriman on a variety of issues. He wanted to engage the Socialist political hopeful in a public debate, a verbal duel complete with attendants and witnesses. Harriman rose to the challenge, agreeing to meet Gibbon at the end of November to debate such major campaign issues as the Los Angeles aqueduct and the San Fernando Valley syndicate (Gibbon was a prominent, if secret, member). Gibbon went into the debate as the representative of the good government forces in Los Angeles.

Gibbon just as forcibly reacted against the efforts of Lincoln Steffens to ameliorate the obvious tensions between capital and labor in the city. Or so he recalled years later. Nine years after the destruction of the *Times* building, Gibbon recalled that he opposed Steffens's attempts to plea-bargain a fifteen-year term for both brothers should they plead guilty. "Of course, I refused to take any hand unless the sentence of the man who set off the bomb should be for life, but it was perfectly evident in his discussion of the matter with me and others that he had no conception of the moral character of the act which sent twenty human beings into eternity, and left a lot of widows and orphans behind them. His attitude in the matter was altogether the most astonishing thing I ever saw."[51]

On a somewhat related front, Gibbon's regard for human lives, always filtered through an attitude of noblesse oblige, could verge on social control (score one for the progressive checklist!). Gibbon's turn-of-the-century tenure on the police commission illustrates this tendency and provides an apt sketch of progressivism's paternal stance toward "our" workers, a stance often codified through regulatory legislation. Gibbon and others on the commission pushed the so-called Gothenberg plan for saloons. The plan would limit the number to two hundred through a simple licensing maneuver and would keep saloons out of the working-class residential districts beginning to pop up along streetcar lines outside the city. "One beneficent effect of this regulation is shown in the matter of relieving the working population of the City of temptation. Inasmuch as our working men nearly all live in small homes located on the outskirts of the City, where land is cheap, if the working man when he gets his week's pay desires to spend some of it for drink, he is compelled to leave his home and go several miles in order to get the opportunity to do so."[52]

Gibbon was equally proud, if not more so, of his and other like-minded reformers' efforts at clearing prostitution from the streets of Los Angeles. His faith in policing efforts evinces a classic sense of progressive optimism. Once a problem had been defined, it could be erased, simple as that. As gentleman reformer, he apparently made quite a study of the prevalence of prostitution in the city. In a letter to a like-minded Bay

Area reformer in 1911, he applauded the efforts of the Los Angeles police: prodded by the civic virtue of the city's citizens, the police had virtually eliminated prostitution. "I have for my own information, taken
some care to personally investigate the matter . . . and I can say that I
am positively convinced that it does not exist on the streets."[53]
    We are left to sum up the points raised by this biographical sketch of
a single California reformer. Either Gibbon is not a progressive and
Mowry remains intact, or we can judge Gibbon against the Mowry template and dismiss him as not a progressive. Or—more to the point, I
would argue—he is both enough of a progressive and different enough
to allow us to call for a serious adjustment of Mowry. What is called for
is some measure, some understanding, that allows us to net Johnson,
Heney, Lissner, Weinstock, and Gibbon all at once. Besides, it is more
interesting to argue that Gibbon was indeed a progressive and that we
therefore need to redefine or reconceptualize the model. At the very
least, we ought to be convinced that the boundaries of progressivism
were fluid. Perhaps the essays in this collection that paint with broader
strokes can hint at the diverse social fabric of progressivism more fully
than this simple biographical inquiry can.

HISTORY NOIR

Thanks to the enduring images in brilliantly evocative novels, motion
pictures, and Chandleresque detective stories, much of the Los Angeles
past reads like a gritty inventory of the human condition. We see Los
Angeles as if through the eyes of Jake Gittes, Philip Marlowe, Louis
Adamic (Los Angeles is "a *bad* place"), Morrow Mayo, or the latest and
most important student of Los Angeles, Mike Davis. This is an often ex-
aggerated view of the city. But it does offer a tantalizing way of ordering
this essay, an examination of one man's Los Angeles during a critical
period in the political history of that city and the entire state of
California.
    Sometime in 1909, probably close to Valentine's Day, Gibbon re-
ceived a peculiar letter from an A. W. Marsh in the Temple Block in
downtown. The letter was clearly a crude attempt at extortion. Mr.
Marsh claimed to be a former railroad detective and expressed his willingness to write newspaper stories for the *Herald.* The stories were to be
about a prominent attorney in Los Angeles, a so-called reformer, who
nonetheless found himself tied tightly to the apron strings of major corporations. His was simply a "Jekyll and Hyde" existence: a devoted

family man with a mistress hidden away in the city; a reformer with
strong ties to the railroad powers in Los Angeles.[54] Maybe Mr. Marsh
knew something we don't? Maybe he was on to something about the
ways in which an "upstanding" member of the community could be progressive and opportunist at the same time?

To conclude, this essay has either simply rescued an important figure
from historical obscurity or, in the process of that task, it has also re-
introduced that individual and his party into a Republican progressive
milieu. If the latter is true, or at least partially true, we must accept the
necessary complement of complexity that comes from muddy, previously calm historical waters. We do not know what progressivism was
or how important it was. But we are finding active Democrats involved
in progressivism, which is more and more looking like that Jekyll and
Hyde world peopled by ambitious climbers such as Thomas Gibbon. As
David Sarasohn has recently pointed out, regarding the Democrats during the Progressive Era, "the early twentieth century Democrats may end
up with nothing more than a historiographical booby prize: recognition
as a much more important element in a much less important
movement."[55]

Journalist William Allen White saw it differently years ago, when he
wrote to a young graduate student about the ideological origins of California Republican progressivism. White saw historical continuity
stretching not only to "the other side" but significantly back in time as
well. As he wrote to Stanford student Alice Rose:

> To get at the real basis of the California insurgency and its contemporary rise
> all over the United States in the first decade of this century, you, of course,
> go back first to what is known as the "Roosevelt policies." When you get into
> that literature you will find that William Jennings Bryan claimed that
> Roosevelt "stole his clothes" while he was swimming. Bryan took his plat-
> form from the Populists of the early Nineties who had theirs from the Green-
> backers of the Seventies and Eighties who got their ideas from the contem-
> porary Grange movement of that era.[56]

What White's thesis may say about the current Democratic party
malaise, where this essay began, is not at all clear. What it says about the
arena this essay and this book are most concerned with is simply that
we must look beyond insurgent Republican success if we are going to
understand the complex animal of California progressivism, an organism quite unwilling to be corralled into a single-party stall.

NOTES

Source for epigraphs: Wilson quoted in Josephus Daniels, *The Wilson Era, Years of Peace, 1910–1917* (Chapel Hill: University of North Carolina Press, 1946), 11; also in David Sarasohn, *The Party of Reform: Democrats in the Progressive Era* (Jackson: University Press of Mississippi, 1989), xi. Carr quote is from "The Memoirs of William Jarvis Carr," Oral History Project, University of California, Los Angeles, 1959.

1. Thomas Byrne Edsall and Mary Edsall, *Chain Reaction: The Impact of Race, Rights, and Taxes on American Politics* (New York: Norton, 1991), 264.

2. Robert Wesser, *A Response to Progressivism: The Democratic Party and New York Politics, 1902–1918* (New York: New York University Press, 1986), ix.

3. See, for instance, J. Joseph Huthmacher, "Urban Liberalism and the Age of Reform," *Mississippi Valley Historical Review* 44 (September 1962): 231–41, and "Charles Evans Hughes and Charles Francis Murphy: The Metamorphosis of Progressivism," *New York History* 46 (1965): 25–40; John D. Buenker, *Urban Liberalism and Progressive Reform* (New York: Scribner's, 1973).

4. As Michael Kazin has written in reference to the ties between progressive actors and progressive chroniclers (specifically referring to the San Francisco graft prosecutions), "subsequent accounts routinely echo the prosecutors' opinion of themselves." See Michael Kazin, *The Barons of Labor: The San Francisco Building Trades and Union Power in the Progressive Era* (Urbana: University of Illinois Press, 1987), 131.

5. Franklin K. Lane to Charles K. McClatchy, March 20, 1909, in Anne W. Lane and Louise H. Wall, eds., *Letters of Franklin K. Lane: Personal and Political* (Boston: Houghton Mifflin, 1922), 70.

6. Ibid.

7. See the tables in the appendix to William Deverell, "Building an Octopus: Railroads and Society in the Late Nineteenth Century Far West," (Ph.D. diss., Princeton University, 1989).

8. In particular, see the excellent book by R. Hal Williams, *The Democratic Party and California Politics* (Stanford, Calif.: Stanford University Press, 1973). This is a study of the party in the late nineteenth century.

9. From State Central Committee publication in James D. Phelan Papers, Bancroft Library, University of California, Berkeley.

10. John F. Murray, State Central Committee secretary, to James D. Phelan, November 13, 1908, Phelan Papers. Murray claimed that the state had 50,000 unaffiliated voters. "That they are not Republicans is good evidence that they might be reasoned with."

11. See Robert E. Hennings, *James D. Phelan and the Wilson Progressives of California* (New York: Garland, 1985), chap. 3.

12. Lincoln Steffens to Francis J. Heney, [1910], Heney Papers, Bancroft Library, University of California, Berkeley.

13. See Donald Ray Culton, "Charles Dwight Willard: Los Angeles City Booster and Professional Reformer, 1888–1914," (Ph.D. diss., University of

Southern California, 1971), and "Los Angeles' 'Citizen Fixit': Charles Dwight Willard, City Booster and Progressive Reformer," *California History* 57 (Summer 1978): 158–71.

14. Quoted in Culton, "Charles Dwight Willard," 333.

15. See the essays in this volume by, especially, Mary Odem, Judith Raftery, and Sherry Katz.

16. Gibbon address before Los Angeles City Club, June 20, 1908. Copy in author's possession.

17. Ibid.

18. Thomas Gibbon to R. D. List, February 2, 1911, Thomas Gibbon Papers, Huntington Library. These papers have only recently come to light. In spite of his statement here, Gibbon had seriously considered a run for the U.S. Senate in 1910. See Thomas Gibbon to Editor, *Los Angeles Express*, November 2, 1910.

19. Mowry concedes that California progressivism "drew upon" older strains of social and political protest but that its leadership sprang from an entirely different setting—in class as well as geographical terms—than that of populism or Grangerism. See George Mowry, *The California Progressives* (Berkeley: University of California Press, 1951), 88–89.

20. See William F. Deverell, "The Los Angeles Free Harbor Fight," *California History* 70 (Spring 1991): 12–29.

21. Thomas Gibbon to Richard Kerens, August 15, 1902, Gibbon Papers.

22. In 1902, Gibbon estimated his net worth at $150,000. Four years later, he had real estate and stock holdings worth, after discounting for debt, somewhere in the neighborhood of half a million dollars. See Thomas Gibbon to Richard Kerens, August 15, 1902, and Thomas Gibbon to W. C. Patterson, January 20, 1906, Gibbon Papers.

23. See, for instance, Mike Davis's discussion of Chandler, entitled "Harry Chandler's Town," in his stunning *City of Quartz* (London: Verso, 1990), chap. 2, especially 114–20.

24. In what could be a page straight out of Robert Towne's *Chinatown* screenplay, Harry Chandler's August 1909 letter to Gibbon detailed a portion of the San Fernando Valley land scheme. "This, in a few words, is the nub of the proposed deal: We pay $2,500,000 for 47,000 acres of land, which is the cream of the San Fernando Valley. . . . I certainly hope you will be able to make the deal. . . . Gen. [Moses] Sherman, Gen. [Harrison Gray] Otis, H. J. Whitley, and a number of others who do not wish their names used in connection with the deal, have promised to go in and have subscribed. . . . In the meantime it is of vital importance that nobody here shall get an inkling as to what is going on." Harry Chandler to Thomas Gibbon, August 17, 1909, Gibbon Papers.

25. See Thomas Gibbon to Franklin T. Lane, March 29, 1911, Gibbon Papers.

26. See, for instance, Thomas Gibbon to Franklin T. Lane, March 4, 1911 (Gibbon Papers), regarding Republican congressman William D. Stephens: "Mr. Stephens was elected as a progressive Republican, which means as you also know, a very considerable resemblance to a progressive Democrat." Similarly, Gibbon wrote to Delancey Nicoll in New York that in "California we were not so fortunate in electing our Democratic candidates. But we can console our-

selves with the thought that the Republican ticket here was insurgent from top to bottom, and represented very largely the reform ideas for which the Democratic party stands, particularly in the matter of the tariff." Thomas Gibbon to Delancey Nicoll, November 10, 1910, Gibbon Papers.

27. Thomas Gibbon to Franklin T. Lane, June 20, 1910, Gibbon Papers.

28. Thomas Gibbon to Meyer Lissner, November 9, 1910, Gibbon Papers. Lissner is an inexplicably understudied figure from this period in California politics. His papers, housed at Stanford, offer great rewards to the patient scholar. Gibbon wrote to crusading reform journalist Fremont Older that, although he voted the Democratic ticket, he felt that "Mr. Johnson's election may turn out the best thing that could have happened." Thomas Gibbon to Fremont Older, November 19, 1910, Gibbon Papers.

29. *Los Angeles County Democrat,* November 4, 1910, and undated clipping, Gibbon Papers.

30. Thomas Gibbon to Democratic County Central Committee for Los Angeles, September 21, 1910, Gibbon Papers.

31. *Los Angeles County Democrat,* September 23, 1910, copy in Gibbon Papers.

32. Davis, *City of Quartz,* 113.

33. Thomas Gibbon to Franklin K. Lane, September 17, 1907, Gibbon Papers.

34. Thomas Gibbon to Marie George Lobdell, March 15, 1907, Gibbon Papers.

35. Thomas Gibbon to Harrison Gray Otis, April 1, 1907, Gibbon Papers. For a brief overview of the secret Otis connection, see Robert Gottlieb and Irene Wolt, *Thinking Big: The Story of the Los Angeles Times, Its Publishers and Their Influence on Southern California* (New York: Putnam's, 1977), 29–31.

36. Thomas Gibbon to Harrison Gray Otis, December 6, 1907, Gibbon Papers.

37. Marie George Lobdell to Thomas Gibbon, March 5, 1907, Gibbon Papers.

38. Thomas Gibbon to W. P. McGonigle, December 2, 1907, Gibbon Papers.

39. Thomas Gibbon to Marion Cannon, April 27, 1908, Gibbon to Harry Chandler, April 13, 1908, Gibbon Papers.

40. Harrison Gray Otis to Thomas Gibbon, January 27 and October 6, 1909, May 2, 1910, and May 15, 1911, Gibbon Papers. By the fall of 1909, the paper was losing an estimated $10,000 a month.

41. Thomas Gibbon to Harrison Gray Otis, May 5, 1910, Gibbon Papers.

42. United States Commission on Industrial Relations, Final Report and Testimony, Submitted to Congress by the Commission on Industrial Relations, 11 vols. (Washington, D.C.: U.S. Government Printing Office, 1916), 5846–47.

43. See the following letters in the Gibbon Papers: Thomas Gibbon to Harry Chandler, July [29], 1911; Chandler to Gibbon, May 14, 1911; [E. T.] Earl to Gibbon, May 22, 1911.

44. Thomas Gibbon to Frank Wolfe, July 14, 1908, Gibbon Papers.

45. Thomas Gibbon to Meyer Lissner, June 4, 1912, Gibbon Papers.

46. Thomas Gibbon to John D. Works, May 31, 1911, Gibbon Papers.

47. Thomas Gibbon to Fremont Older, November 6, 1907, Gibbon Papers.

48. Remember that this edition came out courtesy of the presses at the *Herald*, the nominally Democratic paper run by Gibbon and the fine hand of Otis.

49. Thomas Gibbon to Charles Wilkinson, October 22, 1910, Gibbon Papers.

50. Thomas Gibbon to Max Thelan, November 10, 1911, Gibbon Papers.

51. Thomas Gibbon to Harold Walker, May 12, 1919, Gibbon Papers. Gibbon seemingly (and not surprisingly) played a critical role in the entire McNamara case, a role unfortunately not documented in any of the relevant manuscript collections. According to Meyer Lissner, political leaders in Los Angeles greeted Steffens's hopes for some sort of rapprochement between capital and labor as a "flight of fancy." Once the suggestion of a confession had been broached, Lissner apparently referred Steffens to Gibbon, who acted as a liaison between Steffens and Harry Chandler, and Harry Chandler then did the same, presumably, between Steffens (and Clarence Darrow, perhaps) and District Attorney John D. Fredericks. See Thomas Gibbon to Meyer Lissner, April 15, 1919, and Lissner's reply, April 16, 1919, Meyer Lissner Papers, Department of Special Collections, Stanford University. The Gibbon Papers have a copy of TEG to ML. The fascinating story of the bombing, the hunt for the McNamaras, the trial, and Darrow's humiliation has not yet been told with as much attention to detail as it deserves.

52. Thomas Gibbon to Senator John D. Works, May 4, 1912, Gibbon Papers.

53. Thomas Gibbon to Carlos White, June 14, 1911, Gibbon Papers.

54. A. W. Marsh to Thomas Gibbon, n.d. [originally filed mid-February correspondence], Gibbon Papers. The *Herald* had begun running a series of front-page stories asking "Is Vice Being Protected in Los Angeles?" and detailing Mayor Harper's connections with underworld figures. It is not far-fetched to imagine that Marsh was put up to his extortion task by some of those embarrassed by the *Herald*'s pages. A paper editorial declared that Mayor A. C. Harper was "the first mayor . . . of the city to introduce the destructive element of the corporation-serving politician into the greatest business commission of the city." Quoted in Albert Howard Clodius, "The Quest for Good Government in Los Angeles, 1890–1910" (Ph.D. diss., Claremont Graduate School, 1953), 167, n. 75. Marsh does appear in the city directories of the period as a private detective.

55. Sarasohn, *The Party of Reform*, xi.

56. William Allen White to Alice Rose, June 19, 1941, in Alice Rose Archives, Department of Special Collections and Archives, Stanford University.

A Penchant for Probity

*California Progressives and the
Disreputable Pleasures*

Gerald Woods

The men and women who created the progressive movement in California and led it to signal victories included people of diverse races, creeds, and colors. The leaders, however, were white, generally born in California or the midwestern states, more likely to be Republican than Democrat, and more likely to be Protestant than any other religion or sect. California progressive leaders tended to be comparatively young—in their thirties and forties—and comparatively successful. Newspaper owners and editors were well represented, as were lawyers, realtors, bankers, doctors, and other professionals. The large majority of leaders had at least one university degree. As a group they were independent, democratic, somewhat nativist, somewhat anti-labor, generally opposed to monopolies, and committed to free enterprise.[1]

Their external motivation was apparent: to reform the political and social institutions of their society. Their inner motivation has been the subject of speculation. George E. Mowry described California progressivism as "an expression of an older America objecting to the ideological and social drifts of the twentieth century." In the same vein, Richard Hofstadter asserted that the progressives responded defensively to "a changed pattern in the distribution of deference and power"; that they were "victims of an upheaval in status"; and that "the yankee ethos of responsibility [became] transmuted into a sense of guilt." Guilt accounted for the evangelical fervor with which progressives attacked social problems.[2]

These provocative theories seem somehow inadequate. It is difficult to perceive California progressivism in such limited, negative terms, as simply a response to unwanted changes in American society. The progressives were young, educated, confident members of the dominant ethnic group and the dominant political party. They grew up in the post–Civil War period, when enormous fraud permeated every level of government and business; but instead of becoming cynical, they turned to reform.

The ills the progressives set out to cure were of old origin. The struggle to reform the nation had been under way since at least the 1880s, when most of those who became progressives were still in school. Benjamin Parke DeWitt observed in 1915 that "although differences in name, in the specific reforms advocated, and in the emphasis placed upon them, have obscured the identity of the movement, the underlying purposes and ideals of the progressive elements of all parties for the past quarter of a century have been essentially the same." DeWitt then pointed out common interests endorsed by the Democratic, Republican, Progressive, Socialist, and Prohibition parties.[3]

One characteristic of the progressives about which most historians could agree was their abiding antipathy toward saloons, prostitution, gambling, slot machines, horse races, prizefights, dancing (especially in nightclubs where black men played jazz music), and liaisons between black or Asian men and white women. In this regard, Spencer Olin noted that "this penchant for probity, this moral absolutism, was part and parcel of the progressive mind." George Mowry pointed out the "middle-class Christian respectability" implicit in the closing of saloons and gambling halls in Los Angeles at the turn of the century.[4]

Both comments are accurate but say little about motivation. Benjamin DeWitt stated the case from the progressive perspective: "if the American city fails, it will fail not because of the work its people do or the places in which they live, but because of the pleasures which they seek. It is vice, high living, and deterioration of moral fibre more than anything else that destroys cities and democracies." For DeWitt, nothing less was at stake than the soul of America.[5]

In California, the crusade against the disreputable pleasures was essentially a tale of three cities. San Francisco and Los Angeles, the north and the south, proudly embodied the poles, respectively, of civic vice and civic virtue. Sacramento, specifically the state legislature, was a relatively neutral ground where proponents of "personal liberty" did battle with neo-puritans to preserve the lurid entertainments that for decades had characterized West Coast cities. In Washington, D.C., progressives in the Congress also warred against evil and won some significant victories.

During the progressive heyday, from 1909 through 1918, a variety of sumptuary laws were passed. At the national level, these included the Mann Act, directed at the transport of women across state lines for immoral purposes; more restrictive immigration regulations and anti–"white slavery" agreements with European governments, to reduce the remarkable migration of foreign prostitutes into the United States; and national wartime prohibition, the Eighteenth Amendment to the U.S. Constitution, and the Volstead Act, intended to close the saloons and end forever the consumption of beverage alcohol by Americans.[6]

In 1909, the state assembly, described by the San Francisco Chronicle as "a legislature of progressive cranks," narrowly passed the Anti–Race Track Gambling Act. The act forbade "wagering or pool selling or bookmaking in any way, shape, form or place." The Local Option Law, allowing prohibition by local option, followed in 1911. This act was known generally as the Gandier Ordinance, after Daniel M. Gandier, legislative superintendent of the Anti-Saloon League. By 1913, nearly one thousand saloons had been closed through the introduction of local prohibition. About half the state went dry. The Red Light Abatement Act, aimed mainly at the owners of properties where brothels were operated, was passed in 1913. It allowed for the padlocking of such premises, thereby denying rental income to the owners.[7]

The progressives did not win easily. Franklin Hichborn, chronicler of state legislative sessions from 1909 until the mid-1920s, declared in 1913 that the Senate Committee on Public Morals (a classic example of progressive thought) was dominated by "the tenderloin element." Although draw poker was added that year to the list of forbidden games, a University Dry Zone Bill, anti-prizefighting bills, and measures against illegal saloons (known as "blind pigs") failed to pass. Eventually, the restrictive bills were guided through the legislature, although the success achieved was less than expected. The reformers could carry state elections and drive legislation through with minimal amendments. Once the laws were in place, however, the state legislature was out of the picture. Local governments could enforce the statutes or ignore them. Hichborn complained in 1915 that, despite the regulations, gambling was wide open during the great San Francisco Exposition. Saloons and brothels also flourished. It had ever been thus in the City by the Bay.[8]

San Francisco had an unsavory municipal government (a "California Tammany") and a wicked demimonde. Brash San Franciscans viewed their town as "the future seat and center of the world's commerce . . . that advertised the notorious Barbary Coast to the world as a symbol of its anti-Puritan tradition." And tradition it had! In the 1880s, the city supported an estimated two thousand saloons and brothels in the Chinatown, Barbary Coast, and tenderloin districts. San Francisco's bawdy reputation was nationwide, and numerous books described the fun to be had in the city that took "uncommon pride in its past sins, real or imagined." Crusades for moral purity might come and go, but, as one prostitute told a reporter, "the police wink at us." When the police did make arrests, judges often dismissed the cases.[9]

Occasionally, San Francisco moral reformers won a round, or thought that they did. After the earthquake and fire of 1906, an enormous brothel housing 133 women was quickly reconstructed. It was described by local wits as "the municipal brothel," because half the profits went to city hall. In 1911, a municipal clinic was established, to ensure that prostitutes maintained good health. For the good progressive folk of San Francisco, this was going too far. Fremont Older, editor of the *Bulletin,* observed that "there was more fuss over the operation of the Municipal Clinic than the Municipal Brothel." The clinic soon was closed. The brothel lasted for several additional years.[10]

In 1913, a reform crusade briefly closed the Barbary Coast and the tenderloin. They soon were back in operation. Herbert Asbury noted that the election of Mayor James Rolph and a new Board of Supervisors put an end to "an unfriendly, if not actively hostile" municipal administration.[11] There were then an estimated 2,800 legal and 2,500 illegal saloons. From 1913 to 1917, "Sunny Jim" Rolph, mayor of San Francisco, and Madam Tessie Wall, the city's most notorious brothel keeper, rode together through the vice districts at the head of an annual parade organized by the entrepreneurs of pleasure. This could not have happened in Los Angeles.

Rolph favored "personal liberty" and had no identifiable interest in moral reform, progressive style. In 1917, however, an anti-vice crusade led by the Reverend Paul Smith, a Methodist from Boston, caused the Barbary Coast and the tenderloin to be shut down. Vice entrepreneurs and defenders of personal liberty argued that the spirited city had been wide open for sixty-nine years but could not carry the day. Although vice operations continued, the two most famous districts never were the same.[12]

Douglas Henry Daniels has pointed out that "a long-established reputation as a pleasure or sin city permitted night life to thrive without gangland violence." Even during the Prohibition Era, when gangs in Los Angeles and other major cities warred for control of the liquor traffic, San Francisco remained relatively calm. Although there was plenty of graft for police and politicians, there were few scandals.[13]

The depredations of Boss Abe Ruef and Mayor Schmitz, during the first decade of the twentieth century, are well known. It was revealed during the trials that Ruef and Schmitz shared in the profits derived from vice. Yet—significantly—the ill-gotten gain was not what the fuss was about, and alone would not have been a likely cause for throwing the rascals out. Charles Rudebaugh, a newspaper reporter, observed that "everyone knew and boasted" that the city was open and that the police took bribes. The mayor's discussing the situation in public, however, was considered bad for the municipal reputation. A private investigator was brought in to gather evidence of misconduct. The investigator took pains afterward to point out that he had been given no mandate to close illegal businesses, because the citizens of San Francisco wanted them open. The issue was the extortion of bribes from vice operators by policemen.[14]

Reformers in San Francisco described themselves as progressives at least as early as 1896. Some of them favored moral reform of the city, including suppression of the vice districts. Associations of Protestants, Catholics, and Jews campaigned against the "adult entertainment" industry for decades. Black and Chinese residents also struggled to suppress open vice in their neighborhoods. Eventually, over a period of four decades, they succeeded. In the short term, they failed. Local-option prohibition was soundly defeated. Legislation such as the Red Light Abatement Act was seldom used. Police would not arrest. Judges would not convict. Vice, per se, apparently was not a serious issue for a majority of voters. As long as the vice districts remained quiet, the tradition of benign neglect could be maintained.[15]

The story was very different in Los Angeles. As with San Francisco, rapid growth in population followed the discovery of gold. Los Angeles became "the toughest town in the West," home to all the traditional frontier amusements. During the 1850s, with a population of fewer than six thousand residents, the city supported about four hundred premises providing gambling, alcohol, and prostitution.[16]

By the 1870s, native-born Protestants had become the dominant political force in Los Angeles. They later boasted that the town contained more churches in relation to population than any other city in the United States. The new middle class exhibited a strong interest in law enforcement and in control of vice operations. They found the town marshals ill-equipped to provide the safe streets and moral order to which they aspired. In 1876, the marshals were replaced by the newly formed Los Angeles Police Department.[17] Thereafter, the police force usually was at the center of local politics, either because it could not be controlled by the municipal government or because it was involved in the protection of illegal enterprises.

At the same time that the LAPD was created, the Los Angeles Common Council issued ordinances limiting the location of vice premises, the type of "personal service" permitted, and the times at which such entertainments could be provided. At first, the ordinances merely forbade vice operations within prescribed boundaries in the central business and residential areas. Later, the council established a legal vice district but soon withdrew the law. An anti-prostitution act forbidding single women to reside on the ground floor of any dwelling was overturned by the state Supreme court. The council also forbade gambling and introduced early-closing hours and Sunday closing for saloons. Consequently, the purveyors of traditional pleasures suddenly made illicit by the council were compelled to bribe the police or the politicians, or both, if they wished to stay in business.

Despite their largely unsuccessful efforts to reform the city, the reformers believed that they might be more successful if the police were removed from politics. (The workings of politics dictated short careers for police chiefs: between 1877 and 1889, at least sixteen men held the post.)[18] To that end, progressives set out to reform the city charter. The Los Angeles city charter was rewritten or revised in 1889, 1902, 1909, 1911, and 1925. In each case, control of the police was a major element. In 1889, the first police commission was established, replacing a council committee, to deal with appointments, promotions, dismissals, and general policy. True to their faith in nonpartisanship, the progressives first tried dividing authority between Republican and Democratic councilmen, who each appointed two members to the commission; the mayor also served but could not be chairman. Depoliticizing lines of authority over the police failed because all the commissioners were political partisans, and their decisions concerning the police force were partisan decisions.

In 1902, progressive voters ratified the initiative, referendum, and recall; established a municipal civil service; and revised the rules governing the police commission and the police. All police jobs were classified except the positions of police chief and secretary to the police chief.

Physical and mental entrance standards and competitive promotional examinations were certified. Salaries were mandated by the charter and could not be reduced by the council. The charter further required that any order having to do with the police must be sent directly to the chief for action. The mayor became chairman of the police commission and could remove other commissioners with consent of the council. By these measures, the progressives hoped to raise the caliber and establish the independence of the individual officer, and place day-to-day control of the department in the chief's hands. The mayor, as chief executive officer, was given greater responsibility for the overall management of the police force.

The charter amendments of 1902 outlawed gambling and prostitution within the city limits. Before these amendments were passed, commercial vice had prospered in "the segregated zone"; indeed, directories were printed that identified brothels by address and the name of the madam, often including words of praise for the comely damsels who "assisted" her. Then two churchmen found "the Ballarino," a building of many narrow cells or "cribs," designed for prostitution. Their anti-vice crusade closed the place and brought calumny upon the police force. Afterward, the progressives won a great victory at the polls.[19]

Whether knowledgeable progressives, hoping to gain political support, guided the two ministers to the Ballarino is not known. What is clear is that the anti-vice crusade became the standard election tactic in Los Angeles for half a century afterward. That vice should be the most volatile political issue over a period of five decades spoke volumes about the electorate, although concerns about vice were not entirely misguided. Despite the will of the voting majority, scandal after scandal occurred. Progressives routinely elected "reform" candidates who abandoned reform after the election.

Between 1904 and 1909, the voters rejected, in one way or another, three mayors accused of misconduct involving liquor and prostitution operations. Meredith Snyder was mayor from 1900 to 1904, during which time the vice district flourished. In 1904, Snyder was defeated by Owen McAleer, "the whisky mayor," who opposed further restrictions on saloons. McAleer served two years and declined to run again. The machine Democrat, Arthur Harper, was elected in 1906 but resigned suddenly in 1909 in the midst of a campaign to recall him. Five police chiefs left in disgrace.[20]

Until about 1905, there was still some frontier-style joie de vivre apparent in Los Angeles, but it was soon to disappear. In 1908, the district attorney closed down the brothel of Pearl Morton, the city's best-known madam. The same year, Mayor Arthur Harper boasted that he did not protect vice, he condoned it, notwithstanding the laws against gambling, prostitution, and after-hours saloons. The Municipal League, formed in 1901 by Charles Dwight Willard, then initiated a recall campaign. Other reform clubs joined in, including John R. Haynes's Direct Legislation League, Edward A. Dickson's City Club, and Meyer Lissner's good government organization.

These groups formed the vanguard of the Lincoln-Roosevelt League, which became a powerful, statewide organization. The progressives could depend also on the Anti-Saloon League, the Anti–Race Track Gambling League, the Sunday Rest League, and the League of Justice. Mayor Harper resigned before the recall election. The reason was not made public, but the rumor at the time was that the payoff book detailing the mayor's profits from the tenderloin had been obtained by a local newspaper.

Between 1900 and 1909, Los Angeles's population tripled, to 300,000 residents. Most of the newcomers apparently were native Protestants of progressive sentiments. In the 1909 election, the progressives won all twenty-three elective offices. Subsequently, charter amendments were approved that abolished the ward system and installed nonpartisan election laws. These laws, in effect, eliminated the municipal Democratic party. The great victory of 1911 also initiated the destruction of the movement for political reform, since it witnessed the progressive/ conservative coalition built to thwart the challenge from the left. By 1915, although control of the city remained in the hands of Protestant Republicans, the reform coalition was in ruins. With it went the integrity of the police force.[21]

For the six years between 1909 and 1915, nevertheless, vice had been virtually suppressed. In this effort, the police had been aided by a platoon of ministers sworn in as special constables and by the Morals Efficiency League, also staffed by clergymen. Artistic censorship had been introduced, not only for motion pictures but for dance and drama as well. Isadora Duncan had been forbidden to dance. Eugene O'Neill's play *Desire under the Elms* was not allowed to open. Racetrack gambling and prizefighting had been abolished. To ensure the conviction of prostitutes, a local ordinance forbade sexual relations between persons not married to one another.

Willard Huntington Wright, a local author, watched bitterly as the once exciting city was made "chemically pure." Wright described the general atmosphere as "a frenzy of virtue." Pleasure seekers found themselves "thwarted by some ordinance, the primary object of which is to force Middle West moralities on every inhabitant. Puritanism is the inflexible doctrine of Los Angeles." Wright later was echoed by the district attorney, a Roman Catholic, who denounced "pussy-footing, publicity-seeking, religious despots." The ministerial rebuttal praised the Ku Klux Klan "for the enemies they have made."[22]

Worse or better was in store, depending on the point of view. The moral reformers who provided the voting strength of the progressive movement supported a new mid-teens coalition, led mainly by Protestant ministers. They continued the struggle to suppress vice. The various groups were vociferous and determined. They "raided" dance halls and roadhouses, and sometimes had them closed. They held tumultuous press conferences, often in the offices of the mayor or the police commission. They attacked mayors and got police chiefs ousted. They were influential on voting day (for example, the Gandier Ordinance was passed in 1916 with no real difficulty), and they forced further restrictions on anyone whose idea of fun differed from their own.

In the early 1920s, reformers persuaded the police commission to restrict the conduct of dancers. Dancing with the cheek or head touching one's partner was forbidden. The male could place his hand only on his partner's back, between shoulder and waist. The female could place her hand only in her partner's left hand. No music "suggestive of bodily contortions" could be played. Moreover, women were forbidden to smoke in any room or place adjacent to a ballroom or dance academy. One minister led a campaign against a female candidate for the school board because the woman smoked tobacco. The candidate promised to quit if elected, but the reformers were adamant. She was defeated.[23]

For twenty-five years, the second wave of reformers campaigned for civic purity. They constantly harassed the police by publicly identifying premises where various illegal enterprises were operated. They held press conferences and large church meetings. They wrote pamphlets. They sat in court to find out which judges convicted vice operators and which ones did not. They voted overwhelmingly for charter revisions to reform the police department. Nevertheless, vice operations continued.

The success of these reformers was minimal because the police department was again at the beck and call of officials who owed their support to one or another corrupt interest. The ministerial associations and federations of laity lacked the cohesion and efficiency of the good government organizations. More important, perhaps, they lacked the financial support of philanthropic progressives such as Meyer Lissner and E. T. Earl. Political campaigns required money, but civil service regulations curtailed patronage, nonpartisan election laws vitiated precinct organizations, and abolition of vice eliminated the most generous contributors.

The electoral victories of 1902–1915 proved that the numerous and potentially all-powerful reformers could not be ignored. They could be circumvented, nevertheless. Every political candidate of the time styled himself or herself a progressive. Since the reformers would not or could not finance a municipal slate of preferred candidates, they were compelled to support the most promising of those who stood for office. Consequently, the venal politicians and purveyors of vice, the so-called underworld combination, regained influence by financing ostensible reformers who, once in office, cooperated with corrupt interests, especially by manipulating the police department. The department operated as a sort of licensing and inspection bureau for organized vice operations. Those approved by the combination were protected; independents were put out of business.

The market for disreputable pleasures grew enormously after 1910. The number of transient males—the most likely "consumers"—increased substantially with the opening of the Panama Canal, the construction of the Los Angeles harbor, and the onset of World War I. The city had a seaport, a naval station, and an army camp. New industries attracted more workers. "Factories in the fields" employed many laborers. The large, continuing migration to the area required thousands of tradesmen to construct houses and services. Transients aside, the population rose from 100,000 in 1900 to 576,000 in 1920, and to 1.3 million in 1930.

Concurrently, local prohibition in 1916, followed by the Eighteenth Amendment, created a law enforcement crisis of unprecedented proportions. Opportunities for graft exceeded anything previously known. The number of police officers and other officials eager to share in the bonanza increased as profits increased. With the vice lords ascendant, the reformers concerned themselves almost entirely with moral issues.[24]

In 1925, the last great progressive city charter went into effect. Again, police administration was an important consideration. The new charter (still in effect in 1992) provided for a five-member board of appointed police commissioners. The commissioners, responsible for general policy and for disciplining the chief when necessary, were appointed by the mayor and could be dismissed with consent of the council. The five-year terms were staggered, so that (in theory) only one member could be replaced each year—the idea being that an incoming mayor would not be able to replace the entire board of commissioners.

Like all previous revisions, the charter of 1925 made no substantive difference. Organized, protected commercial vice remained a staple of nightlife in Los Angeles for another fifteen years. Almost all elected representatives were corrupt. The police force reached unexampled depths of infamy. Between 1915 and 1933, Charles Sebastian, Frederick Woodman, Meredith Snyder, George Cryer, and John Porter took office as reform mayors and left in disgrace. A dozen police chiefs came and went. Only in 1938, when the police intelligence squad tried and failed to murder an investigator hired by reformers, did the significant forces unite to unseat the mayor and reform the police department.

It was typical of Los Angeles that the detective was hired to investigate protected commercial vice, of all possible evils, and fitting that he was employed by Clifford Clinton, a Protestant, Republican, progressive businessman and moral reformer. The defeated vice entrepreneurs then moved to Las Vegas, which they had been developing since 1931. The subsequent relative purity of Los Angeles was generally credited to the departed criminals, acting in their own self-interest to suppress commercial vice in the City of the Angels. Thus, it could be argued that even in Los Angeles the progressives failed to impose moral order.[25]

On the surface, the similarities between San Francisco and Los Angeles were quite marked. Both had manufacturers' associations opposed to organized labor. Both had men's and women's service clubs devoted to economic prosperity and the improvement of public morals. Both accepted municipal socialism with respect to public utilities. Both engaged in successful struggles for charter reform. Both were bumptious, rapidly growing, polyglot communities dominated by white, native-born Republicans. Both were progressive. Both had stringent anti-vice laws, flourishing tenderloin districts protected by police and politicians, and crusading religious leaders opposed to commercial vice.

Why, then, did the two cities diverge so widely where "adult pastimes" were concerned? The reason seems to be that the differences between the two cities, though fewer than the similarities, were far more significant. The simplest but most cogent explanation combines religion and ethnicity: San Francisco was a Catholic and Irish city; Los Angeles was a Protestant and evangelical midwestern city, "the capital of Iowa" moved west.

Catholic churchgoers outnumbered Protestant churchgoers in San Francisco by about a five-to-one margin. Most came from countries where the consumption of wine or beer was a part of the national way of life, or they were descended from immigrants from such countries. These people generally opposed restrictions on personal behavior. The politically active and astute Irish dominated municipal politics. Block and precinct headquarters usually were located in saloons.

The Protestants of San Francisco did favor measures for moral reform and would have passed them if they could. George Kennan (the explorer and journalist) mourned for the prosperous and successful city because it emphasized "material achievement and business prosperity rather than civic virtue and moral integrity. But what shall it profit a city if it gain the whole world and lose its own soul?"[26] Similarly, there were Catholic anti-vice crusaders and Catholic progressives in San Francisco. But no temperance campaign ever succeeded there. San Francisco state representatives voted twelve to one against the Gandier Ordinance. Eighty-three percent of voters opposed local-option prohibition. The city was "wet" during the entire period of national prohibition. Los Angeles voters, on the other hand, voted for local prohibition in 1916 and approved other laws intended to suppress gambling and sexual promiscuity.

In retrospect, it is easy to ridicule the progressives' belief that one can reform a community by changing its laws. In truth, progressives believed more in good people than in good laws. They believed that police officers of good moral character, intelligent, educated, well trained, well paid, with tenure of office and adequate pensions, could and would enforce good laws and rid their communities of moral blight.

This ideal, never completely realized, still sustains civic reformers, as well it should. In Los Angeles, when honorable men and women held municipal office, the police enforced the laws, protected commercial vice was virtually eliminated, and the disreputable pleasures were reduced to an acceptable level. Charters, no matter how well drafted, could not achieve those goals.

The nonpartisan public service is an enduring legacy of the progressive movement. The police in particular have responded to the drive to professionalize every human vocation. Intelligence tests, mental health examinations, educational requirements, competitive promotional examinations that favor candidates with advanced education, physical health and strength regulations, even requirements to employ females and members of ethnic minorities—all these things are in the progressive tradition. When the ideal of impartial public service is violated, it is a matter of personal choice, not the failure of an institution or a law.

Fortunately for their place in history, the California progressives were more than puritanical moralists, although without their religious zeal their movement might have been less significant. A poet has said "When I am sick then I believe in law." The line expresses a very progressive and very American view. The progressives saw that their society was sick, and they moved to cure it with laws prohibiting certain kinds of personal, political, and economic conduct. They succeeded to a limited degree in every area, and their inheritors have generally followed the same path.

Frederick C. Howe mused wisely upon the Progressive Era in *The Confessions of a Reformer:*

Early assumptions as to virtue and vice, goodness and evil, remained in my mind long after I had tried to discard them. This is, I think, the most characteristic influence of my generation. It explains the nature of our reforms, the regulatory legislation in morals and economics, our belief in men rather than institutions and our messages to other peoples. Missionaries and battleships, anti-saloon leagues and Ku Klux Klans, Wilson and Santo Domingo are all part of that evangelistic psychology that makes America what she is.[27]

NOTES

1. Alfred D. Chandler, Jr., "The Origins of Progressive Leadership," in Elting Morrison, ed., *The Letters of Theodore Roosevelt*, (Cambridge, Mass.: Harvard University Press, 1954), 8: 1462–65; Otis Pease, *The Progressive Years: The Spirit and Achievement of American Reform* (New York: Braziller, 1962), "Introduction," especially 7–10; George E. Mowry, *The California Progressives* (Berkeley: University of California Press, 1951), chap. 4, "What Manner of Men: The Progressive Mind," 86–154.

2. Mowry, *California Progressives*, 101; Richard Hofstadter, *The Age of Reform: From Bryan to FDR* (New York: Knopf, 1955), 134–36.

3. Benjamin Parke DeWitt, *The Progressive Movement: A Non-partisan, Comprehensive Discussion of Current Tendencies in American Politics* (New York: Macmillan, 1915), viii.

4. Douglas Henry Daniels, *Pioneer Urbanites: A Social and Cultural History of Black San Francisco* (Philadelphia: Temple University Press, 1980), 145–55; Spencer C. Olin, Jr., *California's Prodigal Sons: Hiram Johnson and the Progressives, 1911–1917* (Berkeley: University of California Press, 1968), 55; Mowry, *California Progressives*, 38.

5. DeWitt, *The Progressive Movement*, 362–63.

6. William Issel and Robert W. Cherny, *San Francisco, 1865–1932: Politics, Power, and Urban Development* (Berkeley: University of California Press, 1986), especially 106–60.

7. Franklin Hichborn, *Story of the Session of the California Legislature of 1909* (San Francisco: James H. Barry Co., 1909), 52–67; Robert Glass Cleland,

California in Our Time, 1900–1940 (New York: Knopf, 1947), 48; Olin, *California's Prodigal Sons*, 53–55. For a comprehensive treatment of the anti-liquor struggle, see Gilman H. Ostrander, *The Prohibition Movement in California, 1848–1933* (Berkeley: University of California Press, 1957); and Peter H. Odegard, *Pressure Politics: The Story of the Anti-Saloon League* (New York: Octagon Books, 1966).

8. Franklin Hichborn, *Story of the Session of the California Legislature of 1913* (San Francisco: James H. Barry Co., 1913), 284–86, and *Story of the Session of the California Legislature of 1915* (San Francisco: James H. Barry Co., 1915), xi–xiv.

9. Mowry, *California Progressives*, 23–56; Cleland, *California in Our Time*, 7–8 and passim; William A. Bullough, *The Blind Boss and His City: Christopher Augustine Buckley and Nineteenth Century San Francisco* (Berkeley: University of California Press, 1979), 108–11; Curt Gentry, *The Madams of San Francisco: An Irreverent History of the City by the Golden Gate* (Sausalito, Calif.: Comstock, 1964), 190–200, 255; Daniels, *Pioneer Urbanites*, 145.

10. Herbert Asbury, *The Barbary Coast: An Informal History of the San Francisco Underworld* (Long Beach, Calif.: Brown and Nourse, 1949), 268; Fremont Older, cited in Gentry, *The Madams of San Francisco*, 228.

11. Asbury, *Barbary Coast*, 299.

12. Ibid., 299–313; Gentry, *The Madams of San Francisco*, 216.

13. Daniels, *Pioneer Urbanites*, 145–49; quote in text on p. 145.

14. Fremont Older, *My Own Story* (New York: Macmillan, 1926), 34–48; Cleland, *California in Our Time*, 11; Gentry, *The Madams of San Francisco*, 240–48, 194–95; Issel and Cherny, *San Francisco*, 106–10.

15. Eugene B. Black, *The Immortal San Franciscans for Whom the Streets Were Named* (San Francisco: Chronicle Books, 1971), 195; Issel and Cherny, *San Francisco*, 107, 139–64; Cleland, *California in Our Time;* Asbury, *The Barbary Coast*, 313; Royce D. Delmatier, Clarence F. McIntosh, and Earl G. Waters, eds., *The Rumble of California Politics, 1848–1970* (New York: Wiley, 1970), 169–74; Gentry, *The Madams of San Francisco*, 246–48.

16. For descriptions of the "toughest town in the West" see Homer B. Cross, "Out of the Past," In *The Guardian* (Los Angeles: Los Angeles Police Department, 1937), 17; Horace Bell, *Reminiscences of a Ranger* (Los Angeles: Yarnell, Castile, and Mathes, 1881), and *On the Old West Coast: Being Further Reminiscences of a Ranger* (New York: Morrow, 1902); Harris Newmark, *Sixty Years in Southern California, 1853–1913* (New York: Knickerbocker Press, 1916); J. Albert Wilson, *History of Los Angeles County* (Oakland: Thompson & West, 1880); Charles Dwight Willard, *A History of Los Angeles City* (Los Angeles: Kingsley-Barnes and Neuner, 1901); J. M. Guinn, *Historical and Biographical Record of Southern California* (Chicago: Lewis, 1902); Leonard Pitt, *The Decline of the Californios* (Berkeley: University of California Press, 1966). See also E. Caroline Gabard, "The Development of Law Enforcement in Early California" (M.A. thesis, University of Southern California, 1960); Patricia A. Poos, "The Era of Do-It-Yourself Justice: The First Twenty-one Years of the Los Angeles County Sheriff's Department" (Senior Project, California State Poly-

technic College, Pomona, 1972); and Arthur W. Sjoquist, "From Posses to Professionals: A History of the Los Angeles Police Department" (M.A. thesis, California State University, Los Angeles, 1972).

17. Los Angeles Common Council, *Minutes*, vols. 11–13 (1876); City of Los Angeles, *Records*, vol. 11 (1876); Marvin Abrahams, "The Functioning of Boards and Commissions in the Los Angeles City Government" (Ph.D. diss., University of California, Los Angeles, 1967), 12.

18. "Police Chiefs of Los Angeles," n.p., n.d.; George Wilson, "History of the Los Angeles Police," typescript, n.d. See J. G. Woods, "The Progressives and the Police" (Ph.D. diss., University of California, Los Angeles, 1973).

19. For a fictionalized account of these events, see two books by Sydney C. Kendall; *The Soundings of Hell* (Los Angeles: W. J. Phillips, 1903) and *Queen of the Red Lights* (Los Angeles: W. J. Phillips, 1906). The factual story is in the *Times*, June through December 1902.

20. W. W. Robinson, *Tarnished Angels: Paradisaical Turpitude in Los Angeles* (Los Angeles: Ward Ritchie Press, 1964), 13–21.

21. The best account of the growth of population is Robert M. Fogelson, *The Fragmented Metropolis: Los Angeles, 1850–1930* (Cambridge, Mass.: Harvard University Press, 1968), especially chap. 4, "The Great Migration," 63–84. See also Remi Nadeau, *Los Angeles: From Mission to Modern City* (New York: Longman's, 1960), 59–82, 142–60.

22. Willard H. Wright, "Los Angeles, the Chemically Pure" (*The Smart Set*, 1913), in Burton Rascoe and Graff Conklin, eds., *The Smart Set Anthology* (New York: Reynal & Hitchcock, 1934), 90–102; *Record*, November 21, 1922; Woods, "The Progressives and the Police," 31–43.

23. *Record*, September 5, October 4 and 11, November 21, December 1 and 6, 1922, June 4, 6, 11, and 13, 1923; see especially the front-page article, "Shuler at the Mob Organ," June 12, 1923. See also Los Angeles Police Commission, *Minutes*, April 5, 1921, January 24 and March 8, 1922; and Edmund Wilson's description of two of the city's religious extremists, reprinted in *The American Earthquake: A Documentary of the Twenties and Thirties* (Garden City, N.Y.: Doubleday Anchor Books, 1958), 379–96.

24. James H. Richardson, *For the Life of Me: Memoirs of a City Editor* (New York: Putnam's, 1954), 94–103; Woods, "The Progressives and the Police," 44–83.

25. Ernest Chamberlain, "The CIVIC Committee of Los Angeles, Its Background, Activities and Accomplishments," and "The Revolt of the Angelinos," E. R. Chamberlain Collection; Shaw Scrapbooks, passim; Clinton Papers, passim—all in Department of Special Collections, UCLA. See also Woods, "The Progressives and the Police," 357, 359–72.

26. Michael P. Rogin and John L. Shover, *Political Change in California: Critical Elections and Social Movements, 1890–1966* (Westport, Conn.: Greenwood, 1970), 38–51; Issel and Cherny, *San Francisco*, 139–64; George Kennan, "Criminal Government and Private Citizens," *McClure's* 17 (November 1907): 71.

27. Frederick C. Howe (1925), quoted in Hofstadter, *The Age of Reform*, 206.

PART TWO

What Manner of Men?

Women and the Progressive Impetus

Socialist Women and Progressive Reform

Sherry Katz

After the enfranchisement of California women in 1911, socialist women joined the mainstream woman movement in increasing numbers and with great enthusiasm. Socialist women believed that organized womanhood was emerging as a "revolutionary" cross-class social force, dedicated to "incorporat[ing] the mother spirit, the democratic spirit, in the institutions of society" and to "further[ing] the interests of the people as against the interests of property." These women wanted to "combat the terrible degenerating evils of a man-made class system, of which the bondage of women [was] only one manifestation." The woman movement—as a united and well-organized coalition of female voluntary associations, with a specified political agenda, a cadre of skilled lobbyists, and the votes of the newly enfranchised female electorate—possessed great power to enact humanitarian legislation. If other women reformers could be convinced—as socialist women were—that "our androcentric society" was also a "society of classes," requiring fundamental "economic reorganization," they might become "a tremendous constructive force."[1]

Within these nonpartisan female voluntary associations, socialist activists carved out a special role for themselves as representatives of wage-earning and working-class women and as socialist educators. They championed issues that combined their commitments to women's emancipation, to the empowerment of the working class and organized labor, and to "civic maternalism." Socialist women proved especially active in the areas of "child-saving," women's labor, and sexual emancipation. As the "left wing" of both the woman movement and broader reform coalitions, radical women advocated reforms they believed would prove "underminingly ameliorative," able to empower the working class and/or women and to prefigure conditions under a socialist (and feminist) state. Their influence on the legislative proposals advanced by mainstream women's groups helps explain why California was at the forefront of social welfare legislation for women during the Progressive Era.[2]

SOCIALIST WOMEN: A COLLECTIVE BIOGRAPHY

A sizable and well-organized socialist women's movement flourished in California from the 1890s to World War I.[3] During the late nineteenth century, the state provided fertile ground for the growth of indigenous protest movements that sought to combat the harsh consequences of corporate capitalism. California's speedy economic development, accompanied by glaring economic inequalities, nurtured an openness to radical ideas and political alternatives. During the 1890s, several generations of women active in suffrage and temperance crusades, including many older veterans with strong ties to abolitionism, spiritualism, or labor reform, found in the "Cooperative Commonwealth" the basis for an egalitarian society guaranteeing women's freedom. As these women developed dual commitments to the emancipation of women and of the working class, they came to believe that the struggle for human freedom had to be waged by women working alone and also by women and men working together in a shared commitment to socialism.[4]

After the turn of the twentieth century, local activists built a network of autonomous socialist women's clubs, under the umbrella of the Woman's Socialist Union of California (1902–1911), and worked within both the male-dominated socialist movement and the mainstream woman movement. The "dual strategy" of separatism and integration allowed socialist women to create within each movement a distinctive presence that advocated a special set of concerns and exerted substantial influence. Demonstrating both loyalty and independence, these women brought their organizational skills, leadership abilities, and woman-centered political demands to the state's Socialist party. They also played a prominent role in the California suffrage movement. They helped to expand the movement's base among working-class women, garner support from trade unions, broaden arguments for enfranchisement, and provide new militancy and modern methods. For nearly twenty years, radical women participated in the Socialist party and the woman movement from an independent base that supported their distinct identity as political agents and provided networks that sustained their activism.[5]

The Woman's Socialist Union (WSU) represented hundreds of the most active feminist socialists in the state. A number of like-minded radical women remained independent but developed close ties to their sisters in the WSU. From information gathered on thirty-five state and local leaders of the WSU, I was able to develop a social portrait of the leadership cadre of the socialist women's movement. Most were born in the United States in the 1860s and 1870s, attained either stable working-class or middle-class status, and came to the socialist women's movement through participation in the woman and left movements of the 1890s. Many of these activists had been raised in Protestant households, had married and borne one or two children, and were surrounded by family members who considered themselves socialists. Relatively well educated, they worked in professional or clerical occupations, particularly in teaching and newspaper work, for at least part of their adult lives. They were joined by a number of veteran activists born in the United States between the 1820s and the 1840s who had had formative political experiences in abolitionism, early women's rights, and spiritualism. A younger generation of women born in the United States in the 1880s and 1890s joined the socialist women's movement around 1910.[6]

THE CALIFORNIA "WOMAN MOVEMENT": A BRIEF HISTORY

By the mid-1890s, California possessed a well-organized woman movement based in San Francisco and Los Angeles. This movement had been built primarily by white, middle-class, native-born, Protestant women who settled in California after 1848. Like their sisters in the East and Midwest, the state's activist women felt deeply disturbed by the social dislocation and human suffering caused by industrialization and believed that women had a special role to play in ensuring both social order and social justice. Consequently, they created many of the same kinds of single-sex voluntary associations that flourished elsewhere, including benevolent institutions, temperance organizations, professional associations, civic groups, and women's clubs. These organizations focused on improving the lives of women and children, advancing moral reform, and promoting "municipal housekeeping." As organized women encountered opposition to their reform initiatives and began to gain a sense of political power, they increasingly demanded equality for their sex. By the late 1890s, members of women's voluntary associations joined their sisters in suffrage organizations in demanding the vote as a means to advance women and their public activism. During the first decade of the twentieth century, the suffrage movement broadened its base, gained grater public support, implemented new tactics, and won enfranchisement for California women in 1911.[7]

During the postsuffrage period, the California woman movement expanded its mission and its size. Both old and new women's associations dedicated themselves to "equipping the women with a knowledge of government and civics," studying "public questions," endorsing legislative measures, and providing nonpartisan forums for the discussion of party platforms and controversial issues.[8] Women's organizations now placed greater emphasis on questions of "social betterment" and "public welfare"; they urged women to use their collective power as enfranchised citizens to vote for "humanitarian legislation" that would protect women and children, enlarge civic housekeeping, and benefit the "race."[9] Politically active women sought to create a nonpartisan body of women voters, who would, through voluntary associations and at the ballot box, support a gender-specific political agenda.

To coordinate the reform efforts of all women's organizations in the state and to consolidate a women's presence in the legislative and electoral arenas, the California Federation of Women's Clubs (CFWC)—the most important women's association in the state, with over 25,000 members in 318 affiliates—called for the establishment of a Women's Legislative Council (WLC) in the fall of 1912. Fifty-three women's organizations signed on as charter members of the council, including the Woman's Christian Temperance Union (WCTU), the Young Women's Christian Association (YWCA), the Association of Collegiate Alumnae, the California Congress of Mothers (CCM), the National Child Labor Committee, state teachers' and nurses' associations, garment and laundry workers' unions, local and regional women's clubs, and women's committees of the Democratic, Progressive, and Socialist parties. The council endorsed a number of bills during each legislative session and operated a headquarters for women in Sacramento. Bills given highest priority promoted the welfare of women and children, the extension of women's legal equality, and the health and well-being of the community.[10] The woman's lobby proved effective: the legislature enacted social and moral legislation partly in response to what socialist Alice Park called a "united demand of women voters."[11] The remainder of this essay will explore socialist women's contributions to the development of organized womanhood's reform agenda.

MAJOR REFORMS ADVOCATED
BY WOMEN ACTIVISTS

MOTHERS' PENSIONS

As prominent members of women's clubs, civic associations, and other voluntary groups, socialist women became some of the most vocal advocates of child-saving legislation and programs, and they helped put the welfare of working-class women and children at the top of the political agenda of California's Women's Legislative Council. Alongside their non-socialist counterparts, radical women campaigned for restrictions on child labor, for the provisions of "wholesome" public amusements for poor children and young adults, and for mothers' pensions. Radical women's unique contributions to the child-saving work of the California woman movement lay primarily in the realms of internal debate and policy formation, where the implications of child-saving for class relations, women's emancipation, and social change were contested. Mainstream clubwomen argued for minimalist programs designed to rescue the poorest children and to protect society from their possible "delinquency" and "immorality." Socialist women, by contrast, proposed that child-saving programs serve as the seed for the development of a comprehensive welfare state committed to providing economic support to all its members. They saw in child-saving measures the potential to empower both the working class and women, and they used discussions of child-saving to challenge the class and ethnocentric fears of mainstream clubwomen.

Mothers' pensions emerged as a central demand of the state's organized women in 1912 and 1913. During those years, the Women's Legislative Council made the passage of a mothers' pension bill a major priority. A host of women's voluntary associations drafted bills and expressed their dedication to the issue. Grass-roots support proved enormous.[12]

California women were not alone in their enthusiasm for mothers' pensions. Beginning in 1909, the issue of mothers' pensions captured the attention of female reformers throughout the country. Middle-class women led the struggle for mothers' pensions as part of their attempt to assist working-class women and their children. Some of these activists were college-educated members of the settlement house movement, who sympathized with the cause of labor; others, less well educated and less identified with labor, were homemakers who belonged to affiliates of the General Federation of Women's Clubs and the National Congress of

Mothers. Noting that the efforts to enact such legislation proved especially vigorous in states where women had already been enfranchised, political scientist Barbara Nelson argues that such legislation emerged as an important part of women's "drive for political incorporation." While California was one of the first states to enact a mothers' pension bill, by 1919 thirty-nine states had passed similar measures.[13]

In California, well-educated progressive and socialist leaders of the club movement led the campaign for mothers' pensions. Socialist women helped to draft the legislative proposals and participated actively in the discussion surrounding the necessity and meaning of mothers' pensions. Los Angeles socialists Caroline Foster, Emma J. Wolfe, and Sara Wilde Houser and San Francisco party member Lucy Goode White played central roles in drafting mothers' pension bills on behalf of a number of organizations, including the Friday Morning Club of Los Angeles, one of the oldest and most reform-minded clubs in the state, and the short-lived California League for the Protection of Motherhood. Many other radical clubwomen, such as Frances Nacke Noel, Agnes H. Downing, Mila Tupper Maynard, and Elvina Beals, were outspoken in their support of mothers' pensions.[14]

Most progressive clubwomen favored mothers' pensions as a way to provide relief for destitute mothers and their children. Pensions would "save," "protect," and "help" poor children by keeping them at home with their mothers, who could devote themselves to child raising instead of wage earning. Equally important would be the effect of pensions in protecting the state from "delinquent children and an ignorant vote." Juvenile delinquency and crime could be avoided if mothers trained their children "to be good citizens." Progressive clubwomen did not believe that all indigent mothers were "worthy" of such support, however. Only "respectable mothers," women "of good character," should be able to qualify for the pensions. Grace Simons, a leader of the Friday Morning Club, captured these sentiments: "No opportunity that we can give children equals that of the training of a *good mother* in their own home. The State should realize that an investment in *good mothers* pay its interest in the production of good citizens [emphasis mine]." Clearly, many progressive women envisioned mothers' pensions not as a right of the indigent but as a means of providing government assistance to the "worthy" poor and of protecting society against the "unworthy" poor.[15]

Socialist women agreed with progressive clubwomen that the provision of state assistance to poor children and their mothers would help keep working-class families intact, thereby increasing the mental, physical, and moral health of indigent children and society at large. The beliefs underlying this position were different for socialist and non-socialist women, however. Socialist women wanted to fortify the working-class family not because they viewed its breakdown as a potential menace to middle-class society but because they identified with laboring people and wanted to strengthen the working class and weaken capitalism. They resisted the distinctions between the worthy and unworthy poor, demanding mothers' aid for all in need and identifying such support as a right of the poor and an obligation of the state under capitalism. Some radical women also linked the mothers' pension issue to women's emancipation. They argued that the state should support child rearing because it was socially important labor, and they pointed out that mothers' pensions would enable women to leave oppressive relationships and gain economic and emotional freedom from men. Socialist women pushed for the most comprehensive pension plans and argued against the exclusion of so-called unworthy mothers.

Like their mainstream counterparts, socialist women expressed a deep concern for the well-being of women and children, and argued for mothers' pensions as a means to provide poor children with a nurturing and supportive home life. Despite their commitment to women's emancipation through wage earning and economic independence, they still advocated "home life for the child." Although they themselves, with careers in the paid labor force or in social reform, often developed alternative child-care arrangements, they believed it best for young children to be raised by attentive mothers instead of overworked female wage earners or uncaring institutions. They probably envisioned that mothers' pensions would primarily fund poor mothers with very young children, for whom simultaneous wage earning and child rearing would be extremely difficult. Agnes Downing argued that mothers' pensions "would permit many boys and girls to begin life better . . . and would mean the difference between good, efficient citizens and half starved slum children," who, neglected by their overworked single mothers, "are marked by crime and physical inefficiency before they are of age."[16]

As Downing's remarks indicate, socialist women shared the belief of their mainstream counterparts that poverty fostered crime and interfered with the development of "good, efficient citizens." But radical women also expressed a deep faith in the ability of all working-class parents to raise their children properly when they had adequate financial resources. As mentioned, mainstream female reformers wished to support only worthy mothers, believing that many indigent women lacked proper education and morals because of their lower-class backgrounds; in contrast, socialist women supported pensions for all indigent mothers without male breadwinners "as a matter of simple justice." Downing wanted "honorable" pensions for "every woman who is dependent on her own efforts, and has a baby to raise." Responding to the suggestions that "ignorant mothers" should not receive mothers' pensions, Frances Noel argued that all mothers needed professional training, regardless of their class status. She recommended pensions for both married (including widowed) and unmarried mothers, and did not define one group as upstanding and the other as morally deficient because of their differing marital statuses. Although Noel defined sexual relations outside marriage as "irregular," she placed the blame for such relations on poverty, not on individual or class immorality.[17]

While many mainstream women supported mothers' pensions as a limited form of poverty relief for worthy indigents, socialist women envisioned mothers' aid as part of a large, democratic, and genuinely redistributive social welfare system provided by a state committed to economic equality. To Caroline Foster the "chief cause of deterioration in both boys and girls" was the "unendurable poverty" created by "our profit taking society." State support of mothers with young children was part of the insurance and pension system needed to "protect the weak and ensure industrial justice." Ultimately, poverty could be eliminated only through an overhaul of "our established industrial system." Emma Wolfe also argued that only socialism would eliminate poverty, but she proposed that the state, in the meantime, had an obligation to pension the widows, and support the children, of its "industrial soldiers." When socialist women emphasized society's obligation to further "industrial justice" for the male breadwinner and his family, they inherently, and probably unintentionally, advocated an indirect relationship between women and the state mediated by male workers. Such a mediated relationship ultimately supported what historian Susan Pedersen has called "men's right to maintain" and reinforced women's economic dependence.[18]

Some socialist women advocated a direct relationship between women's economic contributions, their right to maintain families, and state support. Frances Noel and Elvina Beals, for example, argued that the state had an obligation to support women in return for their reproductive labor, for performing the essential social task of rearing future citizens. They wanted to use mothers' pensions to elevate the status of women's unpaid labor in the home to the level of socially important work that should be remunerated. Noel referred to mothers' pensions as a way to "invest motherhood with dignity" and as a "mother's right." Beals believed that mothers' pensions would recognize women for their great "use to the state in properly raising and caring for the coming citizen."[19] Such remuneration would ensure both economic justice and economic independence for women, and would contribute to women's emancipation. For Frances Noel, mothers' aid represented "the first step toward an economically-free motherhood." Noel argued that state support for mothers would allow women in unhealthy or abusive relationships to leave them and to achieve a measure of economic self-sufficiency. "Those women will free themselves under a mothers' pension law, and bring their children up in peaceful homes, free from intoxication and tyranny as soon as the state makes it possible."[20] Noel and Beals stood for a mothers' pension system that provided assistance to all women with children, regardless of their economic status, as a right of women to remuneration for their economic contributions to society and as a right of economic self-determination.

These last two arguments regarding the obligations of the state were problematic in that they relied on women's differences from men to determine women's relationship to the state and defined citizenship rights in gendered terms. Yet, in the context of mothers' pension debates within the California woman movement, both arguments were farsighted in advancing the notion of a redistributive welfare state responsible for ensuring economic justice. Socialist women clearly stood behind the most comprehensive mothers' pension proposals. While Noel wanted pensions for every mother, most socialist women were willing to settle for the pensioning of all "self-dependent" women with children, whether they were widowed, deserted, never-married, or had spouses in prison or with physical or mental disabilities that prevented them from working in the paid labor force. Some socialist women wanted support for wage-earning mothers during periods of "enforced idleness," as well as a system of care for prospective mothers. Radical women also desired a pension large enough to provide a "living wage" and to raise a family out of poverty. Although radical women generally stood behind the most inclusive legislative proposals, some eventually compromised their ideals and supported measures more likely to gain legislative approval. These bills contained residency and citizenship requirements, as well as restrictions based on the moral fitness of the mother and her home.[21]

While all political parties in the state supported mothers' pensions and Governor Hiram Johnson made such aid part of his ten-point legislative program for 1913, much controversy arose over the twenty mothers' aid bills drafted by various women's groups, juvenile court judges, and state agencies.[22] In examining this controversy, one can easily imagine why socialist women felt compelled to support restrictive mothers' pension bills to ensure that at least some mothers received immediate aid. Many of the proposals submitted by women's associations were charged with being improperly drafted and, in some cases, too "radical." Charity workers led the opposition to the bills, in part because they wanted to retain control over the relief of the destitute, and they were joined by both male and female progressive reformers.[23] Some of the harshest criticisms of the proposed measures came from progressive clubwomen who strongly endorsed the idea of mothers' pensions. Progressive reformers feared that some of the more inclusive mothers' aid plans would establish a comprehensive system of pensions for all mothers in need, and that such a system would be too expensive and would lead to guaranteed government support for the poor. Charles Dwight Willard, an editor of California's progressive weekly, the *California Outlook,* warned that if the mothers' pension scheme was "carried out on the wholesale scale that has been suggested, it would be like laying the foundations of a new social order." Reformers also discredited the goal of the "most ardent advocates" of mothers' aid, that "all mothers, regardless of circumstances," receive state support for their labors, as both too costly and outside the responsibilities of the state.[24]

These objections were reinforced by complaints that any plan to pension mothers was illegal, since the state constitution failed to provide for such action. Only indigent orphans, half-orphans, and abandoned children could be funded. Finally, reformers, especially the state's clubwomen, expressed concern about potential abuses of such a system of relief, decrying possible "fraud, patronage, and pauperism." They objected to the funding of the unworthy, fearing improper care of children by uneducated or employed mothers and support for "alien" women and the destitute from other states, who had "no legitimate claim except that of a common humanity for relief." Many prominent clubwomen agreed with the state's "experienced legislators" that the proposed bills were problematic; and they recommended a "calm, sober" state commission to "work out a better plan of relief."[25] Mainstream reformers proved cautious in dealing with legislators, possessed limited reform goals, lacked an urgent desire to reform capitalism, opposed substantive changes in class or gender relations, and feared the creation of broad-based social welfare services for the poor as a step toward the creation of socialism in California.[26]

While controversy raged over the scope and implications of mothers' aid, the fact that the concept continued to have widespread support among the state's organized women, and that legislators from all political parties desired to please newly enfranchised women voters, ensured the passage of a mothers' pension proposal. Many progressive reformers must have been satisfied with the action taken on mothers' pensions by the California legislature in 1913. The principal mothers' aid bill approved by the legislature was submitted not by women's organizations but by the California Board of Control. It made no attempt to alter state law and was probably the most limited of all the proposals.[27] An amendment to the Orphan Aid Law, which already provided support for orphans and half-orphans in institutions, the new measure allowed state monies to be used to fund the children of impoverished, "deserving" widowed mothers in their homes. Funds were to be allocated only to mothers who could provide "proper home[s]." The law also contained a new residency requirement, which stipulated that parents who were not citizens of California had to reside in the state for three years before they could receive aid. The amendment funded three Children's Agents to "investigate the families to which such funds are given."[28] A second bill created a state commission to collect data and make recommendations for legislation regarding old-age and mothers' pensions. This commission did not actually function until 1915, when its focus was expanded to the study of "social insurance." The body focused primarily on state-supported health insurance, never returning seriously to the mothers' aid issue.[29]

Socialist women expressed great disappointment with the mothers' pension laws approved by the legislature. They argued that the legal obstacles to the pensioning of (at least poor) mothers could and should be overcome, and they were irate that the compromise bill funded the child but not the mother. They also believed that the level of funding was far too low to lift women and their children out of poverty. Emma Wolfe complained bitterly that the constitutionality issue was the "stone wall against which we are thrown when we attempt to do anything for the mothers. I supposed some day they will say the mothers are unconstitutional, at least they may well say many of them have no constitution."[30]

PROTECTIVE LABOR LEGISLATION FOR WOMEN

In the area of women's labor issues, socialist women placed protective labor legislation on the agenda of the California woman movement and elicited active backing of eight-hour-day and minimum wage measures. They also played significant roles in debates regarding the nature and meaning of reforms intended to assist wage-earning women. In fact, socialist women became some of the most vigorous proponents of wage-earning women's concerns within the state's women's clubs and civic groups after 1911. They struggled to make the woman movement more responsive and open to working-class women, to convince non-socialist female reformers of the benefits of unionization for women, and to promote understanding of the needs and aims of the working class as expressed through organized labor. They also tried to elevate protective labor legislation for wage-earning women to a major legislative priority.

Socialist women sought to accomplish these goals by working within women's groups as self-defined representatives of wage-earning women. In Los Angeles, radical women also established a branch of the National Women's Trade Union League (NWTUL), which united female trade unionists and clubwomen more directly. In these efforts to make the woman movement more sensitive to and representative of working-class women, socialists were joined by a small, but vocal, group of labor-oriented progressive clubwomen. Among the most prominent spokespersons for protective labor legislation and female unionization were Socialist party members Frances Nacke Noel, Emma J. Wolfe, Caroline Foster, Mary E. Garbutt, Mila Tupper Maynard, and Marion Louise Israel, and progressive clubwomen Katherine Philips Edson, Grace Simons, Mary S. Gibson, and Helen V. Bary.[31]

Across the nation, organized women in the early twentieth century turned their attention to labor issues, especially the health and well-being of female wage earners. Beginning in 1908, a variety of women's organizations attempted to secure protective labor legislation for working women. In addition, pro-labor clubwomen, settlement house workers, and radicals of all stripes helped organize women into unions, promoted their integration into the labor movement, and worked to increase support within the woman movement for working women and their concerns, through the NWTUL and other reform organizations.[32] While socialist and labor-identified progressive clubwomen in California did not achieve much success in organizing wage-earning women or in bringing them into the woman movement, they led organized womanhood's efforts to secure protective labor legislation and helped pressure the legislature to enact some of the first and most comprehensive eight-hour-day and minimum wage bills for women in the country.

Socialist women looked to protective legislation to improve the lot of the vast majority of the state's wage-earning women because they believed the state should help to ensure social and economic welfare and because few women workers in California had been organized into labor unions. While socialist women felt a tremendous excitement over the strikes and unionizing drives of female garment workers in the East and

Midwest in 1909 and 1910, no comparable uprising seemed imminent in California. Despite the efforts of women within the labor movement to push the California State Federation of Labor (CSFL) to place special emphasis on organizing women, no such campaign was forthcoming. In the first two decades of the twentieth century, unionized women workers constituted between 4 and 9 percent of all female wage earners in the state.[33]

As early as October 1909, female trade unionists, socialist women, and labor-identified progressive clubwomen set their sights on securing an eight-hour day for women through legislative action. Led by Frances Noel, the California branch of the Woman's International Union Label League (WIULL) presented a resolution in favor of such a bill at the CSFL convention. To secure adequate backing for the proposed law, the WIULL pledged to "communicate with and request the aid of all the women's organizations" in the state. The CSFL endorsed the league's resolution and made the bill establishing an eight-hour day for women part of its legislative agenda in 1911.[34] By this time, the political atmosphere in California seemed ripe for the passage of wage-and-hour legislation for women. The Socialist party was gaining in popularity, a majority of progressives had been elected to the legislature, and Governor Hiram Johnson, an "insurgent" Republican, seemed interested in courting organized labor and the working-class vote.[35]

While the CSFL and female trade unionists from San Francisco lobbied and provided testimony for the eight-hour-day-for-women bill in Sacramento, socialist women worked hard behind the scenes through women's and labor organizations. Mary Garbutt and Laura Locke made the bill one of the legislative priorities of the Southern California Woman's Christian Temperance Union (WCTU), and the organization circulated petitions and sent them to the legislature. Frances Noel, through the Los Angeles branch of the WIULL, performed "splendid work" for the bill by securing endorsements of many Southern California reform and women's groups.[36] The measure, amended early in the legislative process to exclude women employed in the production and canning of perishable fruits and vegetables, prescribed an eight-hour workday and forty-eight-hour workweek for women employed in manufacturing, mechanical, and mercantile establishments; laundries; hotels; restaurants; telegraph or telephone establishments; and express or transportation companies. The bill passed both houses of the legislature and was signed into law, despite encountering stiff opposition from the owners of department stores, laundries, hotels, and confection, cotton goods, and cracker factories.[37]

After the passage of the women's suffrage amendment in October 1911, the state's organized women made protective labor legislation for women a higher priority. The California Federation of Women's Clubs (CFWC) and its affiliates, the WCTU organizations of Northern and Southern California, and other women's groups advocated the enforcement and extension of the eight-hour-day-for-women law and the enactment of legislation that would set minimum wages for women workers. Socialist and labor-oriented progressive clubwomen led the upsurge in activism on labor-related measures. In 1912, Emma Wolfe put the enforcement of the eight-hour bill on the agenda of the California Congress of Mothers (CCM). Wolfe, the head of the CCM's child labor department, was particularly concerned about an enforcement provision that required female employees to file and sign their complaints. "This puts the burden of exposure just where it should not be," noted Wolfe, "on the one in a position to suffer through the revenge of the employer." Wolfe argued that if the state was to make an "honest effort" to "remedy labor abuses," it had to investigate anonymous complaints. Socialist women active in the Berkeley Center of the California Civic League likewise made enforcement of the law one of the organization's priorities. Elvina Beals, a Berkeley center leader who ran for assembly in 1912 on the Socialist party ticket, placed the development of an adequate enforcement mechanism for the eight-hour law at the top of her list of campaign pledges.[38] In 1913, organized labor and organized womanhood successfully amended the eight-hour law to cover women employed in public lodging houses, apartment houses, hospitals, and places of amusement, workplaces not explicitly included in the original law. Despite problems of enforcement and a lack of coverage for all women wage earners, scholars now regard California's eight-hour law for women as one of the "first effective and the most comprehensive" laws of its kind enacted during the Progressive Era.[39]

In 1913, a bill establishing a minimum wage commission, empowered to regulate the wages and working conditions of women and children wage earners, was endorsed by the CFWC, the California WCTUs, and the Women's Legislative Council. This bill, proposed to Governor Johnson by Katherine Edson, became part of Johnson's ten-point legislative program. The CSFL strongly opposed the bill because it feared that the measure would place a ceiling on women's wages, and would, in turn, bring down men's earnings and undermine the union scale. Most employers and employer associations joined with labor to combat the bill. Nevertheless, the bill passed rather easily because of Johnson's support and the legislature's desire to do something about the presumed connection between women's low wages and prostitution, then a topic of intense national concern.

California's minimum wage bill was one of the first in the United States. The bill established an Industrial Welfare Commission (IWC) with broad powers to investigate wages, hours, and working conditions of women and children. Once these data were collected, the commission could then set minimum wages, maximum hours of work, and standard working conditions in order to ensure the "cost of proper living" and the "health, morals or welfare" of women and minor workers. In the fall of 1914, with the backing of the California woman movement, the Los Angeles labor movement, and progressive reformers of all stripes, an amendment to the state constitution was ratified. This amendment served as an enabling act for the IWC, granting the state broad powers to establish and enforce minimum wages for women and child workers.[40]

Socialist women vigorously endorsed the minimum wage bill and worked for the ratification of the enabling constitutional amendment by California voters through women's and labor organizations, including the Southern California WCTU, the Woman's Political League of San Francisco, and the newly established Women's Trade Union League of Los Angeles (LAWTUL).[41] In May 1914, the socialist-led LAWTUL sent a circular letter to all trade unions in California, requesting that they support protective labor legislation, especially the new minimum wage law, which many of them had opposed. When the league got little response from organized labor, it conducted a campaign to register Los Angeles's working-class women to vote and to gain their backing for protective labor legislation. The LAWTUL sponsored mass meetings where its members gave wage-earning women information (in both English and Spanish) on the labor-related initiatives appearing on the 1914 ballot, especially the IWC's enabling amendment.[42] Socialist women also championed the amendment during their campaigns for local office on the party ticket. Estelle Lawton Lindsey, for example, spoke for the amendment at a well-attended Los Angeles debate during her race for state Assembly in September 1914.[43]

Although socialist and progressive clubwomen worked together to promote mothers' pensions and protective labor legislation for women workers, their arguments for such laws rested on different premises, as was the case with mothers' pensions.

Labor-oriented progressive clubwomen supported protective labor legislation out of both a genuine concern for the well-being of workers, especially wage-earning women, and a deep fear that current employ-

ment conditions would destroy the health, family life, morality, and stability of the working class and therefore harm the nation as a whole.
Socialist women also feared for the health and well-being of the poor,
but they viewed protective labor legislation as a tool to increase the
physical, economic, and political strength of the working class and as a
means to help women achieve economic and social equality. For radical
women, protective labor legislation represented a step toward the creation of a "Cooperative Commonwealth," which would ensure class
and gender equality through the fair distribution of social wealth by a
democratically controlled state.

Progressive leaders of the protective legislation fight urged clubwomen to remedy the dire conditions faced by wage-earning women,
whom they regarded as less fortunate sisters in need of "justice and
mercy." They suggested that middle-class women become "our sisters'
keepers" by campaigning hard for legislative measures that would "protect this weakest and most helpless class."[44]

The mainstream champions of protective legislation seemed even
more concerned, however, about saving the nation from the "dreadful
unrest, the immorality and unhealthy social conditions" that challenged
their conception of social order. They wanted to ensure the physical
and moral health of future generations, protect the home, preserve
women's primary social role as mothers, and maintain the peace and
stability of a country torn by class conflict. They supported protective
labor legislation for women because they believed that such legislation
would help "safeguard" the home and "California's potential motherhood." Fearing that low wages would undermine the health and morals
of the nation's future mothers and their children, they advocated a minimum wage intended to provide "the least amount on which a girl
[could] support herself decently and honestly,"[45]—presumably, until
she could eventually assume her proper place as a non-wage-earning
wife and mother.[46] Progressive clubwomen also hoped that protective
labor legislation would safeguard the "general social welfare." Frightened that an "enormous influx of cheap labor" from southern and eastern Europe and irresponsible employers who underpaid workers would
threaten the health and stability of the working class, these women
called for state enforcement of decent pay and working conditions in
order to stabilize class relations and help build a law-abiding, self-
sustaining, and Americanized working population.[47]

Socialist clubwomen advocated protective labor legislation for women as a means to achieve greater "justice" for workers under capitalism. These women strongly identified with the laboring classes, espe-

cially with wage-earning women. They regarded such legislation as a tool to increase the economic strength and political militancy of the working class and to help women gain economic equality in the labor market. Protection for women workers, they believed, could serve as "a strong entering wedge" for legislation to improve labor conditions for all workers.[48] Such legislation would empower and protect workers until the time when "an enlightened [public] conscience . . . [would] abolish utterly this moloch of capitalism."[49]

While socialist women argued that gender-neutral protective laws were needed to promote social justice and strengthen the working class, they also advocated gender-specific laws based on their belief in women's social and biological differences from men. They argued that women's physical and moral health was particularly vulnerable to the strains of wagework as it was organized under capitalism. Although they did not consider themselves their sisters' keepers, socialist women did believe that the "ever-swelling arm[ies] of [wage-earning] children and young women," socially and biologically vulnerable and largely unorganized by unions, were "utterly defenseless, except as society defends them." Radical women championed protective legislation for women as a means to redress women's biologically, socially, and economically disadvantaged position in the labor market.[50]

Although socialist women argued that wage labor could be detrimental to women's moral and physical health, they did not suggest, as did some of their progressive counterparts, that women belonged in the home and that men should be the sole breadwinners. Instead, radical women believed that the achievement of women's emancipation and autonomy depended upon economic independence attained through wage labor. They argued that protective laws would help to eliminate the economic distinctions between the sexes in the labor market. Elsa Untermann, writing under her pen name, Eleanor Wentworth, was particularly outspoken in criticizing the "difference of wages for men and women for the same labor performed." This difference, she believed, stemmed from women's inability "to protect their labor and demand for it a fair remuneration," their lack of equality before the law, their historical exclusion from the paid labor force, and their valuation of marriage over wage earning. Wentworth argued that minimum wage legislation would help to raise women's wages to approach men's. Equivalent wages would "eliminate the distinction between female labor and male labor"—namely, the cheapness of women's labor—and enable women to "enter all fields of activity." In addition, equal wages would make paid labor more attractive to women, prompting them to choose wage earning over unpaid labor in the home, and ensuring that household labor would become socialized and remunerated. In the end, protective legislation would help women obtain equal wages, break down the sexual division of labor, and achieve economic independence and social equality.[51]

Mila Tupper Maynard argued that protective legislation would enhance women's ability to balance work and home roles, and thus contribute to women's participation in modern society as social equals. She believed that shorter hours and good pay were essential if women were to combine child rearing and wage labor. "When women can work for short hours at good pay," Maynard wrote, they would be able to combine "home duties and interests" with "the trade, profession, or social task, which . . . [they have] chosen for a life-work." Maynard hoped that hours legislation would reduce the time women and men devoted to paid labor, so that both sexes could engage in their "life-work" and in shared parenting.[52]

Ironically, while socialist women linked protective labor legislation to women's emancipation, they failed, for the most part, to demand a living wage for women sufficient to support children, a necessity if women were to ever achieve economic independence from men. Marion Israel was one of the few to argue explicitly that women, as well as men, should be paid a "family wage." Believing that women's wages were kept at low levels so that men could support their non-wage-earning wives and children, Israel called for an end to "this scheme of female dependence . . . maintained by working women." She envisioned the opportunity for all women to work for decent and equal wages and to have "the joy of wifehood and motherhood."[53]

In practice, protective labor legislation failed to live up to the promises it held in the minds of socialist women. At the time the minimum wage law was enacted, radical women criticized it in two ways. They expressed outrage and dismay that the law failed to set actual minimum wage rates for women, and they argued that the process set up for determining wage scales would favor employers, not workers. Not only would working people feel no immediate relief; they would also lack power in determining future wage levels. Even as socialist women supported the establishment of the Industrial Welfare Commission, they knew that the apparatus would never aid the working class in its struggle with capital. Indeed, while the minimum wage law probably resulted in higher wages for some of the lowest-paid female workers in the state, it would not accomplish socialist women's more fundamental goals.[54]

Shortly after legislative approval of the minimum wage bill in 1913, socialist women proclaimed that the "complete failure of the State Legislature to offer the least relief to the working women of California in the passage of a minimum wage law brand[ed] that 'progressive' body as an organization that should be ha[u]led into court . . . for obtaining votes under false pretenses." Unlike many progressive clubwomen—who had, from the beginning, favored creating a commission that would study wage-earning women's economic situation before recommending a minimum wage—socialist women favored the immediate establishment of a minimum wage for female wage earners. In response to the legislature's "complete failure" to guarantee women workers a decent standard of living, radical women in Los Angeles attempted to enact a city ordinance addressing the problem of women's wages. Socialist and union women founded a short-lived, nonpartisan Women's Wage League in April 1913. Backed by the Socialist party's county executive committee, the Central Labor Council, and the state Socialist party's organ, the *California Social-Democrat*, the league circulated a petition demanding that the city pass an ordinance establishing a Woman's Living Wage Investigation Board. Although the proposed board could not have set wage rates, it would have been empowered to "investigate all matters pertaining to the hours, wages, or earnings of the women of Los Angeles"; to compile a public record of all places of employment that failed to pay women more than eight dollars a week; and to post placards on all such establishments. The league then planned to boycott the workplaces that did not provide what the state's own Bureau of Labor Statistics considered a living wage for women workers. While the ordinance never passed, the campaign demonstrated socialist women's commitment to raising the standard of living of wage-earning women and their families by redistributing social wealth through immediate state action.[55]

In objecting to the creation of the Industrial Welfare Commission, socialist women also expressed reservations about whether the commission's structure would allow it to serve workers' interests. Unlike progressive reformers, socialist women were not interested in balancing "competing interests within a capitalist democracy," but, rather, in empowering workers to take command of the state and restructure the economy and class relations. The five-member commission—with one representative from organized labor, one from unorganized labor, two from business, and one "neutral" participant—was to set wage rates and other standards in collaboration with industry-specific wage boards (which were also made up of representatives of labor, employers, and the general public). This cumbersome process allowed employers to play a large role, and it put unorganized women workers at a disadvantage. Clearly, socialist women believed that state action on minimum wages and maximum hours should be determined by working people organized into a solid political force capable of affecting legislation. Marion Israel called for a "political awakening of women to the end that the women workers themselves could determine what should constitute a minimum wage."[56]

Interestingly, socialist women also failed to consider the possibility that protective labor legislation might hinder the achievement of gender equality. Indeed, they overestimated the power of such legislation to improve women's position in the labor force and promote women's right to work outside the home. The protective statutes governing women's labor adopted by many states relied on a conception of women as weak and secondary workers. In practice, they confirmed and helped institutionalize women's secondary place in the labor force.[57]

Throughout the state, the number of non-socialist clubwomen genuinely interested in the cause of labor and willing to make wage-earning women's issues a priority proved small. Nonetheless, socialist and labor-identified clubwomen found a way to bring labor issues into the woman movement and to make protective labor legislation for women more of a priority, and they helped to enact some of the first gender-specific labor laws in the nation. But although the laws providing mothers' pensions and regulating women's working hours and wages improved the lives of some working-class women and their families, they failed to challenge class and gender relations or to bring about a redistributive welfare state.

In summary, socialist women clearly played a vital role in constructing and fighting for the social welfare agenda of the California woman movement. From their positions of power within the state's women's clubs and voluntary associations, they called on organized womanhood to champion protective labor laws for women and a broad-based mothers' pension program. Along with their labor-oriented progressive sisters, socialist women agitated for greater sympathy with organized labor and increased activism on behalf of wage-earning women. They also challenged progressive clubwomen to expand their thinking about the responsibilities of the state toward both workers and women under capitalism, and they demanded greater respect for the indigent. The fact that the measures they helped to enact ultimately proved to be merely ameliorative, not "underminingly" so, should not obscure their radical challenges to class and gender relations or their success in establishing a significant left-wing tendency within organized womanhood. Future research will determine whether socialist women's place in the California woman movement was unique and whether their contributions have, until now, gone largely unrecognized by scholars of women's political activism and of progressivism.

NOTES

1. Eleanor Wentworth, "Feminism and the Trend Towards Democracy," *Western Comrade* 1 (February 1914): 336 and (March 1914): 375; Eleanor Wentworth, "The Significance of Women's Organizations," *Western Comrade* 1 (July 1913): 138. See also Marion Louise Israel, "Why I Am a Socialist," *Women's Bulletin* 2 (July–August 1914): 10–11.

2. For the quote on reform see Sara [Bard Field] to [Charles Erskine Scott Wood], April 8, 1913, box 270, Charles Erskine Scott Wood Collection, Huntington Library, San Marino, California. The term *civic maternalism* was coined recently by Seth Koven. See Nancy F. Cott, "What's in a Name?" The Limits of 'Social Feminism'; or, Expanding the Vocabulary of Women's History," *Journal of American History* 76 (December 1989): 829. I have adopted Cott's model of women's political consciousness in analyzing socialist women's commitments and activities.

3. For a full discussion of socialist women's political commitments, strategies, and contributions to the California woman movement, see Sherry Jeanne Katz, "Dual Commitments: Feminism, Socialism, and Women's Political Activism in California, 1890–1920" (Ph.D. diss., University of California, Los Angeles, 1991).

4. Ibid., chap. 1.

5. Ibid., chap. 2 through chap. 4.

6. Ibid., chap. 2.

7. Gayle Ann Gullett, "Feminism, Politics, and Voluntary Groups: Organized Womanhood in California, 1886–1896" (Ph.D., diss., University of California, Riverside, 1983), especially 1–10, 329–32; Donald Waller Rodes, "The California Woman Suffrage Campaign of 1911" (master's thesis, California State University, Hayward, 1974); Katz, "Dual Commitments," chap. 1 and chap. 4.

8. A Committee of Women of Southern California, "Woman Suffrage: Address in Favor of an Amendment to the Constitution of the United States Extending the Right of Suffrage to Women," *Woman's Bulletin* 2 (December 1913): 12; College Equal Suffrage League of San Francisco, "California Women Have Made Good," *Woman's Journal*, August 24, 1912; Mrs. Seward A. [Grace] Simons, "Bills in the Next Session of the Legislature," *Woman's Bulletin* 1 (October–November 1912): 23; [Estelle Lawton Lindsey,] "Some Results of California's Recent Election," *Woman's Bulletin* 3 (November 1914): 6; Mary Roberts Coolidge, *What the Women of California Have Done with the Ballot* (San Francisco: California Civic League, 1916); Mrs. Charles Farwell [Katherine] Edson, "The Actual Operation of Woman Suffrage in California," *Woman's Bulletin* 1 (September 1912): 29.

9. [Clifford Howard,] editorial, *Woman's Bulletin* 1 (June 1912): 6; Grace Simons paraphrased in [Elizabeth L. Kenney], "First Legislative Conference of

California Women," *Woman's Bulletin* 1 (December 1912): 14; [Clifford Howard,] "Greeting," *Woman's Bulletin* 1 (June 1912): 4; [Clifford Howard,] "Women as Officeholders," *Woman's Bulletin* 1 (September 1912): 5; Committee of Women of Southern California, "Woman Suffrage," 14; Florence Collins Porter, "From a Woman's View-Point," *California Outlook*, June 1, 1912.

10. Mary S. Gibson, *A Record of Twenty-five Years of the California Federation of Women's Clubs, 1900–1925* (Los Angeles: California Federation of Women's Clubs, 1927), 182–209; Mrs. Seward A. [Grace] Simons, *A Survey of the Results of Woman's Suffrage in California* (Los Angeles: California Federation of Women's Clubs, May 1917); San Francisco Center of the California Civic League, *A Summary of the Activities of the San Francisco Center, January 1913–November 1918* (San Francisco: San Francisco Center of the California Civic League, 1918?), 3, League of Women Voters Collection, California Historical Society, San Francisco.

11. For Park's sentiments, see Alice Park, "Team Work of California Women Voters," *Woman's Journal*, August 2, 1913. For more on women's influence in the legislative arena, see Franklin Hichborn, *Story of the Session of the California Legislature of 1913* (San Francisco: James H. Barry Co., 1913), 13–14, 110, 320–44; Mrs. Charles Farwell [Katherine] Edson, "Woman's Influence on State Legislation," *California Outlook*, June 14, 1913.

12. Gibson, *A Record*, 194–95; Mrs. F. E. [Emma] Wolfe, "Report of the California Member of the National Committee on Child Labor," in Mrs. M. C. Kennedy, *History of the California Congress of Mothers* (Pomona, Calif.: California Congress of Mothers, 1914), 89–90; Mary E. Garbutt, "Women with the Ballot in California," *Progressive Woman* 6 (March 1913): 4; "First Legislative Conference of California Women," *Woman's Bulletin* 1 (December 1912): 14; Florence Collins Porter, "From a Woman's View-Point," *California Outlook*, January 25, 1913; Mrs. Seward A. [Grace] Simons, "Equal Suffrage," *Woman's Bulletin* 1 (October –November 1912), 23–24; Helen Bary, "Bills before California's Legislature," *Woman's Bulletin* 1 (April 1913): 8.

13. Barbara J. Nelson, "The Gender, Race, and Class Origins of Early Welfare Policy and of the Welfare State: A Comparison of Workmen's Compensation and Mothers' Aid," in Louise A. Tilley and Patricia Gurin, eds., *Women, Politics, and Change* (New York: Russell Sage Foundation, 1990), 425–26. Also see Ann Vandepol, "Dependent Children, Child Custody, and the Mothers' Pensions: The Transformation of State-Family Relations in the Early 20th Century," *Social Problems* 29 (February 1982): 230–31; Mimi Abramovitz, *Regulating the Lives of Women: Social Welfare Policy from Colonial Times to the Present* (Boston: South End Press, 1988), 190–206; Mark H. Leff, "Consensus for Reform: The Mothers'-Pension Movement in the Progressive Era," *Social Service Review* 47 (September 1973): 398–401; Mary Madeleine Ladd-Taylor, "Mother-Work: Ideology, Public Policy, and the Mothers' Movement, 1890–1930" (Ph.D. diss., Yale University, 1986), chap. 4; Theda Skocpol, *Protecting Soldiers and Mothers: The Political Origins of Social Policy in the United States* (Cambridge: Harvard University Press, 1992), chap. 8.

14. For California socialist women's involvement, see "Socialists Demand Relief for Mothers in Bill for Pensions," *California Social-Democrat* (Los An-

geles), February 1, 1913; Garbutt, "Women with the Ballot"; "First Legislative Conference of California Women"; *California Outlook,* August 17, 1912; Gibson, *A Record,* 194–95; "Friday Morning Club," *Woman's Bulletin* 1 (March 1913): 23; "Legislative Committee of Club Reports," *Los Angeles Tribune,* [February ?] 12, 1913, and February 26, 1913, Friday Morning Club Scrapbook no. 1, Friday Morning Club Scrapbooks Collection (Ephemera), Huntington Library.

15. For Simons's sentiments, see Mrs. Seward A. [Grace] Simons, "Equal Suffrage," *Woman's Bulletin* 1 (October 1912): 24. For arguments asserting mothers' pension as a form of relief for destitute women and their children, see Florence Collins Porter, "From a Woman's View-Point," *California Outlook,* January 25, 1913; Elizabeth L. Kenney, "Some of the Bills California Women Wish to Bring before the Coming Session of the Legislature," *Woman's Bulletin* 1 (January 1913): 9–10. For arguments that emphasized the need for raising good citizens, see Mary S. Gibson, "The Immigrant Woman," *California Outlook,* May 9, 1914; Katharine C. Felton, "Preliminary Report on Aid to Widows with Young Children," November 7, 1915, box 26, John Randolph Haynes Papers (Coll. 1241), Department of Special Collections, University Research Library, University of California, Los Angeles. For the stress on funding only "worthy" mothers, see Gibson, *A Record,* 194–95; Felton, "Preliminary Report."

16. Frances Noel in Estelle Lawton Lindsey, "State Will Be Gainer as Well as Individuals by Mothers' Pension Law," *Los Angeles Record,* [1913,] folder 13, box 5, Frances Noel Papers (Coll. 814), Department of Special Collections, University Research Library, UCLA; Agnes Downing, "Pensions for Mothers," *Progressive Woman* 4 (January 1911): 7. See also Elvina Beals quoted in "Pensioning Parents of Dependent Children," *World* (Oakland), October 19, 1912; Sara Wilde Houser reported in "First Legislative Conference of California Women."

17. Downing, "Pensions for Mothers"; Frances Noel quoted in Lindsey, "State Will Be Gainer."

18. Mrs. E. K. (Caroline) Foster, "Children's Rights," *California Outlook,* July 18, 1914; Emma Wolfe quoted in Estelle Lawton Lindsey, "Woman's Ignorance and Child Labor: These Will Stand or Fall Together," *Los Angeles Record,* [1912,] Woman's Suffrage Scrapbook, compiled by Mrs. M. A. Holmes, Pasadena Historical Society, Pasadena, California; Susan Pedersen, "The Failure of Feminism in the Making of the British Welfare State," *Radical History Review* 43 (Winter 1989): 102. See also Elvina Beals quoted in "Pensioning Parents of Dependent Children," *World,* October 19, 1912.

19. Frances Noel quoted in Lindsey, "State Will Be Gainer"; Elvina Beals quoted in "Pensioning Parents of Dependent Children."

20. Noel quoted in Lindsey, "State Will Be Gainer."

21. For socialist women's views, see Lindsey, "State Will Be Gainer"; Downing, "Pensions for Mothers." Elvina Beals quoted in "Pensioning Parents of Dependent Children." For the bills socialist women helped draft, see note 14; *California Outlook,* September 14, 1912; Florence Collins Porter, "From a Woman's View-Point," *California Outlook,* January 25, 1913.

140 Sherry Katz

22. See "Mothers' Pensions," *Woman's Journal*, November 2, 1912; "1300 Bills Passed by 40th Legislature," *Los Angeles Record*, May 12, 1913.
23. On the role of charity workers in opposing the bills, see C[harles] D. W[illard], "The State and the Mothers," *California Outlook*, February 15, 1913; Katherine C. Felton, "Insurance in Lieu of Pensions," *California Outlook*, February 15, 1913; Katherine Felton reported in "First Legislative Conference of California Women"; Kenney, "Some of the Bills."
24. For the fear of creating a large welfare state, see W[illard], "The State and the Mothers," *California Outlook*, February 15, 1913. See also Felton, "Insurance in Lieu of Pensions." For the objections to funding motherhood, see E. A. Dickson, "Mothers' Pensions," [*Los Angeles Express*,] February 13, 1913, box 161, Haynes Papers. See also Kenney, "Some of the Bills."
25. For a discussion of state law and mothers' aid, see Dickson, "Mothers' Pensions." On the "improper" use of funds, see Kenney, "Some of the Bills"; Florence Collins Porter, "From a Woman's View-Point," *California Outlook*, January 25, 1913.
26. The fear of socialism was especially pronounced for those reformers aligned with progressive forces in California who believed that the Socialist party was a real political threat.
27. Some female activists, including Foster and Wolfe, attempted to shape the final form of the McDonald "administration" bill. See "Legislative Committee of Club Reports," *Los Angeles Tribune*, [February?] 12, 1913; *Los Angeles Tribune*, February 26, 1913, Friday Morning Club Scrapbook no. 1, Friday Morning Club Collection; report of Foster as chair of the special subcommittee on mothers' pensions in "Friday Morning Club," *Woman's Bulletin* 1 (March 1913): 23.
28. For the amended law see State of California, *The Statutes of California* (Sacramento: California State Printing Office, 1913), chap. 323, 629–32.
29. For the commission's late start, see Katherine C. Felton to Frances M. Noel, December 29, 1914, folder 7, box 10, Noel Papers; *California Outlook*, January 2, 1915. On the expansion of the commission's mission in 1915, see the following documents in the Noel Papers, "CHAPTER 275: An act authorizing the governor to appoint a commission to investigate and report at the forty-second session to the legislature concerning the adoption of a system of social insurance and making an appropriation therefor," May 17, 1915, folder 1, box 5; Katherine C. Felton to Frances N. Noel, September 23, 1915, and John Frances Neylan to Frances N. Noel, September 18, 1915, folder 9, box 10.
30. Mrs. F. E. [Emma] Wolfe, "Report of the California Member of the National Committee on Child Labor," in Kennedy, *History of the California Congress of Mothers*; Mrs. E. K. [Caroline] Foster, "Human Conservation," *Woman's Bulletin* 3 (April 1915): 7. Socialist women were no doubt also disappointed in the results of the program in the long-term. As in other states, California's legislation ultimately supported a small number of white, native-born, working-class widows deemed morally fit to raise their children. See California Board of Control, Children's Department, *Report of the Children's Department, State Board of Control* (Sacramento: California State Printing Office, 1919).

31. Katherine Philips Edson referred to the effort to gain support for trade unionism and wage-earning women within the woman movement as an uphill "fight for organized labor." See [Katherine Philips Edson] to Mary Anderson, May 10, 1922, folder 12, box 1, Katherine Philips Edson Papers (Coll. 235), Department of Special Collections, University Research Library, UCLA.

32. Alice Kessler-Harris, *Out to Work: A History of Wage-Earning Women in the United States* (New York: Oxford University Press, 1982), 165–66, 187–88, 195–96, 203–5; Sara M. Evans, *Born for Liberty: A History of Women in America* (NY: The Free Press, 1989), 147–51, 156–60; Nancy Schrom Dye, *As Equals and as Sisters: Feminism, the Labor Movement, and the Women's Trade Union League of New York* (Columbia: University of Missouri Press, 1980); Robin Miller Jacoby, "The Women's Trade Union League and American Feminism," *Feminist Studies* 3 (Fall 1975): 135–38; Diane Kirkby, " 'The Wage-Earning Women and the State': The National Women's Trade Union League and Protective Labor Legislation, 1903–1923," *Labor History* 28 (Winter 1987): 54–74; Elizabeth Anne Payne, *Reform, Labor, and Feminism: Margaret Dreier Robins and the Women's Trade Union League* (Urbana: University of Illinois Press, 1988); Mari Jo Buhle, *Women and American Socialism, 1870–1920* (Urbana: University of Illinois Press, 1981), chap. 5.

33. Jessica B. Peixotto, "Women of California as Trade-Unionists," *Publications of the Association of Collegiate Alumnae* series 3, no. 18 (1908): 40–49; Katherine Philips Edson, *Minimum Wage Constitutional Amendment* (Los Angeles: n.p., 1914?), folder 5, box 7, Edson Papers.

34. For the WIULL resolution and plans to push the eight-hour bill, see California State Federation of Labor, *Proceedings of the Tenth Annual Convention* (San Francisco?: CSFL, 1909), 33; Frances N. Noel to [Mary A.] Strachan, [October? 1909,] folder 5, box 11, Noel Papers.

35. On the Socialist party's growing electoral strength, see Ralph Edward Shaffer, "A History of the Socialist Party of California" (master's thesis, University of California, Berkeley, 1955), 83–93. On the 1910 elections and Johnson's support for legislation of specific interest to the working class and/or organized labor, see George E. Mowry, *The California Progressives* (Berkeley: University of California Press, 1951), 129–34; Spencer C. Olin, Jr., *California Politics, 1846–1920: The Emerging Corporate State* (San Francisco: Boyd and Fraser, 1981), 58–71.

36. For the labor movement's lobbying efforts, see Clara M. Beyer, "History of Labor Legislation in Three States," in U.S. Department of Labor, Women's Bureau, *Bulletin of the Women's Bureau*, no. 66 (Washington, D.C.: U.S. Government Printing Office, 1929), 124. For the work of Noel and the WIULL of Los Angeles on behalf of the eight-hour bill, see Maud Younger to [Frances] Noel, January 8 and February 9, 1911, Knox Mellon Collection (privately held papers of Frances Noel). For Garbutt and Locke's role, see Mary Alderman Garbutt, *Victories of Four Decades: A History of the Woman's Christian Temperance Union of Southern California* (Los Angeles: Woman's Christian Temperance Union of Southern California, 1924), 105–6, 127; "W.C.T.U. Indorses Union Measures," *Citizen* (Los Angeles), June 2, 1911.

37. Franklin Hichborn, *Story of the Session of the California Legislature of 1911* (San Francisco: James H. Barry Co., 1911), 247–60; Beyer, "History of Labor Legislation," 122–24; Earl C. Crockett, "The History of California Labor Legislation," 1910–1930" (Ph.D. diss., University of California, Berkeley, 1931), 8–12; California State Federation of Labor, *Proceedings of the Twelfth Annual Convention* (San Francisco?: CSFL, 1911), 80–81, 93–94. In 1915, the U.S. Supreme Court upheld the constitutionality of the original eight-hour law for women and the amendments to it passed in 1913.

38. Report of Mrs. F. E. Wolfe in Kennedy, *History of the California Congress of Mothers*, 89; Emma Wolfe in Lindsey, "Woman's Ignorance and Child Labor," Suffrage Scrapbook; *World*, May 25, 1912; Elvina Beals quoted in "Woman Nominee Interviewed," *California Social-Democrat*, July 27, 1912.

39. Crockett, "History of California Labor Legislation," 15, 19–20; Beyer, "History of Labor Legislation," 120, 125; Kessler-Harris, *Out to Work*, 187–88.

40. Katherine Edson in Gibson, *A Record*, 191–92; Crockett, "History of California Labor Legislation," 64–83; Beyer, "History of Labor Legislation," 128–31; Norris C. Hundley, Jr., "Katherine Philips Edson and the Fight for the California Minimum Wage, 1912–1923," *Pacific Historical Review* 29 (August 1960), 271–77; State of California, *Statutes of California*, chap. 324, 632–37.

41. Garbutt, *Victories of Four Decades*, 105–6, 127; Los Angeles WTUL circular, "A Word to Union Men and Women," May 15, 1914, folder 10, box 3, Noel Papers; [Katherine Philips Edson] to [Walter G.] Mathewson, October 14, 1914, Edson Papers; "$6 a Week for Girls Too Little to Live," *San Francisco Examiner*, March 27, 1913.

42. On the appeal to organized labor, see "Woman's League Plans Great Future at Successful Get-Together Supper," *Citizen*, April 17, 1914; LAWTUL circular, "A Word to Union Men and Women," May 15, 1914, folder 10, box 3, Noel Papers. On the local registration and educational activities, see "Men and Measures," *California Social-Democrat*, September 26, 1914; "Working Women to Organize for Big Campaign," *Los Angeles Record*, September 24, 1914; and Los Angeles Committee of the NWTUL meeting notice, October 27, 1914, folders 10 and 12, box 3, Noel Papers. Many of the LAWTUL's meeting notices were translated into Spanish.

43. "Big Debate Tonight," *Los Angeles Record*, September 14, 1914.

44. Katherine Philips Edson, *California Minimum Wage Constitutional Amendment* (Los Angeles: 1914?), folder 5, box 7, Edson Papers; Beyer, "History of Labor Legislation," 130. Also see Katherine Philips Edson, "Industrial Problems as I See Them," [1914?], folder 5, box 7, Edson papers; Mrs. J. B. Stearns, "Labor and Its Laws," *Woman's Bulletin* 1 (February 1913): 10; [Frances Noel,] typescript of speech or article, [1922,] folder 2, box 1, Noel Papers; Mrs. Seward A. [Grace] Simons, "Equal Suffrage," *Woman's Bulletin* 1 (February 1913): 27.

45. See the following documents by Katherine Philips Edson in folders 4 and 5, box 7, Edson Papers: "Industrial Problems as I See Them"; speech or report to organized womanhood [1922?]; and *Minimum Wage Constitutional Amendment*. See also "Minimum Wage," *Woman's Bulletin* 1 (June 1913): 19.

46. Edson, "Industrial Problems as I See Them"; Stearns, "Labor and Its Laws."

47. Ibid.

48. Frances N. Noel, "Woman's Appeal to Women," [June? 1912,] folder 8, box 1, and Los Angeles WTUL circular, "A Word to Union Men and Women," May 15, 1914, folder 10, box 3, Noel Papers; Mary E. Garbutt, "Labor Laws Affecting Women," *Labor Clarion*, November 3, 1911. See also Agnes H. Downing, "Unions for Girls," *California Social-Democrat*, April 25, 1914.

49. Garbutt, "Labor Laws Affecting Women."

50. Noel quoted in undated clipping [April 28–May 2, 1914] from the *Citizen*, Mellon Collection; Mary E. Garbutt, "Writer Reviews Protective Laws," *California Social-Democrat*, October 18, 1911. Socialist women, like their mainstream counterparts, were particularly concerned that low wages would cause women to become prostitutes. See Garbutt, "Writer Reviews Protective Laws"; Fanny Bixby, "How I Became a Socialist," *Woman's Bulletin* 2 (June 1914): 10; Mila Tupper Maynard and Frances Noel, "Women Tell What They Will Do if Put in Council," *California Social-Democrat*, April 26, 1913.

51. Eleanor Wentworth, "Woman, Wages, and the Ballot," *Progressive Woman* 6 (March 1913): 4.

52. Mila T. Maynard, "Why Women Are for Shorter Day," *California Social-Democrat*, February 22, 1913, and "What Socialism Means to Women," *California Social-Democrat*, March 15, 1913. See also Eleanor Wentworth, "Feminism and the Trend Towards Democracy," *Western Comrade* 1 (February 1914): 335–36.

53. Marion L. Israel, "Gender of the Pay Envelope," *California Social-Democrat*, February 14, 1914.

54. For the commission idea, see Roy Lubove, *The Struggle for Social Security, 1900–1935* (Cambridge, Mass.: Harvard University Press, 1968), 33. For the problems inherent in setting wage rates through such commissions and the specific results of the IWC's efforts, see Kessler-Harris, *Out to Work*, 196–7; Crockett, "History of California Labor Legislation," 84–6, 92–4.

55. On the Women's Wage League, see "No Relief for Working Women from Legislature," *California Social-Democrat*, April 19, 1913; "New League Formed Here Seeks to Aid All Working Women," *Los Angeles Record*, April 2, 1913; "Women Ask Real Investigation of Labor Conditions," *Los Angeles Record*, April 18, 1913; "City Briefs," *Los Angeles Record*, May 5, 1913.

56. For the progressive view, see Katherine Philips Edson, "Effect of Limited Hours and Minimum Wage on Women in Industry," *California Outlook*, May 2, 1914. For Israel's views, see *Citizen*, April 17, 1914.

57. For a fine critique of protective labor legislation, see Kessler-Harris, *Out to Work*, chap. 7. Also see Dye, *As Equals and as Sisters*, 159–60.

Los Angeles Clubwomen and Progressive Reform

Judith Raftery

Beginning in the 1880s, California women began developing a reformist political culture through women's clubs. In doing so, against all odds, they worked through a series of complex networks to play a significant role in shaping statewide progressive programs. Women's clubs flourished both as cultural clubs for self-betterment and as agencies of reform. Most women joined the clubs for self-improvement, but those who came to further reform did so in an attempt to reshape a society they perceived as corrupted by modernization and its concomitant: industrialization, immigration, and urbanization. Many of these women also hoped to create a more public role for themselves, and eventually for all women, whence they would share civil and political rights with men. Indeed, a few remarkable leaders emerged out of the clubs and became effective lobbyists for reform and female equality. Among the most prominent of them in Los Angeles were Caroline Seymour Severance, Mary Simons Gibson, and Katherine Philips Edson. Through their lives we can explore the links between women's clubs and progressive reform in California.

"Organized womanhood," as clubwomen called their network, began after the Civil War and reached an apex during the Progressive Era. Caroline Severance and Jane Cunningham Croly were largely responsible for the growth of these clubs. In New York in 1868, journalist and women's rights advocate Croly founded Sorosis. That same year in Boston, Severance gathered reform-minded women to found the New England Woman's Club. These organizations were exclusively for women.

The founders feared that if men became active members, they would take over, just as they had taken over many reform movements—most notably, perhaps, abolition and temperance.[1] Women's political culture grew from these nascent organizations. Within a short time, women's clubs attracted a wide variety of women. Most, however, were middle- and upper-middle-class white women, mainly Protestant. Although some clubs accepted Catholic and Jewish women, organized woman- hood rarely crossed the color line.[2]

Reform-minded clubwomen became known as municipal housekeep- ers, transferring their responsibilities as moral guardians of their homes to work for civic betterment. As mothers, they and others believed, they knew what best suited the needs of their children, family, and commu- nity. The leaders who emerged carried these ideas forward and had an impact on the law and on political parties. In an attempt to gain greater political access, clubwomen formed a national organization in 1890, the General Federation of Women's Clubs (GFWC), and shortly thereafter states organized affiliates. California clubwomen founded the California Federation of Women's Clubs (CFWC) in 1900. The national organi- zation and state affiliates provided clubwomen with a large network from which to pool resources.[3] Black women, excluded from the GFWC, organized their own societies, such as the National Federation of Afro- American Women and the National Association of Colored Women's Clubs, where they concentrated on issues that had more to do with race betterment than with women's rights.[4]

Los Angeles club members who saw their role as municipal house- keepers campaigned directly for reform measures. They established dis- cussion programs to educate members and then set out to educate the public by giving lectures, publishing and distributing literature, and holding forums to discuss the issues. At the same time, they lobbied at the city, county, and state levels to have their reforms turned into law. Legislation that established pure-milk standards, brought kindergartens into public schools, and set up classes in English for immigrant women grew out of this type of direct action. Clubwomen supported reforms in other ways also. They held fund-raising events such as theatricals and musical performances. Some members contributed by donating money for local club–sponsored charities; others gave financial support for long-term legislative campaigns. Through these means many club- women became active participants in reform.

Often the line between philanthropy and reform was blurred. For in- stance, through their financial support, clubwomen on the board of the

Los Angeles College Settlement Association enabled the settlement workers to devote their energy to establishing a juvenile court for the city and county of Los Angeles. Clubwomen also paid salaries of kindergarten teachers at kindergartens catering to poor children and the salaries of workers who successfully lobbied for and then set up the city's visiting nurse program and the city's park commission. Without clubwomen's support, programs that became part and parcel of progressive reform would not have been realized. So successful were clubwomen in effecting reforms, including suffrage for California women, that during his first term Republican governor Hiram Johnson picked six clubwomen to serve on state boards or commissions.[5]

Indeed, clubwomen had become so active in California's political life that many people held them responsible for the failure of the Republican presidential candidate in 1916. A few days after the reelection of Woodrow Wilson, clubwoman and state commissioner of industrial welfare Katherine Philips Edson wrote a series of letters to prominent progressive women who had worked on the national campaign for his opponent, New York governor Charles Evans Hughes. California women, having gained the vote in 1911, were said to hold the balance in what had been predicted to be a close presidential election. Now many blamed them for Hughes's defeat. Edson, an active campaigner for Hughes, felt obligated to explain why she and other Hughes workers had not delivered the women's vote to the Republicans, and why women could not be expected to vote as a block. Writing to Florence Kelley, head of the National Consumers League, she explained it this way: "As you know, solidarity is about the last development in human nature, and as a friend of mine remarked—'women and dogs have been trained for eons to be loyal to man and disloyal to each other.' " She continued, "I don't suppose the six month campaign can overcome the training of generations. I know you have worked long enough to be patient, but some of the rest of us are learning the lessons."[6]

Nevertheless, the role of organized womanhood in California reform has been overlooked by most scholars who study the period. In part this oversight may be attributed to George Mowry, the preeminent historian of California's Progressive Era.[7] Mowry sought to answer puzzling questions about the progressives: Who were they? What motivated them to act as they did? And what did they think they had accomplished? In *The California Progressives*, Mowry characterized upper- and middle-class men who led the movement. Women played no part in his construct. He ignored the hundreds of women's organizations throughout the state, from the coastal cities to rural interiors. In the following essay I take issue with this methodology by drawing attention to three club-women who actively engaged in progressive reform efforts during the 1870s through the 1920s.

Through women's clubs, these people created a network where women who shared many of the same values relied on each other. Their lives are illustrative of the changing challenges clubwomen faced in the late nineteenth and early twentieth centuries as they moved from the world of female reform to mainstream political activities.

CAROLINE SEYMOUR SEVERANCE

Born in 1820, Caroline Seymour Severance lived for nearly a century, and during most of those years she worked for reform. She began her reforming strategies in Cleveland and Boston and brought her learned talents to California in 1875. She participated in the major reform move-ments of the 1840s: abolition, temperance, and women's rights. Because of her longevity, she also participated in many of the reforms associated with the Progressive Era: women's suffrage, peace, social purity, and municipal and school reform. Severance represents the first generation of women to move into the public arena. She founded the New England Women's Club in order to make reform efforts work more efficiently. Years later, because of that first club, she would be called the "Mother of Women's Clubs."

Caroline Severance moved to Los Angeles with her banker husband, Theodoric, just ahead of the Southern Pacific Railroad. Theodoric came from a reform-minded Cleveland family and had committed himself to many of the same movements as his wife had, including abolition and women's rights. To the cosmopolitan Severances, Los Angeles (with a population of less than 11,000) must have seemed a frontier town but, nevertheless, a place ready for molding. Utilizing their considerable tal-ents, they brought some eastern amenities to the far western frontier. They organized a Unitarian church, and in 1878 Caroline organized the first women's club in Los Angeles. By 1890 a revised version of the 1878 club, the Friday Morning Club, had become one of the most successful clubs in the state.[8]

Through her women's clubs Severance achieved her most far-reaching reforms, and in these clubs she embraced a separate, female po-litical culture. Yet she was not opposed to seeking the support of men friendly to her reforms when she felt they would help her cause. Her greatest political commitment was to women's suffrage, and many other of her activities were ancillary to that goal. She considered herself a poor platform speaker and rarely gave public lectures, a decision that caused suffrage leaders to criticize her. But no one faulted her organizing skills. Behind the scenes, in committees of women's clubs, she pushed and prodded uninitiated women into public action.[9]

Well aware that most women viewed her most cherished reforms, particularly women's rights, as too radical, Severance moved with deliberate gradualism in order not to antagonize potential converts. She gently nudged women into action by educating them through lectures and descriptive literature.[10] To attract the largest number of members, she divided the club into committees of interest. Many committees were purely for self-betterment through such activities as literary discussions and theatrical or musical presentations; others were clearly aimed at reform: temperance, suffrage, education. By appealing to a variety of interests, she brought many women together into a single club where they might be influenced by the more militant members. Her organizational genius enabled her to raise funds, gain publicity for her causes, set her projects into motion, and step aside and move on to another cause. Mary S. Gibson said that Severance was "born without vanity" and eschewed the limelight.[11]

One of her many causes, kindergartens, demonstrates her importance in progressive reform. Kindergartens represent the beginning of progressive innovations in public schooling. They illustrate the extent to which progressive reform affected all segments of society, and they bridge the gap between philanthropy and reform in public schools. Kindergartens ushered in a myriad of social services, such as school lunch programs, day-care centers, after-school playgrounds, summer schools, and medical and dental services, all aimed at mitigating the harsher aspects of urban life for children. Most of these services were either established or funded by clubwomen.

Severance assumed that the Los Angeles club would replicate the work of the New England Woman's Club, and she began a campaign to put a woman on the school board, establish a kindergarten and a training school for kindergarten teachers, and continue her work for women's suffrage. The New England Woman's Club had been in the forefront of the movement to initiate kindergartens for middle-class children in Boston in 1860. Severance herself was a proponent of school reform and taught at the experimental Dio Lewis School in Boston after the Civil War.[12] American reformers thought kindergartens would relieve the austerity of traditional childhood schooling by introducing play into early-childhood education. Within a short time reformers began to view kindergartens as instruments of amelioration and Americanization for poor immigrant children. In St. Louis in 1873, kindergarten became a part of the public schools in the city's slums.[13]

Severance began her kindergarten project for middle-class children in Los Angeles before her permanent move west. She had arranged with a Boston textbook dealer to have a set of German books shipped to California for the training school in 1874.[14] Then, in 1876, the year after the Severances had settled in, Caroline enticed Emma Marwedel, a German kindergartner, to move to Los Angeles.[15]

With Marwedel on her way west, Severance began her search for prospective students for the training college as well as for parents willing to send their children to the new school. She traveled to Santa Barbara and convinced the impressionable Kate Douglas Smith (later Kate Douglas Wiggin) that she was "born" to do pioneer service. Severance made all the arrangements. She found two other young women to sign up for the nine-month training course, convinced families to put their children in the care of the German teacher, and opened the class with twenty-five children ages five to seven.[16] The kindergarten itself lasted only two years, but the training school continued its independent operations until the kindergarten curriculum became part of teacher training at the State Normal School at Los Angeles in the 1890s.[17]

Controversy surrounded the pioneer kindergartens everywhere they were established, and this controversy may explain why the first Los Angeles school closed. Americans disliked the "Germanness" of the instructors and curriculum. Also, the notion of turning over very young children to others for instruction seemed wrong-headed to conventional society. Moreover, the liberal Protestant views of reformers such as Severance and Wiggin, who emphasized the importance of play for children and rejected the older theological views of childhood education, went against the grain of many traditional American families. Finally, the economic depression of the 1870s reached southern California by 1877, and many families may have found more pressing needs for their money than paying tuition for early-childhood education.

By the mid-1880s, when Severance and women's club members launched a drive to introduce kindergartens into public schools, many of the most objectional aspects of kindergartens had been modified. In particular, the development of many kindergarten training schools throughout the country produced American-born trained kindergartners; and the introduction of the Massachusetts-based Milton Bradley Company, which manufactured "occupational" materials for kindergarten classrooms, eliminated much of the Germanness from the schools. Also, there was a wider acceptance of play as an important factor in molding young minds and bodies, and middle-class parents had become more amenable to sending their youngsters to schools that implemented the new theories.[18]

Moreover, by the mid-1880s Los Angeles had recovered from the hardships of the 1870s, and the anticipated arrival of the Santa Fe Railroad, the second rail link to eastern markets, brought newcomers to the city in record numbers. In 1890 the population would stand at 50,000, and by 1900 it would reach over 100,000. The number of poor and immigrant children grew apace and made apparent the scarcity of institutions available to assist needy families.

To fill one void, the Los Angeles Woman's Club established the Free Kindergarten Association. Club members sponsored a tuition-free kindergarten, supported by donations, in a Protestant church in the poorest area of town. Reformers saw kindergartens as opportunities to provide charity and the essentials of food, child care, and clothing along with moral training to needy children.[19] The Los Angeles version was based on San Francisco's Silver Street model, organized in 1878 and superintended by Kate Douglas Wiggin. Also during these years, a tuition kindergarten began its operation, and the stage was set to make kindergartens part of public schooling.[20]

Severance's work for kindergartens fit nicely with her campaign for women's rights. She wanted to put women in policymaking positions in city government and help those few already in positions to retain them. She worked to keep a woman as city librarian, retain the city's first female superintendent of schools, and have a reform-minded woman serve on the Board of Education.[21]

Severance carried out her political strategy through the women's club. As she had done for the kindergarten training school, she chose the club's key committee members with care. Jane E. Collier was on the Education Committee in 1885, and Caroline wanted her to remain there. Recognizing that there was a "clamor" for Collier on the literature committee, she wrote, "I think your place in the Education Committee is equally important." With Collier on the Education Committee, Severance felt that clubwomen would be in a better position to help elect a woman to the Board of Education. Moreover, she needed someone she could trust "to take up" some of the "shortcomings" of both private and public kindergartens.[22]

Working through the women's club during the summer of 1886, Severance intensified her efforts. She had begun fund-raising and brought wealthy patrons to the "cause" through what she termed "educating" the public. Dr. Dorothea Rhodes Lummis, a newly arrived physician and wife of the flamboyant newspaperman and self-promoter Charles Lummis, offered her office as a meeting place for the "cause of kindergarten." To increase the interest of club members, she invited prominent visitors to speak before club meetings. These included Dr. Horatio Stubbens, the highly regarded minister of San Francisco's First Unitarian Church and a supporter of kindergartens in San Francisco, and Miss Nettie Stewart, a kindergarten teacher at the state school in Berkeley for the deaf. Severance hoped that their visits would create the publicity to win supporters.[23]

Through correspondence with Wiggin, Severance knew that it would be difficult to persuade the Board of Education to finance kindergartens. During the past three years, the San Francisco board had cut back the number of public school teachers and reduced their salaries. Yet Wiggin sent her old friend encouragement. "I think you can do more with [the] public school question in Los Angeles than we can here."[24] Wiggin may have been correct, because shortly thereafter Los Angeles initiated a program that provided for kindergartens in public schools in some of the poorer districts of the city.

Kindergarten supporters held important positions on the school board. Frank A. Gibson, kindergarten advocate and husband of Mary Simons Gibson, served as president. In this capacity, Gibson had authority to ensure that, in 1889, a new city charter granted the board power to establish kindergartens. That same year city bond sales provided funding.[25] Severance could not hide her pleasure. "We gather once more to congratulate ourselves," she wrote in 1891; "kindergartens were no longer an experiment rather a natural course of human development."[26]

After the success of kindergartens, Severance spent her last years as she had done previously, pushing and prodding clubwomen into becoming reformers. Through her efforts the Friday Morning Club grew into the most influential women's club in Southern California and built its own clubhouse. She founded the literary and reform Ebell Club, served as honorary president of the Equity League to promote women's suffrage, and also served on boards of the city's first Protestant orphanage and settlement house. The Severance Club, a new group that included men as well as women, became a meeting place for the city's progressive-minded citizens. She continued her suffrage work and organized and lent support to younger, more vigorous women. She remained in touch with Susan B. Anthony and Anna Howard Shaw and hosted them whenever they came to Los Angeles.[27]

During these years her own political views had changed. While she had rejoiced over Ohioan James A. Garfield's victory in 1880, by the close of the century she grew wary of Republican leadership. It has been suggested that after Theodoric's death in 1894 Caroline became more radical.[28] It may be more accurate to say that a series of circumstances turned her away from conservatives within the Republican party. She endorsed Cleveland mayor Tom Johnson's plan to help the homeless by giving them city land on which to support themselves by growing food for city institutions. Indeed, she thought well enough of the plan to en-courage its implementation in Los Angeles. Like many progressives, she advocated peaceful solutions to international conflicts and questioned government responses that led to the Spanish-American War.

Her many affiliations included membership in both the Socialist Re-form Union and the League of Christian Socialists, and she supported educational projects of the Socialist Party of America. By 1906, and per-haps as early as 1898 as a member of the Union Reform League, she en-dorsed William Jennings Bryan and began referring to herself as a Chris-tian socialist or an "opportunity socialist."[29] When the city of Los Angeles hosted the naval fleet in 1907, she contended that the $25,000 spent on that fete would be better served to feed the unemployed. She detested Theodore Roosevelt's bellicose stance and openly criticized his views on "race suicide," noting that "when there is peace" women will consent to have children and not fear that their sons "will be cut down in budding manhood."[30] She did not support the national Progressive ticket in 1912, but it is not clear whether she supported Woodrow Wil-son. She worked with Los Angeles progressives John Randolph Haynes and Meyer Lissner on local reform issues and relied on them to support her projects.[31] But it is also unclear whether she promoted the 1910 gu-bernatorial bid of Hiram Johnson, whose support for women's suffrage was never more than lukewarm. When California women did win the vote in 1911, suffrage leaders honored her. She was the first woman in Los Angeles to register to vote, and friends and supporters throughout the country sent their congratulations for her nearly sixty years of con-tinuous effort for the cause.

Severance had arrived in Los Angeles with an agenda for reform, which she executed through women's clubs. Although she was more interested in political issues, she designed the clubs to attract the largest number of women by making available all levels of participation. The success she achieved came through her organizational ability and her gift of involving others in her projects. Her legacy was to set up the club structure in a way that made it easier for other women to work for reform.

MARY SIMONS GIBSON

Mary Simons Gibson worked with Severance on many reform projects. A few years after Severance's death, the Friday Morning Club asked Gibson to write the club's memorial to Severance. The memorial was dedicated to the members of the International Kindergarten Union Convention, which was held in Los Angeles in 1925.[32] The year before her friend's death in 1914, Gibson had set aside her role as fund-raiser and campaigner for progressive reforms and moved to a prominent position as a commissioner on the Immigration and Housing Commission (IHC). She served in that capacity until 1921. Thirty-five years younger than Severance, Gibson participated in government as a full-fledged citizen in a way that Severance could not.

Born in 1855, Mary Simons moved to Los Angeles from her native Santa Clara Valley in 1878 to join the fledgling corps of city schoolteachers.[33] She left teaching in 1881 to marry Frank A. Gibson, and devoted herself to household duties and civic work.[34] They had four children, but only one son, Hugh, survived. During these years she worked with her mother-in-law to found the city's first Protestant orphanage and served as its secretary. She was part of the nucleus that founded the Los Angeles Woman's Club and the Friday Morning Club; and, along with the Severance family and Kate Douglas Wiggin, she raised money for the city library and later the Unitarian church. Frank died in 1902, and after a proper period of mourning, Mary renewed her vigorous life in philanthropy and reform.[35]

As a member of the Friday Morning Club, Gibson had focused on women's suffrage, municipal reform, and education as her main interests. She believed that clubs should not serve personal gain or "personal culture" but, instead, should serve "constructive social work."[36] By the turn of the century, she joined civic organizations, campaigned for a single moral standard of "social purity," and worked for birth control. She supported progressives and Hiram Johnson for governor in 1910. In 1911, at age fifty-six, she raised $10,000 in short order, a "tremendous sum for women's issues," and campaigned throughout the state for the suffrage bill, amazing her friends and worrying her son. Writing from his diplomatic post in Havana, her son implored her to slow down.[37] During the 1912 presidential election, she chaired the Women's Rally Committee Chorus, often referred to as the Southern California Jane Addams Chorus. The chorus, named for one of the nation's foremost progressives and a staunch supporter of the Roosevelt-Johnson ticket, was composed of women dressed in white garments who performed at rallies coordinated by Gibson during her campaign travels.[38] The Roosevelt-Johnson Progressives won in California—nationally Progressives carried only five states—and many pundits attributed its success to the work of newly enfranchised clubwomen such as Gibson.[39] Her loyalty and ability were brought to Governor Johnson's attention, and he appointed her to the Immigration and Housing Commission (IHC) in 1913.

Pushed into action by progressive supporters, in particular Sacramento businessman and social reformer Simon Lubin, Johnson established the commission to study immigrant problems in employment and housing. The anticipated opening of the Panama Canal in 1915 provided some urgency, for the canal was expected to increase the already growing numbers of southern and eastern Europeans in California. Lubin, an assimilationist, expected the commission to find ways to ease the process of immigrant adjustment, an idea he shared with Gibson.

Gibson's beliefs in assimilation had been influenced by Jane Addams and Frances Kellor.[40] The General Federation of Women's Clubs had provided access for women in different regions of the country to form strong networks based on mutual interest and shared values. Gibson was in contact with Addams through correspondence and had incorporated her version of Addams's "immigrant gifts" into her work with California immigrants. Chester Rowell, a leading progressive and editor of the *Fresno Republican*, noted that Gibson intended Americanization to enhance, rather than diminish, the cultures that immigrants brought with them. She believed, Rowell said, that immigrants would "broaden us also to the things they might contribute to our lives."[41] Gibson viewed adequate housing, access to education for children and adults, and citizenship training as prerequisites for assimilation. Assuming these tasks as her primary responsibilities on the commission, she conducted investigations and obtained help from civic organizations, including the YMCA and women's clubs.

Central to Gibson's commission work was current information on the housing and education of California's immigrants. Because of her club affiliations, she had access to that information. Investigations and surveys conducted by clubwomen had revealed inadequate housing and health services. In Los Angeles these studies resulted in tenement house legislation, city-appointed visiting nurses, a juvenile court system, and a playground commission to build and maintain city playgrounds. In her correspondence with Lubin, Gibson readily acknowledged the help clubwomen had given her and made him aware that through their efforts the commission, and therefore the state, had been spared great expense in obtaining the data. Gibson presented these studies to the full commission.[42]

Armed with the club members' statistics and their model for new social legislation, Gibson began her program to modify what she perceived as one of the worst elements of immigrant life—the breakdown of the family. She set in motion a project to aid immigrant families by bringing education to foreign-born mothers. That project became the basis for the Home Teacher Act of 1915.[43]

Gibson appealed to middle-class Americans' notion of the "cult of domesticity"—the prescribed role women were to play in the family—and then she molded it to fit immigrant mothers as well. The immigrant process, she claimed, had robbed mothers of their children's respect and, therefore, their control over them. "The Americanization of the children in public schools often adds to [a mother's] difficulty."[44] While husbands and children might move about freely in American society, learn English, and participate in urban life, mothers, shut in at home, often lacked contact with the larger society. Even when they worked outside their homes, they rarely mixed with groups other than their own. Gibson introduced studies that reinforced her theories on family breakdown—notably, that a majority of juvenile delinquents came from the ranks of immigrant communities.

Gibson also appealed to the middle-class fear of radicalism. Radical groups, such as the Industrial Workers of the World, had made inroads to the heart of immigrant societies. To underline the urgency of her plea, she pointed to the IWW's involvement in the 1913 Wheatland riots, where police authorities had shot down striking agricultural workers in Southern California. As an antidote to radicalism, a program such as the

Home Teacher Act, which would bring teachers into immigrant homes and workplaces, would provide opportunities for mothers to become Americanized and regain their rightful position as moral guardians within the family structure.

Gibson began a lobbying campaign to win legislation for her program. She called for help and received it from women's organizations throughout the state. The California Federation of Women's Clubs had organized a legislative committee, the Women's Legislative Council of California, to promote its programs, and Gibson called it into action. After six weeks of intense lobbying in Sacramento, the council persuaded the legislature to pass the Home Teacher Act.

Gibson used her position as commissioner to expand the Home Teacher Act and introduce the program into more cities. Her strategy was simple: she convinced city leaders that the Home Teacher Act would save money. Using information based on the surveys her commission had conducted, Gibson told her audiences that money spent on immigrant education programs, particularly the Home Teacher Act, was an efficient way of taking care of the "immigrant problem."[45]

With the passage of the 1915 Home Teacher Act, Gibson's political reputation soared. Edson referred to her in 1916 as "the most important woman in Southern California politically" and perhaps in the state.[46] Frances Kellor had "besieged" Gibson to come east and organize a Woman's Republican League, but Gibson declined.[47] She had many things to do in California.

One of the first items on her list was to provide special training classes for home teachers. Within a short time Gibson convinced influential Californians that the Home Teacher Act represented a positive addition to education. By the summer of 1919, the University of California and the newly organized campus in Los Angeles, the southern branch, offered teachers classes in immigrant education. Some of the earliest teachers trained in Americanization techniques through the Home Teacher Act became sought-after spokeswomen of immigrant education and lectured throughout the state.[48] Meanwhile the programs expanded. Gibson wrote in 1926 that nearly 50,000 immigrants had been reached by the classes.[49]

Nevertheless, the program had flaws. Gibson attributed some of the problems to lack of funding. The act had no state appropriations, and city school districts, the sole source of the act's funding, were slow to provide teachers and materials. Gibson looked to the federal government to give immigrant education a permanent home and joined in the drive to create a Department of Education. To facilitate that drive, she became chairwoman of the Immigrant Committee of the General Federation of Women's Clubs in 1918.[50] As with her previous campaign, she relied on clubwomen to furnish her with statistics from their surveys and planned a propaganda campaign to enlist an army of clubwomen in a national Americanization program. But opposition to a cabinet-level Department of Education was stronger than Gibson and supporters suspected, and their efforts came to naught.[51]

She had more success in California. There she managed to put one of her staff members on the Immigration Committee of the State Board of Education in 1920 and, in this way, tried to ensure that the programs of the IHC would be continued. Nevertheless, the progressive impulse in California politics had faded. Governor Friend Richardson began his term in 1923; and he, along with Republican regulars, tried and eventually succeeded in dismantling most of the state commissions that had been the cornerstone of progressive legislation. Gibson resigned in 1922. By the time the IHC was dissolved in 1927, it had long since lost its power.[52]

Several years before Gibson resigned from the IHC, she had become disillusioned with the Republican party. In 1918, she responded to Will H. Hays, then head of the Republican National Committee, who had called for a conference of Republican women to discuss the best way to put women to work for Republican candidates. She would not be patronized, and she told him in no uncertain terms that she was angry with her party for its undervaluation of women. Republican men, she argued, failed to put women in leadership roles that they clearly deserved. She sent Hays a copy of a resolution—prepared and passed by several organized women's groups, including the General Federation of Women's Clubs—that stated what the women expected the government to do.[53]

After the 1920 election, Gibson left the Republican party. She rejected Johnson's bid for presidential nomination that year because of his stand against the League of Nations. As a peace advocate, she believed that the League of Nations offered the best hope for lasting postwar peace. When Republican leadership in Congress voted against joining the league, she announced that she would no longer be a Republican.

Gibson remained active. Progressives hailed her as the fairy godmother of immigrant women; and in 1925, still interested in immigrant education, she proudly wrote of the accomplishments of the Home Teacher Act. But she no longer held any state position. Instead, she turned her energies to projects advocated by her late husband and joined John Randolph Haynes in his work with California's Indians. She served as one of the original trustees of the Haynes Foundation. In 1927 Gibson compiled the history of the CFWC, and included in it a modest account of her own achievements. She founded the League of Women Voters in California, and her peace work led her to raise money for International House at the University of California, a facility designed to promote world understanding through programs that brought foreign and American students together. Shortly before her death in 1930, she supported the Cause and Cure of War Conference in Washington and, closer to home, celebrated the passage of the Kellogg-Briand Pact with a reception at the Friday Morning Club.[54]

Women's clubs and the network of women who shared the same values were central to Gibson's work as a reformer. Women's clubs gave her a forum as well as contacts to voice and spread her ideas. As did Severance, Gibson drew upon particular men for help for her projects, and like Severance she had the support of many progressive men. Lubin had brought her into state government. Yet it was her club affiliations that provided her with the resources she called upon when she became a commissioner. Her last project was directed at compiling the record of organized California women, and her friends held her memorial at the Friday Morning Club.

KATHERINE PHILIPS EDSON

Katherine Philips Edson had the most public profile of the three women in this study—partly because she was born in 1870, fifty years after Severance and fifteen after Gibson. Thus, many of the battles these older women had fought were won before Edson came of age. Furthermore, Edson was young enough to participate fully in the public arena after California women received the vote. She first made her reputation as a competent organizer through the Friday Morning Club, where she served as treasurer and vice president and chaired two important committees, Public Health and Industrial and Social Conditions. After she moved from local to state and then to federal positions, her reliance on women's clubs lessened. In any event, solidarity within organized womanhood had diminished after passage of the Nineteenth Amendment in 1920.

Katherine Philips met Charles Farwell Edson in Chicago in 1889. An Ohioan, she planned to study voice in the big city and prepare for a musical career. Katherine's father, a physician well known in Ohio for his interests in raising health standards, supported her desire for further education. Charles, a native-born Californian, had gone to his mother's family home in suburban Chicago to attend Lake Forest College. But he soon abandoned his academic studies and was studying music at the time he met Katherine. After their marriage, the couple came to California and settled in with Charles's parents on their almond orchard in the Antelope Valley in 1891. Eight years later they moved to Los Angeles.[55]

Within a short time their new home in Los Angeles became a center of cultural activities. Charles imagined he could support his growing family, which came to include three children and his widowed mother, by giving music lessons. Charles was well connected through his Farwell relatives. One uncle served as U.S. senator from Illinois; another had made a fortune in the dry goods business. Two of his female cousins were accomplished; one was a writer, another owned a bindery, and both had married men of distinction in literature and music. Several of his cousins had been part of a small group of literary people who, in the 1890s, founded a Paris-style salon in Chicago named "the Little Room." Charles could expect to use his connections to build up a fashionable clientele.[56]

In Los Angeles it seemed natural for Katherine to seek membership in the stimulating atmosphere of the Friday Morning Club. While she lived on the Edson family ranch, she had participated in the unsuccessful 1896 women's suffrage campaign; now, as a member of the Friday Morning Club, she could combine her interest in music with that of women's suffrage. At the club she met and worked with prominent Angelenos, including Severance and Gibson. Influenced by the political activities of many club members, she began to combine her suffrage work with other reform measures.

By 1908, Edson settled on a reform that would launch her career as one of the most active women in California progressive politics. Through the Friday Morning Club she began a crusade aimed at providing adequate health inspections to ensure that the milk sold in the city came from cows free of bovine tuberculosis. In 1911 she became chairwoman of the club's Public Health Committee. The committee conducted studies on successful pure-milk campaigns in Chicago, New York, and Baltimore. Its members inspected dairies in Los Angeles and publicized their findings in a monthly bulletin, identifying those dairies that sold milk with bacterial counts higher than experts considered safe. Members lobbied for measures to guarantee that only untainted milk would be sold in Los Angeles.[57]

Edson's efforts on behalf of pure milk brought her an appointment on the Los Angeles County Medical Milk Commission, as the only commissioner without a medical background, and an appointment on the Los Angeles Charter Revision Committee in 1910. In 1912, the General Federation of Women's Clubs endorsed Edson's recommendation to make pure milk a national issue.[58]

Edson's political reputation grew. She helped coordinate the southern and northern branches of the Political Equality League. She became known as an effective progressive campaigner during the 1910 gubernatorial election and worked with Meyer Lissner, Chester Rowell, and Edward A. Dickson. Rowell and Lissner remained her lifelong friends. During the 1911 drive to give women the vote, she and the other leading clubwomen led lobbying efforts to get the bill passed in the legislature and then campaigned throughout Southern California for passage of the state amendment.

As a reward for her dedication, Hiram Johnson—in spite of his longstanding belief that women did not belong in politics—appointed her to the state Bureau of Labor Statistics for Southern California. Almost immediately Edson focused her investigation on working conditions of women and children in industry. The results of her investigation revealed a pattern of low wages and wretched conditions. From the information she gathered for the bureau, she campaigned for a minimum wage law for women and children.

Even though Edson was sensitive to the conditions of working women and children, she believed that forcing these groups into the work force was wrong. Rather, she thought that men should assume their roles as head of household by supporting their families. Nevertheless, if necessity mandated that women and children work, then they needed protection. She herself now experienced the need to earn money. Charles had not found the financial success he had expected in Los Angeles; therefore, Katherine's salary on the Bureau of Labor Statistics served as a critical ingredient in maintaining her career. She kept her job on the bureau in order to ensure that she would have a salary after she had moved on to other appointed state positions.[59]

Soon after the legislature granted women suffrage, Edson met with five members of the California Federation of Women's Clubs and agreed to form a central legislative body to coordinate legislative proposals originating from women's organizations. To avoid duplication and save expenses, they planned to bring together each club's experts on particular issues. The federation accepted their plan and allowed them to open a headquarters in the Sacramento Hotel a block from the capitol. The Women's Legislative Council of the CFWC was ready for business by 1913 and presented its platform of seventeen proposals to the legislators.[60] The council had done its job well. In 1913 ten of the council's proposals passed, and Edson was directly responsible for two of these ten bills: minimum wage and a pure-milk law.[61]

As a consequence of her persistence, the pure-milk bill Governor Johnson signed into law gave the state power to regulate by certification all dairy products produced and sold in California. The 1913 minimum wage law for women and children was more complicated. It required an agency to enforce it and, to ensure the constitutionality of such an agency, called for an amendment to the state's constitution. With the CFWC to provide education and publicity, the amendment passed with a majority of 84,000 votes. It now included not only minimum wages but also a provision for the "comfort, health, safety, and general welfare of any and all employees."[62] The new amendment also authorized the governor to establish an Industrial Welfare Commission (IWC) to set and enforce the provisions of the law. The amendment mandated that one of the five commissioners be a woman, and Johnson appointed Edson. She served on the commission from 1914 to 1931.[63]

Edson became the most influential member of the IWC. Her age—forty-three in 1913—ambition, and vitality allowed her to surpass Gibson as the most visible female progressive in California.[64] As a commissioner Edson worked to provide higher wage rates for workers in manufacturing industries, hotels and restaurants, motion pictures, laundries, and canning and packing industries throughout the state. Opposition to her work came from business as well as organized labor. AFL leaders feared that state-set minimum wages would lead to state-set maximum wages, thereby inhibiting labor's bargaining power. Edson was more concerned over the plight of working women, whom the AFL ignored. Although the IWC continued to regulate workers' hours and wages, its constitutionality came under question. In 1923 the United States Supreme Court took under review a Washington, D.C., case, *Adkins v. Children's Hospital,* and ruled that minimum wage laws were unconstitutional. Edson refused to back off and continued to enforce the IWC policies until Governor James Rolph forced her resignation from the IWC in 1931.[65]

Edson's reputation as a successful organizer and outspoken progressive had brought her into contact with leading Republicans. She participated in the Women's Auxiliary Alliance, organized in 1916 for Governor Hughes's election, and she joined the "National Campaign Train" in Washington State, giving speeches for Hughes from Spokane to Los Angeles. In Portland hecklers nearly caused her talk to be canceled. She did not blame the hecklers, female members of the Industrial Workers of the World, for the outrage as much as she did the Republican party. The National Democratic Committee dubbed the train the "millionaires of Wall Street," and Edson wondered whether the Republican leadership had been wrong-headed in its choice of speakers sent to tell the "Western people how to vote." As an example of Republican miscalculations, Edson noted that they had sent Mrs. Guggenheim as part of the train. She reminded friends that in the West Guggenheim meant "Colorado mining operations of a pretty shady character," and it was no wonder the train had done little to win votes for Governor Hughes.[66]

The 1916 election proved particularly painful for progressives such as Edson and Gibson, who had been disappointed when Johnson did not receive the nomination. They had supported Hughes because of his reform politics in New York, not because of feelings of loyalty toward the regular Republicans. Both women were with Johnson at the Virginia Hotel in Long Beach when Hughes's entourage neglected to meet with the California governor. Throughout his California trip, Hughes failed to acknowledge Johnson's progressive reform program; and his campaign committee ignored most of the state's leading progressives, including Gibson and Edson.[67] This egregious error had cost the Republicans a win in California. The national Republicans had over and over misjudged the westerners and were insensitive to the differences in politics and custom in the West. Edson tried to convey this oversight to Florence Kelley in her letter after Wilson's reelection. Solidarity, Edson knew from personal experience, was hard to come by. Her sister, a high school teacher in Los Angeles, had voted for Wilson.

Despite Hughes's loss, Edson's reputation continued to grow. Democrats wanted her support. Wilson's chairman of the War Labor Policies Board, Felix Frankfurter, asked her to serve with him to help enlist women in the war effort. But her IWC activities kept her in California, and by the time she could leave her duties, the war had ended. Edson continued to work for a national suffrage amendment, although her limited financial resources did not allow her to spend much time outside of California. In 1920 she represented California as one of Johnson's delegates to the national Republican convention in Chicago. Edson seconded her old friend's nomination. Only one other women had had the honor before, when Jane Addams seconded Theodore Roosevelt's nomination in 1912.[68]

For the second time Edson felt disappointment when Johnson did not receive the Republican nomination. Edson also lost a faithful ally in Mary Simons Gibson, since she and Gibson had parted political ways. Gibson supported Herbert Hoover over Johnson because of Johnson's anti–League of Nations position. In a letter to Chester Rowell, Edson noted that clubwomen had played an important role in Republican party politics; later, referring to Gibson in particular, she remarked on the loss of many clubwomen because of what she termed their "peace propaganda."[69]

Nevertheless, Edson joined Warren Harding's camp after he assured her that he would support the spirit of the League of Nations and told her that he was eager for such a body to be formed.[70] She campaigned for Harding, and after his election he asked her to serve as one of four women on the American advisory delegation to the International Conference for the Limitation of Armaments. This conference laid the groundwork for the Five Power Naval Treaty of Washington, signed in 1922. In an advisory capacity, Edson worked as a lobbyist just as she had worked in Los Angeles for the pure-milk campaign and then in Sacramento for a minimum wage law. Unlike Severance or Gibson, Edson did not actively participate in any peace movement, but she redefined her views on the minimum wage to bring them in line with disarmament. "Raising wages of working people," she wrote, "will raise their hopes and will do more to bring peace on earth and goodwill toward men than scrapping every battleship afloat."[71]

Edson had become openly more xenophobic than either Severance had been or Gibson was. There is no indication that either would have supported the California Federation of Women's Club membership in the Japanese Exclusion League as Edson did. Although she had remained silent during the 1913 debates on the California Alien Land Act, by 1918 she expressed her thoughts on further Asian and Mexican immigration. Conducting a survey for California's Women's Council of Defense, she concluded that the state's agricultural areas would soon be overrun by "Mexicans and Orientals" unless something were done. To protect the state from "coolie labor, she went so far as to suggest that middle- and upper-middle-class women and children join in as farm laborers."[72] A few years later she attempted to explain the "California viewpoint" on Japanese exclusion to easterners. Writing in a late 1921 issue of *The Women Citizen*, the National League of Women Voters' periodical, she outlined her ideas. Using the familiar rhetoric of exclusionists, she voiced fears of "orientalization" of the West Coast; at the same time, she tried to quiet her critics by noting that her objection to the

"Oriental Tide" was based on economic interests. Japanese laborers drove out white workers from California orchards and farms. She had promised to write a second article the next month, but, ironically, her appointment as an adviser to the International Conference for the Limitation of Armaments—where Japan would play a key role—kept her from it.[73]

After her work in the conference ended, she returned to California and continued her work on the IWC until 1931. She remained active in the California Federation of Women's Clubs and the newly formed League of Women Voters, but by this time she suffered from renewed bouts of cancer, and her health had begun to deteriorate. Her marriage had also deteriorated, and in 1925 she and Charles divorced. She lived another nine years, succumbing to cancer in 1933.[74]

Edson's political career began through women's clubs; and her quick rise from club-centered politics to state and national arenas is, in part, attributable to the structure of the club Severance had designed. Severance created an atmosphere where activists such as Edson could join in established committees or begin new ones. As Edson moved into mainstream politics, she depended less on club support than did Gibson and certainly Severance. She became a public figure during the time when California women won suffrage, and she had greater opportunities in public life than did the two older women.

THE CHANGING ROLE OF WOMEN
AND WOMEN'S CLUBS

After obtaining suffrage, California women had more opportunities to participate in politics, and women's clubs no longer served as centers of public activities. The previous separation from men, which had bound women activists together and enabled them to build a political culture during the Progressive Era, seemed less relevant. Even before 1911 many chose to collaborate with politically powerful men in order to influence power.[75] Caroline Severance had depended on Reverend Stubbens and school board president Frank Gibson in her efforts to make kindergartens part of public schooling.

Enfranchised women expected to join men on all levels of politics and relied less on their own organizations to affect political reform. Yet many kept their club ties and continued to use their club networks to further reforms. In the late 1910s, when Mary Gibson directed the General Federation's national drive to organize a federal Department of Education, she proposed courses for clubwomen so that they could become trained teachers in programs of immigrant education.

Clubwomen used their clubs to bring about reforms well into the 1930s. Through their efforts, a separate women's state prison at Te-hachapi, long a goal of women reformers, was constructed in 1935; and the following year an amendment to the state constitution established a separate governing board for female prisoners. But by the 1930s, women had several agencies other than clubs for their activities. Moreover, the solidarity that held middle-class women together during the Progressive Era had been based on the overriding goals of suffrage and temperance. In the 1920s, following the seeming achievement of these goals, much of that solidarity evaporated. In fact, differences in approaches to solving post–World War I problems often led to acrimonious encounters, as exemplified by the split between two of the best-known political activists, Florence Kelley and Alice Paul, during the 1923 *Adkins v. Children's Hospital* debate.[76] In California, progressive Republicans Edson and Gibson parted ways over support of the Republican candidates during the 1920 election.

The Republican party had been home to most reformers in the nineteenth century. But just as Severance had broken her allegiance, perhaps as early as 1898, Gibson, and to a lesser degree Edson, demonstrated that by the 1920s the Republican party had surrendered much of its appeal to reformers. Gibson's letter to Hays in 1918, demanding that women be given some positions of leadership, had done little to change his or the party regulars' minds. Two years later Edson commented on Hays's continued unwillingness to include women in any meaningful policy-level conferences. In a letter to Chester Rowell, she expanded on how much women resented their exclusion from mainstream party politics. Hays was guilty of the easterners' syndrome: he did not know that western women would not be "corralled."[77]

Even Edson had considered abandoning ship. While President Harding's decision to bring women in as advisers to the Disarmament Conference did much to keep Edson in the Republican camp, still she voiced her apprehension. Writing to Rowell in 1928, she described her support for the Herbert Hoover candidacy but confided that if the Republicans "defeat him for the nomination," she would "vote for Al Smith."[78] Women's solidarity had been destroyed by the vagaries of politics, and the political culture women developed to further their reforms had fallen by the wayside as voting women demanded entrance into the political world as equal partners.

Severance, Gibson, and Edson represented the changing role of women in the late nineteenth and early twentieth centuries. They moved from a separate sphere of their homes to an extension of home life in the separate world of women's clubs. Severance carried out her programs for philanthropy and reform within the constructs of a female culture she helped create. Gibson serves as a transitional figure who began her political career working in philanthropic reforms and, then, after suffrage, moved to state-level politics, relying on both women and men. Edson moved much more quickly from female networks to the male political sphere, although she continued to rely on traditional women's networks to support legislation. But by 1916 she had moved far beyond the closed circle of women's clubs that had defined female political culture.

The political culture developed by these three California women started with their interest in reform. They began as municipal housekeepers, and after suffrage Gibson and Edson moved into the public sphere as fuller participants. As members of women's clubs, all three had forums for their political activities. Given their achievements and the roles they played in the state's progressive politics, George Mowry's exclusion of these women and of the role of clubwomen in his history of California's progressive reform seems an unfortunate oversight.

NOTES

1. Karen Blair, *The Clubwoman as Feminist: True Womanhood Redefined, 1868–1914* (New York: Holmes and Meier, 1980), 34. During the nineteenth century, women referred to their organizations as woman's clubs. Caroline Severance wrote that the work she and other women had done during the Civil War—for instance, their work in establishing the Sanitary Commission and the Freedmen's Bureau—convinced them of "our own capacity for public effort, and [we] learned the lesson of working harmoniously together for common interests and aims." See Ella Giles Ruddy, ed., *The Mother of Clubs: Caroline M. Seymour Severance* (Los Angeles: Baumgardt Publishing Co., 1906), 22–23. Severance also was influenced by a journal on English women's clubs, *English Woman's Journal*, edited by Emily Faithful.

2. In most cases, African-American women were excluded from white clubs and formed their own organizations.

3. Mary S. Gibson, comp., *A Record of Twenty-five Years of the California Federation of Women's Clubs, 1900–1925* (Los Angeles: General Federation of Women's Clubs, 1927), 5.

4. Rosalyn Terborg-Penn, "Discontented Black Feminists: Prelude and Postscript to the Passage of the Nineteenth Amendment," in Kathryn K. Sklar and

Thomas Dublin, eds., *Women and Power in American History: A Reader* (Englewood Cliffs, N.J.: Prentice-Hall, 1991), 2:132–45. The race issue came to national attention in 1902, when black clubs were excluded from the GFWC. Severance corresponded with Booker T. Washington on the subject, and the renowned educator wrote that he refused to discuss the matter, since his concerns were with the "larger aspects of the problem of race." See Booker T. Washington to Caroline Severance, March 5, 1902, box 24, Caroline M. Severance Papers, Huntington Library, San Marino, California. Severance may have been concerned with the larger aspects of women's issues, and in 1902 her concerns would be with suffrage. Almost all clubs in the South and many elsewhere threatened to pull out of the GFWC if black clubs were admitted. She would not alienate potential supporters at this crucial stage of the battle. When the General Federation of Women's Clubs publicly discussed race and membership of "colored" clubs in 1902, Caroline sided with the majority to exclude black clubs.

5. Gibson, *A Record*, 116; *Report of the College Settlement, Los Angeles, California* (Los Angeles: College Settlement Association, 1905?).

6. Katherine Philips Edson to Florence Kelley, November 18, 1916, box 1, Katherine Philips Edson Papers, Special Collections, UCLA.

7. George Mowry, *The California Progressives* (Berkeley: University of California Press, 1951).

8. Joan M. Jensen, "After Slavery: Caroline Severance in Los Angeles," *Southern California Quarterly* 48 (June 1966): 175–86; Ruddy, *The Mother of Clubs*, 44. The club organized in 1878 was short-lived; another, founded in 1881, met a similar fate. Caroline's extended trips to the East Coast left a void in those clubs' leadership. In 1891 she founded the Friday Morning Club and served as its first president; in 1894 she was elected president emeritus.

9. Ruddy, *The Mother of Clubs*, 14. Severance began her public-speaking career in 1853, when she was "chosen" as the first woman to address the Mercantile Library Association in Cleveland. After moving to Massachusetts in 1855, she had asked Elizabeth Cady Stanton to speak at the Theodore Parker Fraternity Association. Stanton was unavailable, and Severance spoke in her place. She was not particularly pleased with her performance that evening and "from want of gift of voice" did not speak much in public after that. For an overview of Severance's contributions to reform, see the Clipping Collection, box 45, Severance Papers.

10. See Dora Haynes to CS, n.p., n.d., box 18, Severance Papers.

11. Mary S. Gibson, *Caroline Severance, Pioneer* (Los Angeles: Friday Morning Club, 1914), as quoted in Barbara Greenwood, comp., *History of the Kindergarten Movement in the Western States, Hawaii and Alaska* (Washington, D.C.: Association for Childhood Education, 1940), 11.

12. Abolitionist leader Theodore Weld taught at Dio Lewis while Severance was there. Dio Lewis believed that education included exercise for both boys and girls to ensure healthy bodies as well as healthy minds. See Jensen, "After Slavery," 179. The New England Woman's Club established the New England Hospital for Women and Children, ran and officered by women, set up scholarships for university-bound women, lobbied for the Massachusetts law changing "age of consent," put police matrons in institutions where girls and women were

held, raised money for archaeological expeditions in Greece and Egypt, and worked for female dress reform. See Ruddy, *The Mother of Clubs*, 15, 25–26.

13. Ruddy, *The Mother of Clubs*, 31–32; Michael Steven Shapiro, *Child's Garden: The Kindergarten Movement from Froebel to Dewey* (University Park: Pennsylvania State University Press, 1983), 29–63. Caroline's interest in kindergartens grew out of her contacts with Elizabeth Peabody, an honorary member of the New England Woman's Club. Peabody, whom Severance referred to as "Saint Elizabeth" (Ruddy, *The Mother of Clubs*, 26), and other club members had sponsored kindergartens in Boston, opening the first English-speaking kindergarten in 1860. But it was through the pioneering work of the St. Louis superintendent of public schools, William Torey Harris, and kindergarten promoter Susan Blow in 1873 that kindergartens reached into slum areas as part of public schooling.

14. Henry Ivison to CS, January 1, 1874, box 42, Severance Papers. Ivison, a bookseller in Boston and probably an in-law, wrote that he would send the German textbooks Caroline had requested, but he felt that it was unethical for her to request any more. It was better to let California book dealers deal direct. This once he would send them, and he said she should consider them a gift from "Santa."

15. Fletcher Harper Swift, *Emma Marwedel, 1818–1893: Pioneer of the Kindergarten in California* (Berkeley: University of California Press, 1931), 153–55, 161, 167. Marwedel had studied with Friedrich Froebel in Prussia and had been brought to the United States by kindergarten pioneer and New England Woman's Club member Elizabeth Peabody in 1867. Peabody had gone to Germany to learn more about kindergarten training. Marwedel worked briefly in New York and then moved to Washington, D.C., where her kindergarten and private school attracted the attention of public officials, including the future president and friend of Severance, James A. Garfield, whose three children attended Marwedel's establishment.

16. Kate Douglas Wiggin, *My Garden of Memory: An Autobiography* (Boston: Houghton Mifflin, 1923), 88–105, quote on 91. Wiggin dubbed Caroline her "fairy godmother" and agreed to give it a try. She likened her to "Elijah alighted from his chariot" asking her to "accompany her to some unknown Paradise." Shortly after their initial meeting, the "fairy godmother" wrote that she had been studying her without her knowledge and added that "at my age I am a fair judge of the necessary requirements." The training program required a hundred dollars for tuition plus twenty-five dollars for books and materials. The Severances welcomed her as a member of their family for the course period of nine months.

17. Swift, *Emma Marwedel*, 153–55, 161, 167. After its closure, Marwedel moved to Oakland, then to San Francisco and opened a training school and kindergarten class there. She died in 1893, in Oakland, and Severance's oldest son, Seymour, attended the funeral and wrote his mother a full account of the event. Seymour Severance to CS, November 20, 1893, box 1, Severance Collection; *History of the Los Angeles State Normal School, Quarter Centennial, 1882–1907* (n.p., 1907), 9, Huntington Library, San Marino, Calif.

18. Michael Steven Shapiro, *Child's Garden: The Kindergarten Movement from Froebel to Dewey* (University Park: Pennsylvania State University Press, 1983), gives a good account of the reasons kindergartens met with resistance prior to the Progressive Era.

19. Ann Taylor Allen, " 'Let Us Live with Our Children': Kindergarten Movements in the United States and Germany, 1840–1914," *History of Education Quarterly* 28 (Spring 1988): 23–48. Kindergartens had been perceived as agents of moral reform in Germany before they made their appearance in the United States.

20. Kate Douglas Wiggin, *Annual Statement of the Silver Street Kindergarten Society* (San Francisco: C. A. Murdock and Co., 1886), 6–7; Greenwood, *History of the Kindergarten Movement,* 10–14. Silver Street was the first tuition-free kindergarten west of the Rockies to teach hygiene and English along with the regular Froebelian curriculum. From an American viewpoint, by the 1880s some of the more objectionable aspects of kindergartens (derived from their German origins) had been modified and "Americanized." "Americanized" kindergartens also created greater interest among middle-class parents who could afford tuition classes.

21. CS to Margaret Collier Graham, September 27, 1881, box 24, Margaret Collier Graham Papers, Huntington Library. From Massachusetts, in 1881, Severance wrote to Margaret Graham, a teacher in Los Angeles, "in white heat of my indignation" of her frustration when the Los Angeles Board of Education failed to renew the contract of Chloe Jones, the first female superintendent of the public schools. She wished that Graham might be a member but feared that Graham's residence in Pasadena would make it unlikely. But she hoped that "our Board is sufficiently cosmopolitan to accept an able and eminent member from without the sacred precinct and from their loveliest suburb." CS to Margaret Collier Graham, July 15, 1886, box 24, Graham Papers. In 1887 Mrs. Ana S. Averill became the first woman school board member.

22. CS to Jane E. Collier, June 26, 1885, box 24, Graham Papers.

23. Prominent banker I. W. Hellman intended to donate a gift to the "cause." CS to Jane Collier, June 26, 1885, box 24, Graham Papers. Other groups began to follow. The Woman's Christian Temperance Union opened a tuition-free kindergarten.

24. Kate Douglas Wiggin to CS, October 7, 1885, box 24, Severance Papers. Wiggin, now head of the California Kindergarten Training School in San Francisco, wrote, "It's a lucky thing for the San Francisco kindergartens when I married Samuel B. Wiggin." Her marriage enabled her to give "about four hours a day to 'work for humanity' which is a good term I suppose for work done for gratis."

25. Sherman H. Freeman, "Board of Education–Superintendent Relationships in the Los Angeles City School System, 1853–1920" (Ph.D. diss., University of California, Los Angeles, 1951), 154, 223. The superintendent of schools, William Friesner, had visited a tuition kindergarten that his niece attended and apparently had been impressed by what he observed. The bond provided $200,000 to build classrooms, some of which could be used for kindergartens.

Over the next several years, supporters of organized kindergartens (in middle-class school districts as well as in schools for the poor) successfully lobbied for the passage of several enabling ordinances. And the movement flourished. With the signing by Governor Hiram Johnson of the "Petition Law" in 1913, kindergarten supporters statewide succeeded in having kindergartens formally incorporated in public schools by petition. In 1920 kindergartens became part of the state constitution and part of the public school system, thereby obviating the need of petition. Greenwood, *History of the Kindergarten Movement*, 23–24.

26. 1891 Kindergarten Meeting, n.p. but undoubtedly Los Angeles. She begins, "Dear Friends," box 26, Severance Papers.

27. Susan B. Anthony to CS, August 29, 1890, box 14, Severance Papers.

28. Jensen, "After Slavery," 183. After Garfield's assassination, she remained in contact with his widow. Fifteen letters from Lucretia Rudolph Garfield to CS, 1908–14, box 17, Severance Papers.

29. *Los Angeles Record*, May 2, 1906, box 42, Severance Papers. Tom Sitton, *John Randolph Haynes: California Progressive* (Stanford, Calif.: Stanford University Press, 1992), 30–33, 44. Severance was one of a long list of vice presidents of the Social Reform Union. See Mari Jo Buhle, *Women and American Socialism, 1870–1920* (Urbana: University of Illinois Press, 1981), 77–78. Buhle refers to Severance as a "proselytizer for Christian socialism."

30. Clipping file, n.p., n.d., box 42, Severance Papers.

31. Meyer Lissner to CS, December 23, 1909, and Lulu Pile Little to CS, September 8, 1896, box 20, Severance Papers. She probably voted against the Socialists during the city elections in 1911. In that election Republican George Alexander defeated Socialist Job Harriman for mayor. The newspapers carried stories to the effect that women voters had defeated Harriman. One of the articles (box 45, Severance Papers) contains a quote by Severance just after the voting analysis.

32. Gibson, *Caroline Severance, Pioneer*. The convention was held from July 8 through 11, 1925.

33. Little is known of her early years. Severance and Edson both graduated from female seminaries, but there is no indication that Gibson had attended a seminary. Nevertheless, what formal education she had was based on liberal Protestantism, and she later referred to herself as a Unitarian.

34. "Dictation of Frank A. Gibson," n.d., may have been written November 21, 1887, California Dictation Misc., Bancroft Library, University of California, Berkeley. Like Mary, Frank had come to Los Angeles in the 1870s. He served as postal clerk for a short time, then as county recorder for Los Angeles, then as a banker. He was elected president of the Board of Education in the late 1880s. His father, a Methodist minister, was appointed Indian agent on a Mendocino County reservation in the 1870s, and Frank kept the reservation's financial accounts. Through his work on the reservation, Frank developed an awareness of the injustice done to California's Native Americans—sentiments shared by his wife.

35. Friday Morning Club, *Mary S. Gibson, Pioneer* (Los Angeles: Friday Morning Club, 1930), 1–33.

36. Ibid., 33.

37. Ibid., 13–14; quote is from Mrs. Seward A. Simons. Hugh Gibson to Mary S. Gibson, September 23, 1911, box 25, Hugh Gibson Papers, Hoover Institution Archives, Stanford, Calif.

38. Chorus members were drawn mainly from women's clubs representing their towns and cities. Mary Gibson to Jane Addams, undated telegram, probably sent on August 29, 1912, Jane Addams Papers, Microfilm, Reel 6, frame 1547, University of California, Irvine.

39. Progressives won in California, Pennsylvania, Michigan, South Dakota, and Washington. Mowry, *California Progressives*, 189. Mowry does not mention the work of clubwomen during the election.

40. David George Herman "Neighbors on the Golden Mountain: The Americanization of Immigrants in California" (Ph.D. diss., University of California, Berkeley, 1981), 316–72. Lubin, influenced by Jane Addams's and Frances Kellor's plank on "The Immigrant" at the Progressive party convention in 1912, convinced Johnson that California needed a commission along the lines of New York's State Immigrant Commission. Johnson established a temporary Immigration Commission in 1912 with Lubin as its head. The commission studied California's immigrant problems and won organized labor to its cause within the progressive camp after Johnson appointed Paul Scharrenberg, secretary of the California Federation of Labor, to serve on the commission.

41. Friday Morning Club, *Mary S. Gibson*, 23–25. Rowell was one of several who gave eulogies at the memorial for Gibson.

42. Judith Raftery, *Land of Fair Promise: Politics and Reform in Los Angeles Schools* (Stanford, Calif.: Stanford University Press, 1992), 19–40.

43. This move led her beyond the conventional pedagogical wisdom that children's education would generate assimilation into the middle class and adoption of middle-class culture. Reformers had emphasized this theory when they recommended that kindergartens become part of public schooling.

44. California Commission on Immigration and Housing, *Report* (Sacramento: California Commission, 1915), 99.

45. Gibson to Lubin, January 31, 1914, Simon Lubin Papers, Bancroft Library, University of California, Berkeley. If more were spent on education, she argued, less would be needed for other services. Between 1914 and 1915, over $1.2 million had been spent on immigrants in Los Angeles, but only $40,000, or 2.9 percent, of that went for education.

46. Katherine Philips Edson to Harriet Vittum, September 6, 1916, box 1, Edson Papers, Department of Special Collections, University Research Library, University of California, Los Angeles.

47. Edson to Mrs. Raymond Robbins, November 29, 1916, box 1, Edson Papers.

48. Los Angeles Board of Education, *Minutes of the Board*, 1919, 18:399. Ruby Baughman, appointed supervisor of immigrant education for Los Angeles schools in 1917, and Amanda Mathews Chase, the first home teacher in Los Angeles public schools, wrote and lectured throughout the state. Amanda Mathews Chase, "The 'Official' Home Teacher," *Out West Magazine* 43 (January 1916): 33–37; Olive Percival Diary, July 16, 1915, uncatalogued, Huntington Library. Chase was scheduled to take a "new-style" examination to qualify

as a home teacher. The new examination was made possible by the Home Teacher Act. Chase was a known writer and experienced teacher in 1915. She lobbied the California legislature along with Gibson to establish the Home Teacher Act. By having the Daughters of the American Revolution pay Chase's salary for the first year and a half, Gibson was able to bring her into Los Angeles schools to set up the Home Teacher program as a volunteer. After that, the school district paid Chase's salary. Mary Cunliffe Trautwein, "A History of the Development of Schools for Foreign Born Adults in Los Angeles" (M.A. thesis, University of Southern California, 1928), 64. Baughman had experience teaching immigrant children in the mining towns of Butte and Helena, Montana, before she moved to Los Angeles to teach in the Los Angeles State Normal School in 1911. Ruby Baughman, comp., *Elementary Adult Education*, publication 27 (Los Angeles: Board of Education, November 1919), "Elementary Education for Adults," *Annuals of the American Academy of Political and Social Science* 29 (January 1921): 161–68.

49. Mary Gibson, "Schools for the Whole Family," *Survey Graphic*, June 1926, 303.

50. Mary Gibson to Simon Lubin, July 6, 1915, Lubin Papers; Mary Gibson, "A Suggested Program for Americanization, 1918–1920," pamphlet box 43, Clara Bradley Burdette Collection, Huntington Library. Ruby Baughman had pointed to many of the problems when she wrote that school districts were slow to provide teachers and materials. Also, The Home Teacher Act, which had no state funding and relied on city school districts for support, was little more than a band-aid measure. Baughman thought that some of the problems facing immigrants were more serious than the cures proposed by the Home Teacher Act. Chiefly she thought that Americans regarded immigrants as cheap labor and treated them so. Baughman, "Elementary Education for Adults," 161–68.

51. On the drive to create a Department of Education within the federal government, see Lynn Dumenil, "The Insatiable Maw of Bureaucracy," *Journal of American History* 77 (September 1990): 499–524.

52. Gibson, "Schools for the Whole Family," 303. Hiram Johnson had become a U.S. senator in 1917, and most Progressives had returned to the regular Republican party. Richardson had dismissed Lubin and Paul Scharrenberg in 1923. Herman, "Neighbors on the Golden Mountain," 373, 490.

53. Mary Gibson to Will H. Hays, June 25, 1918, Chester H. Rowell Papers, Box 14, Bancroft Library.

54. Friday Morning Club, *Mary S. Gibson*, 13–14, 35. She raised money for the Desert Conservation League and the Women's Athletic Club, which built its own building.

55. I am indebted to Jacqueline R. Braitman for her work on Edson. Most of the background material in my essay is taken from "A California Stateswoman: The Public Career of Katherine Philips Edson," *California History* 65 (June 1986): 82–95; "A Stateswoman in the Age of Reform," in James J. Rawls, ed., *New Directions in California History: A Book of Readings* (New York: McGraw-Hill, 1988), 240–52; and "Katherine Philips Edson: A Progressive-Feminist in California's Era of Reform" (Ph.D. diss., University of California, Los Angeles, 1988).

56. *Dictionary of American Biography*, 6: 294–96; Dale Kramer, *Chicago Renaissance: Literary Life in the Midwest, 1900–1930* (New York: Appleton-Century, 1966), 208–10.

57. Braitman, "Katherine Philips Edson," 83. The Friday Morning Club's bulletin showed which of the dairies had milk with bacterial counts of 1 millimeter per cubic centimeter.

58. Braitman, "A Stateswoman in the Age of Reform," 242.

59. Braitman, "Katherine Philips Edson," 205–9.

60. Gibson, *A Record*, 181–99. A copy of the platform was sent to each of the fifty-three charter members of the Legislative Council, and atop each platform was a quotation from Matthew Arnold: "If ever the time comes when women shall come together simply and purely for the good and benefit of Mankind, it will be a power such as the world has never dreamed" (186).

61. Ibid. The bills that were passed, together called the "Ten Commandments," also included Joint Guardianship, Health Certificate for Marriage, Psychopathic Parole, Injunction and Abatement, Registration of Nurses, School for Girls, Mothers' Pensions, and Civil Service Reform.

62. Braitman, "A Stateswoman in the Age of Reform," 244.

63. Norris C. Hundley, Jr., "Katherine Philips Edson and the Fight for the California Minimum Wage, 1912–1923," *Pacific Historical Review* 29 (1960): 271–85. Her California work brought her national recognition. She had been elected as a member and only woman on the Council of the National Municipal League (Addams was an honorary member) prior to 1913.

64. Although Gibson had become known as the "fairy godmother" for immigrant education, she never outmaneuvered Simon Lubin for power on the IHC.

65. Hundley, "Katherine Philips Edson and the Fight for the California Minimum Wage," 271–85. The United States Supreme Court in *West Coast Hotel v. Parrish* in 1937 ruled the constitutionality of minimum wage.

66. Edson to Mrs. Lyndsay Van Rensselaer, December 2, 1916, box 1, Edson Papers.

67. Ibid.

68. Braitman, "A Stateswoman in the Age of Reform," 248.

69. Braitman, "Katherine Philips Edson," 330, 341; Edson to Chester Rowell, September 17, 1920, box 13, Rowell Papers, Bancroft Library, University of California, Berkeley.

70. Edson to Rowell, September 17, 1920.

71. Braitman, "A Stateswoman in the Age of Reform," 249; *Stockton Record*, November 4, 1921.

72. *Stockton Record*, February 14, 1918; *Oakland Tribune*, February 3, 1918. For a good analysis of Edson's role in California's anti-Japanese campaign, see Frank Van Nuys, "California Progressives and Alien Land Legislation, 1913–1924" (M.A. thesis, California State University, Chico, 1993).

73. Katherine Philips Edson, "California's Japanese Problem," *The Woman Citizen*, November 5, 1921, 9, 16–17, November 19, 1921, 10–11. Drafts of the two articles are located in box 5, Edson Papers. I thank Frank Van Nuys for

bringing them to my attention. *The Woman Citizen* of November 12, 1921, explains Edson's absence from its pages: she had become an advisor to the Arms Limitation Conference and therefore was unable to supply a second article.

74. Braitman, "A Stateswoman in the Age of Reform," 245, 250.

75. Paula Baker, "The Domestication of Politics: Women and American Political Society, 1780–1920," *American Historical Review* 89 (June 1984): 620–47; Sarah Deutsch, "Learning to Talk More Like a Man: Boston Women's Class-Bridging Organizations, 1870–1940," *American Historical Review* 97 (April 1992): 379–404.

76. That case pitted Florence Kelley against longtime suffragist and leader of the Women's Party, Alice Paul. Edson sided with Kelley in that case, which threatened to and did strike down minimum wage. See Joan G. Zimmerman, "The Jurisprudence of Equality: The Women's Minimum Wage, the First Equal Rights Amendment, and *Adkins v. Children's Hospital, 1905–1923," Journal of American History* 78 (June 1991): 189–225.

77. Edson to Chester Rowell, January 15, 1920, box 13, Rowell Papers.

78. Ibid., February 14, 1928.

City Mothers and Delinquent Daughters

Female Juvenile Justice Reform in Early Twentieth-Century Los Angeles

Mary Odem

The Progressive Era was a time of intense public anxiety about the sexuality of young unmarried women. Business leaders, public officials, reformers, and physicians expressed grave concern about the apparent rise in illicit sexuality among young working-class women in American cities. Social experts conducted innumerable investigations and produced a barrage of reports about the serious social and moral consequences of such behavior. In their view, the female "sex delinquent" was a major social problem that demanded a forceful public response.[1]

The great anxiety about female sexuality was a reaction to the growing social independence of working-class daughters in American society. The massive economic and social changes of the late nineteenth and early twentieth centuries, which affected all aspects of national life, greatly expanded opportunities for young women and girls. New forms of employment and recreation drew working-class daughters out of the domestic sphere into a public urban world, where they experienced unprecedented freedom from family and neighborhood restrictions. As they earned wages working in stores, offices, and factories, and spent their leisure hours in dance halls and movie theaters, female youth attempted to establish a social space for themselves outside of their traditional roles as dutiful daughters and future wives.[2]

As the adolescent girl challenged family relations, she became a symbol of social disorder—a magnet for Americans' anxieties about immigration, disease, urban and industrial development, and the consequent disruptions of family and community life. To civic leaders of the early twentieth century, the sexual activity of female youth posed serious moral, social, and biological threats to the rest of society. Reformers, physicians, and public officials perceived an increase in prostitution among young women in American cities and formed vice commissions throughout the country to investigate and do something about the conditions that supposedly led young women to turn to vice.[3]

Eugenicists considered the female "sex delinquent" a major threat to their goal of purifying the American population's genetic pool. They regarded her behavior as a sign of inherent mental defect and asserted that she endangered society through the propagation of defective and degraded children. The eugenics movement took on increasingly racist tones with the influx of immigrants from southern and eastern Europe who, engenicists feared, would pollute the nation's heredity.[4] The female sex delinquent supposedly presented another danger through the spread of venereal disease. Progressive physicians and public health experts launched a national campaign to combat venereal disease through social hygiene education and the repression of illicit sex. Influenced by prevailing social attitudes rather than medical reality, they identified the "immoral" woman as the primary locus of infection.[5]

Social anxieties were not only figuratively projected but practically worked out in the figure of the adolescent girl. Reformers and public officials constructed an elaborate legal apparatus—including juvenile courts, special police, detention centers, and reformatories—that aimed to control sexual misconduct among working-class female youth.

Women reformers and social workers played a leading role in developing social policies aimed at reducing female sexual delinquency. Convinced that family protection was no longer adequate, they increasingly called on the state to regulate the sexual behavior of young women and girls. In calling for state regulation, women reformers specifically envisioned a maternal state. They insisted that women professionals should manage the control and rehabilitation of young female delinquents, in order to provide them with the necessary maternal protection and supervision. Reformers called for the appointment of women police, juvenile court judges, probation officers, and staff to administer all correctional facilities for female youth. As a result, women's authority within the criminal justice system expanded, and a whole new range of professional opportunities was created for educated, middle-class women.

Los Angeles is an ideal place to explore these developments. The activities of an influential group of women reformers placed the city at the

forefront of the national campaign to eliminate female delinquency. Reformers and social workers proved remarkably adept at shaping policies
and gaining control of the female juvenile justice system. They were
among the first in the country to lobby successfully for the appointment
of women professionals in police departments and juvenile courts and
for the establishment of new correctional facilities for delinquent girls.

This clear professional and political victory for middle-class women
carried more ambiguous consequences for the working-class women
and girls now subject to court control. On the one hand, women reformers and professionals challenged the harsh attitudes and methods of punishment that were common in the preexisting criminal justice system.
On the other, they helped to expand and administer a state machinery
that targeted working-class female youth for violating dominant standards of female respectability. In the interest of "protecting" young
women, the new women professionals furthered state surveillance and
control over their lives and social behavior.

A well-organized women's movement in Los Angeles pushed the issue
of female sex delinquency to the center of the progressive political
agenda. At the heart of this movement was a network of women's clubs:
the Friday Morning Club, the Ebell Club, the Woman's Christian Temperance Union, and, after 1911, the Woman's City Club and the Southern California Civic League. Clubwomen were deeply troubled about
the effect of modern urban conditions on the moral development of
working-class daughters. In their minds the circumstances of working-
class lives seemed to encourage sexual delinquency: impoverished
homes exposed adolescent daughters prematurely to sex; new commer-
cialized recreations—dance halls, amusement parks, movie theaters—
exploited their need for diversion and excitement; early entrance in the
work force at low-paying jobs surrounded them with moral dangers and
temptations that all too often resulted in immorality.

The concern about female delinquency was part of a broad program
of social welfare reform that aimed to protect women, children, and the
home from the harmful effects of rapid urban growth and industrial capitalism. In addition to juvenile delinquency, clubwomen targeted a wide
range of issues, such as child labor, unsanitary housing, prostitution,
and low wages and poor working conditions of women laborers. They
believed that women were particularly suited to confront these social ills
and thus demanded a greater role for women in the political sphere as
electors and policymakers. They helped to organize an impressive suffrage campaign in California in the first decade of the century and even-

tually won the right to vote in 1911.[6] With the support of progressive
governor Hiram Johnson and reform politicians in the state legislature,
newly enfranchised women lobbied effectively in the ensuing years for
a range of measures aimed at protecting women and children: mothers'
pensions, child labor reform, compulsory schooling, minimum wages
and limited hours for women workers, and a Red-Light Abatement Act
to eliminate prostitution.[7]

During this period, women reformers also persuaded local and state
officials to implement innovative measures for preventing and controlling female delinquency. They drew upon a nineteenth-century tradition
of women's penal reform in the United States. In the 1840s, women
prison reformers in New York, Massachusetts, and Indiana—in response to the neglect and poor treatment of female inmates in men's
prisons—called for separate institutions for women under the control of
female staff and administrators. They claimed that female prisoners
faced abuse and degradation when handled by male officials and that
women, because of their maternal qualities, were better suited to reform
female offenders.[8] In a similar vein, progressive women in Los Angeles
criticized the existing male-controlled criminal justice system for dealing too harshly with young female offenders and for neglecting their special needs.

Although they followed in the footsteps of nineteenth-century prison
reformers, progressive women differed from them in several important
respects. They envisioned a much broader role for women within the
criminal justice system. They sought to extend female authority to all
aspects of the system, including prevention programs, police surveillance, and judicial processing, as well as correctional treatment. Furthermore, reformers believed that maternal sympathy, while important,
was no longer enough for the effective control and rehabilitation of female delinquency. They were part of a new generation of college-
educated social workers and professionals who increasingly emphasized
the importance of "scientific" methods of diagnosis and treatment.[9] The
women professionals who filled the new positions in the criminal justice
system would attempt to combine maternal values with those of "scientific" social work in their work with young female offenders.

One of the first goals of women reformers was the hiring of women
police officers by the city. The moving force behind this campaign was
reformer Alice Stebbins Wells. In 1910, with the support of prominent
clubwomen, she petitioned Mayor George Alexander to appoint her
as a police officer to do "preventive-protective" work with young

women and girls. Wells argued that she could better address the problems of wayward young women if she had an official position within a police department, instead of working simply as a volunteer for a charity organization. "A volunteer cannot keep order nearly as well as someone with authority," she explained. Under the mayor's instructions, the police department hired Wells on September 13, 1910. With this appointment Los Angeles became the first city in the country to hire policewomen on a permanent, full-time basis. A second policewoman was hired in 1912, and by 1914 five policewomen were patrolling the streets of Los Angeles.[10]

The appointment of Wells immediately attracted national attention and provoked both enthusiastic and hostile responses. Some journalists portrayed her as a masculine, gruff woman with glasses, wearing her hair in a tight bun and grasping a revolver. Despite such caricatures and the staunch opposition of some police departments, her success in Los Angeles generated demands for women police in many other cities. She was asked to speak on the issue by women's clubs, civic organizations, churches, parent-teacher associations, and universities in all regions of the country. By 1915, at least 25 other cities had hired full-time, paid policewomen; and by 1924, more than 145 cities employed women officers. The policewoman had become a permanent presence in the American urban landscape.[11]

Though women officers theoretically exercised full police powers, their actual duties differed significantly from those of male officers. Their primary function, according to Wells, was "protective work for women, children, and the home."[12] "The woman officer does not and should not do the kind of work our police officers are actually doing," explained Chicago settlement worker Edith Abbott. "She is not a 'policeman' engaged primarily in detecting crime; she is a social worker engaged in the most difficult kinds of public welfare work."[13]

The "protective work" of policewomen entailed surveillance, arrest, and detainment of young women and girls suspected of illicit activity. One of their central tasks was monitoring young women in dance halls, amusement parks, and other trouble spots and apprehending those who seemed in moral danger. Aletha Gilbert, one of the first policewomen hired in Los Angeles, described the work of women officers in the following way: "We shall have three women patrolling the streets from 3:30 to 11:30 and when young girls are found standing on street corners ogling men and boys or hanging about theater entrances, they will be taken home. And we will then try to find out why their parents did not know what they were doing." Policewomen performed another important function through the questioning and investigation of young women held in custody. With the appointment of Wells, male officers were prohibited from questioning female offenders. According to Police Chief Charles Sebastian, "Such work is delegated solely to these women assistants, who by their womanly sympathy and intuition are enabled to gain the confidence of their younger sisters."[14]

Women police officers persuaded Chief Sebastian to introduce another novel approach to the problem of female delinquency with the establishment of the City Mother's Bureau in October 1914. Staffed by Gilbert and two policewomen assistants, the bureau was a confidential office where parents might come for advice and assistance without having to file a formal report against their children to the police. It was located apart from the police station in an old school building in the heart of downtown, "so that parents—especially mothers—will not hesitate to confide their troubles to the 'City Mother.' "[15] Chief Sebastian appointed a committee of clubwomen to assist the bureau by raising funds and educating the public about its work. During its first year of operation, the City Mother's Bureau reported that hundreds of parents had sought assistance with disobedient daughters. In addition to meeting with parents and their children, the City Mother conducted numerous investigations of dance halls, movie theaters, vaudeville shows, and various other amusement resorts.[16]

Reformers also aimed to shape policies and extend female authority over delinquent girls in juvenile court. As in other areas of the country, clubwomen and settlement workers in Los Angeles initiated the movement to establish the county's first juvenile court in the early years of the twentieth century. Members of the College Settlement House, the Friday Morning Club, the Ebell Club, and the Woman's Christian Temperance Union organized public meetings and lobbied politicians until the legislature passed the California Juvenile Court Law in 1903. Clubwomen then called for the creation of a juvenile probation department and paid the salaries of the first probation officers until the county agreed to assume the cost two years later.[17]

Considered one of the most significant of progressive penal reforms, the Juvenile Court Law removed children and youth from the adult criminal justice system and handled them in special courts that emphasized rehabilitation instead of punishment. The aim of juvenile courts, in contrast to that of criminal courts, was not to determine guilt or innocence, but to assess the conditions in a youth's life that led to delinquency. Judges and probation officers focused more on the youth's character, habits, family background, and upbringing than on the particular offense he or she had committed.

When the court was first founded in Los Angeles, both boys' and girls' cases were handled by a male judge, Curtis D. Wilbur, and a male probation officer, A. C. Dodds. The growing concern about female delinquency after 1910 led women reformers to demand the appointment of female probation officers and judges to handle girls' cases. As reformer Aletha Gilbert asserted, "No man can do the work that a woman could do. It is a terrible thing for young girls, weighted beneath shame and sorrow, to have to go into a court room and face a man with the story of her life." "A woman," she explained, "a kind woman, who could act as mother and judge, to whom a girl could tell every secret of her heart and from whom she could receive judgement, advice and understanding, could save 90 per cent of the girls who enter the juvenile courts here."[18] In response to such concerns, the county hired female probation officers, most of whom were college-educated women with social work experience. By 1913, six of the court's fifteen paid probation officers were women; at least as early as 1917, the Probation Department had established a separate division for girls under the direction of a female officer.[19]

Not content with probationary work, reformers continued to broaden their demands for female authority by calling for women judges. Clubwomen affiliated with the City Mother's Bureau spoke before various organizations to build public support and consulted with Curtis D. Wilbur to draft a bill to create the position of a woman judge. Mrs. E. K. Foster, member of the Friday Morning Club and head of the Juvenile Protection Association in Los Angeles, lobbied state legislators in Sacramento on behalf of clubwomen to support the bill.[20]

Women reformers in Southern California formed part of a nation-wide effort to secure women judges for young female offenders. Members of the National Association of Women Lawyers, based in New York City, argued strenuously for the cause in a series of articles and editorials published in the *Women Lawyers' Journal* from 1912 to 1915. The writers argued that male judges either handled girls' cases superficially, to avoid the embarrassment of a thorough examination, or they destroyed girls' "feminine modesty" by interrogating them about intimate matters before an audience of men. The attitude of most men toward a girl's immorality, complained one writer, "is far too light and flippant a one." They failed to understand that a girl's "misstep is more vital to the race than destruction of millions of dollars' worth of property, or even destruction of life. It is an attack upon motherhood, it is the poisoning of the sources of life, it requires more immediate, intimate and expert attention than bodily ailments which require the woman physician. Place a man at the task and you dam the mainspring of a better race at its source."[21]

Under pressure from women reformers and their supporters, California legislators amended the Juvenile Court Law in 1915 to create the position of a female "referee" who was invested with nearly all the powers of a judge.[22] With this measure the Los Angeles Juvenile Court became the first in the country to create a permanent position for women judges to preside over girls' cases. Women court workers had succeeded in convincing juvenile court judge Sidney Reeve that "a woman dealing with women would naturally have a better understanding of any given case and a better conception of the method of reformation or correction than a man." In 1915, Orfa Jean Shontz, a lawyer and former juvenile probation officer, was appointed the first female referee of the Los Angeles court. When Shontz resigned in 1920 to become city clerk of Los Angeles, a young social worker, Miriam Van Waters, assumed the position of referee. Through her writings and professional work in Los Angeles, Van Waters became a leading local and national figure in the movement for juvenile justice reform.[23]

When they heard cases, referees sought to avoid any resemblance to a typical criminal court hearing. They held private, informal hearings with girls in Juvenile Hall away from the Hall of Justice, where criminal trials were heard. Referees wore street clothes instead of a robe and sat at a table with the girl and her parents instead of presiding over them from a judge's bench. According to one account, in Shontz's courtroom, "There are good pictures on the walls, curtains, not bars, at the windows; and a big vase of roses, fresh from the garden is in front of the girl." Most important, male court officials were excluded from these hearings; the clerk and bailiff, as well as the judge, were women: "When a girl is brought into this little courtroom she sees only three faces and they are the faces of three of her own sex, whose hope is to aid and not to punish."[24]

The social policies developed by female reformers may have softened the experience of appearing in court for girls, but at the same time they facilitated a more effective prosecution of female juvenile offenders and sanctioned the use of invasive procedures of sexual control. Although intended to shield youth from the severity of the criminal justice system, juvenile court laws also defined whole new areas of deviant behavior that were subject to state control. The California law, for example, subjected minors to arrest and detention for a wide range of activities, including incorrigibility, disobeying parents, associating with disreputable companions, or simply being in danger of leading "an idle, dissolute or immoral life." Under this law female minors were arrested primarily for sexual or moral offenses, which ranged from going to dance halls unchaperoned, to flirting with sailors, to engaging in sex outside marriage.[25] Juvenile court laws provided a broad and far-reaching legal tool for apprehending young women and girls who violated dominant moral codes.

The young women most likely to face arrest and prosecution for delinquency in Los Angeles came from working-class families. An analysis of all girls charged with delinquency in 1920 (220 cases) reveals that most of their fathers (81 percent) were employed in a range of skilled, semiskilled, and unskilled occupations as carpenters, teamsters, tailors, railroad workers, fruit packers, and agricultural laborers. The rest (19 percent) either owned small businesses or farms or worked in low-level white-collar jobs as clerks or salesmen. The mothers who worked outside of the home were concentrated in low-paid occupations as domestics, laundry workers, and janitors. The racial and ethnic backgrounds of the girls brought to court reflect the county's unique population mix in the early twentieth century. Slightly more than half (54 percent) of the girls were native-born whites, and 5 percent were native-born blacks. Approximately two-fifths (41 percent) were either immigrants or children of immigrants. Half of the immigrant families were of Mexican origin; the rest came from a number of different countries, including England, Canada, Italy, Germany, and Russia.[26]

The working-class daughters arrested for delinquency were subjected to invasive procedures of sexual surveillance and control. They were routinely detained at the county detention center, known as Juvenile Hall, where they faced compulsory pelvic examinations to determine if they were virgins. Those with broken hymens were labeled "sex delinquents" and separated from the "innocent girls." Another routine procedure for young female offenders was compulsory testing and treatment for venereal disease. In response to the social hygiene campaign to combat venereal disease, court officials demonstrated great vigilance in tracking down infected female youth. Female physicians tested every girl admitted to Juvenile Hall for syphilis and gonorrhea; those found to be infected were detained and treated at the detention hospital attached to the institution.[27]

The concern with venereal disease was not unfounded, for more than one-third (34.6 percent) of girls in detention in 1920 tested positive. Court policies, however, were sexually biased and unnecessarily harsh. Physicians tested boys, but did not require their quarantine and confinement. In contrast, girls typically were detained in the hospital for the course of their treatments, which generally lasted from one to three months, and sometimes as long as a year. This policy reflected a widespread cultural assumption that young women should be held responsible for the consequences of illicit relations. More than a medical measure, quarantine was a form of punishment for girls who had violated prevailing moral codes.[28]

Once examined and classified, young women faced close questioning by women judges and probation officers about the details of their sexual lives. Although they objected to this form of questioning by male judges, women court officials felt no hesitancy in probing for the intimate details of girls' sexual relations.[29] As women, they felt they were better equipped to get the "truth" from young female offenders in court. As one observer noted, so far in Judge Shontz's courtroom, only one girl had "hesitated in making a clean breast of the whole matter in which she was involved."[30]

In addition to new policies at the court level, progressive women devised new methods of correctional treatment for delinquent girls. Penal reformers in the early twentieth century rejected the prevalent nineteenth-century belief that delinquents were of a single type and best treated through a single program of institutionalization. They sought alternatives to incarceration with prevention programs and, most important, with the use of probation, which aimed to rehabilitate youth in their own homes under the supervision of a probation officer.[31]

In spite of the growing enthusiasm for juvenile probation, reformers and social workers continued to promote institutional commitment for female sex delinquents. Delinquent girls, they thought, more often required institutionalization than delinquent boys for several reasons. In one of the most influential progressive texts on juvenile delinquency, Chicago settlement workers Edith Abbott and Sophonisba Breckinridge explained that the girl's offense was of a far more serious nature. The delinquent girl, they wrote, "is in a peril which threatens the ruin of her whole life, and the situation demands immediate action." The delinquent boy, on the other hand, "is frequently only a troublesome nuisance who needs discipline but who, as the probation officer so often says, is 'not really a bad boy' and 'with a little watching he is sure to come out all right.' " Furthermore, reformers and social workers believed that a girl's delinquency more often resulted from a degraded or inadequate family life and that her rehabilitation demanded prompt removal from such influences. According to Breckinridge and Abbott, "the only hope is to remove her entirely from influences that threaten destruction and to place her in an institution until the critical years are past."[32]

Juvenile court statistics from Los Angeles indicate that girls, in fact, were more likely to be institutionalized and less likely to receive probation than boys. During 1920, one in three girls faced long-term institutional confinement, compared to only one in five boys. The differential treatment is all the more striking when one considers that most girls were charged with status or noncriminal offenses, usually sex-related activities, while most boys were charged with offenses that fell under the adult criminal code, mostly theft and assault. (Higher institutional commitments for girls in juvenile court have been documented for other cities, including Chicago, Memphis, and Milwaukee.)[33]

The growing number of young women arrested for sex delinquency and the reluctance to place them on probation prompted the establishment of new reformatories for girls in Los Angeles and California during the Progressive Era. Prior to 1910, the only institutions for wayward girls in Los Angeles were small homes run by religious organizations— Protestant institutions, such as the Truelove Home and the Florence Crittenton Home, and the House of Good Shepherd, founded and staffed by a Catholic order of nuns.[34] But in the century's second decade, clubwomen began to call on the state to establish reformatories for the control and rehabilitation of delinquent girls. Led by members of the Friday Morning Club and the Juvenile Protective Association, women reformers made a state reform school for girls one of their central legislative demands after the suffrage victory. In response to their concerns, legislators opened the first state reformatory for girls in Ventura, California, in 1915, and the county of Los Angeles opened the El Retiro School for Girls in 1919.[35]

The growth of state reformatories for girls in Los Angeles and California during the early twentieth century reflected a nationwide trend. In the 1910s, the number of publicly sponsored reformatories for girls increased dramatically throughout the country. In the period between 1850 and 1910, an average of fewer than five new facilities were established per decade. By contrast, twenty-three new reformatories were opened in the decade between 1910 and 1920.[36]

In the name of protecting working-class daughters, women reformers and social workers had helped to develop an elaborate state machinery for the regulation of sexual delinquency. In their new official positions as police, judges, probation officers, and superintendents, professional

women assumed the authority to define and enforce a code of moral behavior among working-class female youth.

The approach to female sexual delinquency by progressive women reformers is best exemplified in the career of Miriam Van Waters. She was
part of the generation of university-educated women who pursued professional careers and engaged in reform activities. Van Waters earned a
Ph.D. in anthropology from Clark University in 1913 and worked for
several years with delinquent youth in Boston and Portland, Oregon.
Once in Los Angeles, she played a pivotal role in implementing progressive policies for female juvenile offenders, as superintendent of Juvenile
Hall from 1917 to 1920, as founder of El Retiro in 1919, and as referee
of the juvenile court from 1920 to 1929. She soon acquired national recognition for work in the Los Angeles juvenile justice system and for her
extensive body of writing, which included numerous articles and two
major books, *Youth in Conflict* (1926) and *Parents on Probation* (1927).
In 1927, Felix Frankfurter invited her to take part in the Harvard Law
School Crime Survey; and two years later, President Hoover asked her
to serve on the National Commission on Law Observance and Enforcement (the Wickersham Commission) as a consultant on juvenile corrections. That same year, Van Waters was elected president of the National
Conference of Social Work, the main national organization of social
work professionals.[37]

Her approach to female delinquency rested on a conception of the juvenile court as parent to young offenders. As she wrote in one article,
"In theory this court is parental, a court of guardianship—not a criminal or quasi-criminal court, but a court where the paramount issue is
the welfare of the child."[38] Female juvenile offenders, she argued,
should not be treated as criminals, but as troubled youth in need of maternal guidance and supervision. This model of female juvenile justice
led Van Waters to fight for humane treatment of young female offenders
within existing institutions, but also to sanction extensive state surveillance and control over their lives.

Throughout her years of service in the juvenile justice system, Van
Waters stood firmly against harsh methods of correctional treatment of
young female offenders. In what she described as a "war on force," she
rejected the use of guards, confining walls, uniforms, and corporal punishment in the juvenile institutions she managed. In place of the punitive
approach, she advocated a program of rehabilitation.[39]

In her design of El Retiro, Van Waters incorporated the latest in progressive correctional methods, making the institution a model of its kind

in the country. One of the main functions of the reformatory, in her view, was to create a home environment and to provide girls with the maternal care and supervision they supposedly lacked in their own homes. With this function in mind, she organized El Retiro on the cottage system (as opposed to the congregate system), whereby inmates were divided into individual surrogate "families," each headed by a matron. Influenced by Chicago reformer Martha Falconer, Van Waters introduced a system of self-government. Inmates elected officers; held regular student body meetings, where they aired complaints and planned activities; and exercised a limited role in the institutions's affairs. Van Waters staffed the institution with young college women who administered a program of academic training, cultural development, and recreation.[40] Ethel Sturges Dummer, a major financial supporter of social reform in Chicago, was so impressed with the institution when she visited in 1920 that she commissioned Van Waters to conduct a national survey of girls' reformatories in order to disseminate El Retiro's methods throughout the country.[41]

Van Waters urged those who worked with delinquent girls to dispense with moral condemnation and to focus instead on their particular needs and problems: "By all means, let us let go of the concept of the moral judgment and seek as patiently as social physicians must, the causes that underlie behavior."[42] She challenged a still common view within the criminal justice system that female sex delinquents were permanently "ruined" and a source of moral contamination for the rest of society. She believed that young female offenders were capable of reform through the wise counsel and guidance of trained woman social workers.

The energetic young social worker promoted her ideas and policies about juvenile justice throughout the Los Angeles community. She spoke regularly before women's clubs, churches, and parent-teacher organizations on subjects such as "Preventive Work and the Juvenile Detention Home," "The Woman Judge," and "The New Opportunity of the Juvenile Court." In 1918 alone, she delivered over forty lectures and talks to, among others, the Catholic Bureau of Charities, the Colored Federation of Women's Clubs, the Friday Morning Club, the State Normal School, the Hollywood Christian Church, the Pasadena Methodist Church, and the Boyle Heights Parent-Teacher Association.[43]

As she developed contacts with community organizations, Van Waters also established close ties with other young professional women working within the juvenile justice system. In particular, she formed a close personal and professional relationship with Orfa Jean Shontz. Van Waters and Shontz quickly became allies in the movement to promote progressive juvenile justice. Together they challenged punitive measures taken by police and other officials working with juvenile offenders. They recruited college-educated women with social work training to staff positions in the court, Juvenile Hall, and El Retiro and provided a source of support and companionship for them at the home they shared with two other colleagues.[44] The "Colony," as they called their home, became a gathering place for women professionals to thrash out their ideas and strategies for reform.

With this network of support, Van Waters worked to defend and expand progressive policies within the juvenile justice system in Los Angeles. In the more conservative political climate of the 1920s, however, she encountered greater opposition to the reform agenda from public officials and law enforcement authorities.[45] A continual source of trouble was the district attorney's office. In 1921, District Attorney Thomas Woolwine backed a bill before the state legislature that would have made juvenile offenders subject to criminal court proceedings. With the help of their supporters, Van Waters and Shontz managed to defeat this bill, but they continued to face Woolwine's opposition the following year, when he supported a conservative judge to head the juvenile court, a man whom Van Waters described as "utterly inexperienced and committed to the policy of ignoring the legislation providing for the juvenile court." The progressive group once again blocked the district attorney's plan by getting their candidate appointed to the juvenile department, but, as Van Waters noted, "we are safe" only for another year when election time returns.[46]

Reformers faced another struggle in 1921, this time with county supervisors, over the hiring of a new superintendent of Juvenile Hall. As a political favor to an influential supporter, county supervisors agreed to appoint a certain man to the position who had little training in juvenile corrections. When she learned of their intention, Van Waters worked quickly and effectively to block the plan. In a letter to her father she denounced the supervisors' action and vowed to fight it: "How any sane person could think a man could run an institution for children, one half of whom are girls, and one fourth of whom are suffering and in need of hospital care for venereal infection is more than I can see. . . . Of course I have not the slightest idea of letting them do this, but unless I were here a man would surely go in."[47] She called on prominent local and national women reformers (including Martha Falconer and Dr. Valerie Parker) to write letters to the Board of Supervisors, detailing the problems with male superintendents. In response to the pressure, the board agreed to appoint Margaret Bullen, a young woman whom Van Waters had personally trained and selected for the position.[48]

Van Waters encountered particular hostility to the progressive program of rehabilitation in place at the El Retiro School for Girls. Although she had no official position at the institution, Van Waters continued to shape its administration and hiring decisions throughout the 1920s. She introduced a controversial policy in 1920, when she permitted El Retiro girls to enroll in the local high school in San Fernando. Her reasoning was that reform school girls should be integrated into the community as much as possible in order to remove the sense of shame and isolation they might feel. This action met with stiff opposition from a group of businessmen led by the Chamber of Commerce. They argued before the Board of Education that inmates from El Retiro posed a serious moral threat to the other students and should not be permitted in the school. Van Waters countered businessmen's resistance by meeting with mothers of high school students and speaking with parent-teacher organizations and members of the Board of Education. Persuaded by her arguments and the community support she gained, the board voted a week later to permit El Retiro girls to attend the school.[49]

Some county officials objected to the lenient disciplinary methods and what they considered the "free and easy manners" of the El Retiro girls. At one point the chief of the county probation department threatened to build a fence around El Retiro to tighten security and discipline there.[50] In 1923, when Van Waters fired a staff member for hitting one of the inmates, county supervisors warned her against further interference with the management of the school. Van Waters, however, continued to oversee policies and staff appointments at El Retiro. As she explained to a friend: "But I have made this statement to officials that I simply assume the right to see that the girls are properly treated and that the school maintains its tradition. If they deny that right they must prove that I do not possess it. They must challenge it! The only thing they have done (or can do without a lot of unpleasant publicity which they always fear) is to refuse to pay for the gasoline I burn in making trips!"[51]

As Van Waters battled the opponents of progressive juvenile justice outside of the court system, she exercised far-reaching authority over young female offenders inside the system. While she protested harsh forms of correctional treatment, she never questioned that young women and girls should be apprehended and disciplined for sexual misconduct in the first place. Van Waters assumed that working-class daughters in court needed supervision and rehabilitation and that middle-class women professionals were the ones to provide it.

In her various positions as Juvenile Hall superintendent, founder of El Retiro, and juvenile court referee, she assisted state efforts to monitor and correct sexual delinquency in working-class female youth. An enthusiastic advocate of "scientific" social work, Van Waters made pelvic examinations and venereal disease testing routine procedures for all female inmates when she was superintendent of Juvenile Hall. She defended such measures on the grounds that they were necessary to determine the causes of delinquency and proper methods of treatment. But in practice, these procedures clearly served to segregate and ostracize female sex offenders.[52]

As juvenile court referee, Van Waters exercised firm, often rigorous, authority over the young women and girls who appeared in court. In court hearings, she typically questioned them closely about their sexual lives and did not hesitate to discipline those who failed to give satisfactory answers. In the following exchange, Van Waters pressed a seventeen-year-old girl to reveal the details of her sexual activities:

REFEREE: Now, [Eliza], when you were at the beach how many men or boys did you have intercourse with? . . .

ELIZA: I have not had anything to do with anyone but [Franklin] . . .

REFEREE: How long had you known him when this happened?

ELIZA: 24 hours.

REFEREE: You want us to believe that is the only one you had intercourse with while you were away?

ELIZA: Yes it is so.

REFEREE: [Eliza], you can easily see we don't place reliance on what you have said. You cry now because your father comes in. . . . You tell us the truth now or we will send you back where you came from. You have got to come across now with a clean sheet.[53]

She expected female offenders to reveal all such details because she believed that the court's central aim was to help and protect them. In juvenile court, she argued, youth did not need the legal safeguards used in criminal court to shield defendants from improper questioning and procedures. The juvenile court "can demand the whole truth because it has the power to save, to protect, and to remedy. Its orders or judgements are not penal, but parental."[54] Young women and girls who refused to cooperate with the "parental" authority of the court faced longer periods of detention.

In the position of referee, Van Waters used a range of disciplinary measures to "rehabilitate" female sex delinquents: closely supervised probation in the home of parents or relatives; placement in a private home, usually to work as a domestic; and incarceration in a variety of public and private facilities. As already noted, girls were less likely to receive probation and more likely to be removed from home than boys. Nearly half (47 percent) of the girls who appeared before the court in 1920 were removed from their homes and placed in private homes or institutions, compared to only one-fourth (25 percent) of the boys.[55]

The rigorous methods of control practiced by Van Waters in Juvenile Hall and the court may at first seem inconsistent with her campaign for protection and humane treatment of female offenders. But I would argue that she saw no conflict between these aspects of her work. In a revealing passage, Van Waters told one teenage girl who was in court for sexual misconduct: "We can control you without beating you and if you don't behave we will have to keep you locked up some place. The Court does not exist to punish a girl but to protect her and a girl that has the ideas you have certainly needs protection."[56] Maternal protection ruled out corporal punishment, but often demanded exacting methods of control, including interrogation, detention, and incarceration.

With the support of local women's and civic groups, Van Waters had managed to maintain progressive policies of juvenile corrections throughout most of the 1920s, but the system came under increasing political attack by the end of the decade. Beginning with the reorganization of El Retiro, county officials effectively curtailed her authority within the juvenile justice system. In August 1927, while Van Waters was in Boston working on the Harvard Crime Survey, the Probation Committee, under the direction of the Board of Supervisors, fired the progressive administration of the school. The committee charged the superintendent, Alma Holzschuh, with insubordination and inefficient management, and raised the old complaint of lax discipline in the school. Committee chairman Charles D. Lusby stated that "there was too much freedom without thought of necessary discipline to make for the success of the undertaking." He replaced Holzschuh with Rosemary Good, who dismantled the system of self-government, locked the doors to the girls' rooms, and posted male guards on the grounds.[57]

The committee's action aroused opposition from several corners. The El Retiro inmates staged a walk-out to protest the firing of Holzschuh and the new repressive measures. Two days after Good arrived, all but five of the fifty-four girls at El Retiro left the school en masse and walked almost eighteen miles before they were picked up by county officials. The girls refused to return to the institution unless Holzschuh were reinstated and the principles of the school resumed.[58]

Van Waters and Shontz challenged the committee's charges against Holzschuh and called for her reinstatement. They found support among numerous civic organizations in the county. The Los Angeles League of Women Voters and the California Congress of Parent and Teacher Associations, among others, issued statements endorsing the school's constructive work with delinquent girls and called for a public hearing on the matter.[59] In response to public pressure, the county ordered a grand jury investigation of conditions at El Retiro, and the resulting report urged immediate policy changes or the closing of the school. Rosemary Good was fired and the guards removed from the school grounds. The Probation Committee, however, successfully limited the influence of Van Waters by assuming tighter control of staffing and policy decisions. The committee did not reinstate Holzschuh as Van Waters desired, but selected a social worker from outside of progressive circles to replace Good.

As a result, many of the innovative policies Van Waters had introduced at El Retiro were eliminated. The girls were removed from the local high school and restricted to classes held within the institution; the system of self-government was curtailed, and stricter security measures were enforced. In 1928, Van Waters described El Retiro as one of the repressive types of juvenile institutions: "At El Retiro they are building 'cottages' with tiny rooms, like cells, windows six feet from the floor, tiny slits with bars (I have protested the bars, but they will not alter the size and location of the single windows)."[60]

The erosion of progressive influence was also evident in the construction of the new juvenile detention facility in 1929. Unlike the original Juvenile Hall, the new building was built with bars on the windows and an eighteen-foot cement wall surrounding the institution. Van Waters lamented to her parents that "No prison in the country has a worse wall." By the end of the decade she had become increasingly despondent about the possibility of progressive reform in Los Angeles. Furthermore, she felt that the work she and Orfa Shontz and other women reformers had accomplished was not recognized or appreciated by public leaders and officials: "for 25 years social work in California has gone on slowly building—Orfa has labored 20 years and I 12 and there was no credit given."[61] Finally, in October 1929, Van Waters decided to resign as referee of the juvenile court. That year she moved to Boston to complete her work on the Harvard Crime Survey and soon after accepted a position as superintendent of the Massachusetts Reformatory for Women in Framingham.[62]

Women social workers and reformers in Los Angeles had developed an elaborate institutional network for the regulation of female sexual delinquency, but in the end they were unable to maintain their control over the institutions they had created. They could not ensure that the principles of rehabilitation and maternal protection would continue to operate.

By the end of the 1920s, the progressive spirit in the Los Angeles juvenile justice system had declined in the face of a more conservative political climate and the departure of Van Waters from the city. What remained, however, were the institutions of sexual control—female police and probation officers, the juvenile court, detention center, and reformatories—that would continue to monitor and regulate working-class female sexuality throughout most of the twentieth century.

NOTES

1. Steven L. Scholssman and Stephanie Wallach, "The Crime of Precocious Sexuality: Female Juvenile Delinquency in the Progressive Era," *Harvard Educational Review* 48 (February 1978): 65–95; Mary E. Odem, "Delinquent Daughters: The Sexual Regulation of Female Minors in the United States, 1880–1920" (Ph.D. diss., University of California, Berkeley, 1989); Ruth Alexander, "The 'Girl Problem': Class Inequity and Psychology in the Remaking of Female Adolescence, 1900–1930" (Ph.D. diss., Cornell University, 1990); Regina Kunzel, "Professionalization of Benevolence: Evangelicals, Social Workers, and Unmarried Mothers, 1890–1945" (Ph.D. diss. Yale University, 1990).

2. On the changing social behavior of young working-class women, see Kathy Peiss, *Cheap Amusements: Working Women and Leisure in Turn-of-the-Century New York* (Philadelphia: Temple University Press, 1986); Elizabeth Lunbeck, " 'A New Generation of Women': Progressive Psychiatrists and the Hypersexual Female," *Feminist Studies* 13 (Fall 1987): 513–43; Joanne Meyerowitz, *Women Adrift: Independent Wage Earners in Chicago, 1880–1930* (Chicago: University of Chicago Press, 1988).

3. On the anti-prostitution crusade during the Progressive Era, see Barbara Hobson, *Uneasy Virtue: The Politics of Prostitution and the American Reform Tradition* (New York: Basic Books, 1987), chaps. 6–8; Ruth Rosen, *The Lost Sisterhood: Prostitution in America, 1900–1918* (Baltimore: Johns Hopkins University Press, 1982).

4. On the eugenics movement in the early twentieth century, see Mark H. Haller, *Eugenics: Hereditarian Attitudes in American Thought* (New Brunswick, N.J.: Rutgers University Press, 1963); Donald Pickens, *Eugenics and the*

Progressive Era (Nashville: Vanderbilt University Press, 1968); Daniel J. Kevles, *In the Name of Eugenics: Genetics and the Uses of Human Heredity* (Berkeley: University of California Press, 1985). On the association of mental defect with sexual delinquency, see Ruth Rosen, *The Lost Sisterhood*, 21–23; Lunbeck, " 'A New Generation of Women.' "

5. Allan M. Brandt, *No Magic Bullet: A Social History of Venereal Disease in the United States since 1880* (New York: Oxford University Press, 1985), chap. 1; David J. Pivar, "Women, Sexuality, and the Social Hygiene Movement, 1910–1931," paper delivered at the annual meeting of the Organization of American Historians, April 5, 1984.

6. On progressive women reformers in California, see Sherry Jeanne Katz, "Dual Commitments: Feminism, Socialism, and Women's Political Activism in California, 1890–1920" (Ph.D. diss., University of California, Los Angeles, 1991), chaps. 4, 6, 7; Jacqueline R. Braitman, "Katherine Philips Edson: A Progressive-Feminist in California's Era of Reform" (Ph.D. diss., University of California, Los Angeles, 1988); Mary S. Gibson, comp., *A Record of Twenty-five Years of the California Federation of Women's Clubs, 1900–1925* (Los Angeles: California Federation of Women's Clubs, 1927); Mary Alderman Garbutt, *Victories of Four Decades; A History of the Women's Christian Temperance Union of Southern California, 1883–1924* (Los Angeles: Woman's Christian Temperance Union of Southern California, 1924); Thelma Lee Hubbell and Gloria R. Lothrop, "The Friday Morning Club: A Los Angeles Legacy," *Southern California Quarterly* 50 (March 1968): 59–90.

7. Katz, "Dual Commitments," 493–95; Walton Bean and James J. Rawls, *California: An Interpretive History*, 5th ed. (New York: McGraw-Hill, 1988), 245–59; George E. Mowry, *The California Progressives* (Berkeley: University of California Press, 1951; repr., Chicago: Quadrangle Books, 1963), 46–47; Spencer C. Olin, Jr., *California's Prodigal Sons: Hiram Johnson and the Progressives, 1911–1917* (Berkeley: University of California Press, 1968), chaps. 4–5; Tom Sitton, *John Randolph Haynes: California Progressive* (Stanford, Calif.: Stanford University Press, 1992).

8. Estelle Freedman, *Their Sisters' Keepers: Women's Prison Reform in America, 1830–1930* (Ann Arbor: University of Michigan Press, 1981); Nicole Hahn Rafter, *Partial Justice: Women in State Prisons, 1800–1935* (Boston: Northeastern University Press, 1985).

9. On the development of "scientific" social work among women reformers, see Ellen Fitzpatrick, *Endless Crusade: Women Social Scientists and Progressive Reform* (New York: Oxford University Press, 1990); Freedman, *Their Sisters' Keepers*, chaps. 6–7; Regina Kunzel, "The Professionalization of Benevolence: Evangelicals and Social Workers in the Florence Crittenton Homes, 1915–1945," *Journal of Social History* 22 (Fall 1988): 21–43; Robyn Muncy, *Creating a Female Dominion in American Reform, 1890–1935* (New York: Oxford University Press, 1991); Rafter, *Partial Justice*, chap. 3.

10. Los Angeles Police Department, *Annual Report*, 1912, 40–41, and *Annual Report*, 1914, 26–27; Maud Darwin, "Policewomen: Their Work in America," *Nineteenth Century* 75 (June 1914): 1371–77; Clarice Feinman,

Women in the Criminal Justice System (New York: Praeger, 1980), chap. 4; Mary E. Hamilton, *The Policewoman: Her Service and Ideals* (New York: Frederick H. Stokes, 1924); Chloe Owings, *Women Police: A Study of the Development and Status of the Women Police Movement* (New York: Frederick H. Hitchcock, 1925), 101–2; Margaret Saunders, "A Study of the Work of the City Mother's Bureau of the Los Angeles Police Department" (M.A. thesis, University of Southern California, 1939); Mrs. Mina C. Van Winkle, "The Policewoman a Socializing Agency," *American City* 34 (February 1926): 198–99. Quote from Wells in Darwin, "Policewomen," 1372.

11. Owings, *Women Police,* 104–6; Feinman, *Women in the Criminal Justice System,* 82–84.

12. Quoted in Feinman, *Women in the Criminal Justice System,* 82. On the protective function of policewomen, see also Hamilton, *The Policewoman,* 9; Van Winkle, "The Policewoman a Socializing Agency"; Darwin, "Policewomen."

13. Edith Abbott, "Training for the Policewoman's Job," *Woman Citizen* 10 (April 1926): 30.

14. Estelle Lawton Lindsey, "Policewomen Take Up Cudgel to Protect Girls from Loose Men," *Los Angeles Record,* May 5, 1913; Los Angeles Police Department, *Annual Report,* 1913, 21.

15. Mrs. Aletha Gilbert, "The Duties of a 'City Mother,' " *American City* 226 (March 1922): 239–40; Los Angeles Police Department, *Annual Report,* 1913, 29; Saunders, "The City Mother's Bureau," 45–47.

16. "Advice Bureau to Aid 'City Mother,' " *Los Angeles Examiner,* September 29, 1914, Friday Morning Club Scrapbook no. 3, Friday Morning Club Collection, Huntington Library; Los Angeles Police Department, *Annual Report,* 1917, 23, and *Annual Report,* 1920, 31.

17. Thomas Stuart McKibbon, "The Origin and Development of the Los Angeles County Juvenile Court," (Master's thesis, University of Southern California, 1932), 17–24; Gibson, *A Record,* 213–14; *Report of the College Settlement, Los Angeles, California* (Los Angeles: College Settlement Association, 1905?), 8.

18. "Urge Trial by Woman Judge of All Girl Cases," *Los Angeles Herald,* October 2, 1914, Friday Morning Club Scrapbook no. 3, Friday Morning Club Collection.

19. *Report and Manual for Probation Officers of the Superior Court Acting as Juvenile Court* (Los Angeles: Board of Supervisors of Los Angeles County, 1912), 86; Los Angeles County Probation Department, *Annual Report,* December 31, 1917, 4, and *Annual Report,* December 31, 1920, 1; Francis H. Hiller, *The Juvenile Court of Los Angeles County, California* (Los Angeles: Los Angeles Lithograph Company, 1928), 25–26.

Women probation officers for the Los Angeles Juvenile Court were a well-educated, experienced group. According to a survey conducted in 1927, two-thirds of the twenty-nine women probation officers previously held jobs in social work; all but three were high school graduates, and two-thirds had graduate training (Hiller, *Juvenile Court of Los Angeles County,* 25–26).

20. "Urge Trial by Woman Judge of All Girl Cases"; "Women Discuss Proposed Bills," *Los Angeles Examiner,* December 3, 1914, Friday Morning Club Scrapbook no. 3, Friday Morning Club Collection.

21. "The Juvenile Court and the Girl," *Women Lawyers' Journal* 2 (August 1912): 42; "Our Juvenile Court Problem, the Delinquent Girl—Need for a Woman Judge," *Women Lawyers' Journal* 2 (February 1913): 58; "Give Us Women as Judges for Girls," *Women Lawyers' Journal* 2 (November 1912): 51; "This Court's All Women," *Los Angeles Times,* November 4, 1915.

22. In 1913, the Chicago Juvenile Court appointed Mary Bartelme, a lawyer and settlement worker, to hear girls' cases in the position of assistant to the judge. But it was not until 1923, when she was elected circuit court judge for Cook County, that Bartelme acquired judicial authority over girls' cases. On Bartelme, see "The Ideal Woman Judge for Children," *Women Lawyers' Journal* 2 (May 1913): 67; Estelle B. Freedman, "Mary Margaret Bartelme," in Barbara Sicherman et al., eds., *Notable American Women: The Modern Period* (Cambridge, Mass.: Belknap Press of Harvard University Press, 1980), 60–61.

23. The quote from Reeve is found in Los Angeles County Probation Department, *Annual Report,* 1917, 2. "Orfa Jean Shontz, Referee Juvenile Court, Los Angeles," *Women Lawyers' Journal* 6 (January 1917): 30; "This Court's All Women"; "Dr. Van Waters Made Referee," *Los Angeles Times,* April 4, 1920; Robert M. Mennel, "Miriam Van Waters," in Sicherman, *Notable American Women,* 709–11.

24. Hiller, "The Juvenile Court," 19–20; "Orfa Jean Shontz," 30.

25. Los Angeles County, *Laws of California and Ordinances of the County and Cities of Los Angeles County Relating to Minors* (Los Angeles: Standard Printing Company, 1914), 7–8. In Los Angeles County most girls were arrested for sex immorality under two of sixteen possible behavior offenses defined by the California Juvenile Court Law: "Who is incorrigible; that is, who is beyond the control and power of his parents, guardian or custodian, by reason of the vicious conduct or nature of said person"; and "Who from any cause is in danger of growing up to lead an idle, dissolute or immoral life."

26. For more information on the social backgrounds of young women and girls in the Los Angeles Juvenile Court, see Odem, "Delinquent Daughters," chap. 4.

27. Los Angeles County Probation Committee, "Rules Governing Juvenile Hall and Juvenile Hall Hospital," June 1915, box 16, John Randolph Haynes Papers, Special Collections, Research Library, University of California, Los Angeles; *Report of the Los Angeles County Probation Committee on Juvenile Hall and El Retiro* (Los Angeles County Probation Committee, 1929), 17–19; Dr. Muriel Dranga Cass to Dr. Miriam Van Waters, Superintendent of Juvenile Hall, March 17, 1920, box 141, Haynes Papers.

28. Ibid.

29. My analysis is based on a close reading of case files of all delinquent girls.

30. "Orfa Jean Shontz," 30.

31. On the history of the juvenile court and juvenile justice in the Progressive Era, see David J. Rothman, *Conscience and Convenience: The Asylum and Its*

Alternative in Progressive America (Boston: Little, Brown, 1980), chaps. 6–7; Steven L. Schlossman, *Love and the American Delinquent: The Theory and Practice of "Progressive" Juvenile Justice* (Chicago: University of Chicago Press, 1977); Robert Mennel, *Thorns and Thistles: Juvenile Delinquency in the United States, 1825–1940* (Hanover, N.H.: University Press of New England, 1973); Anthony Platt, *The Child Savers: The Invention of Delinquency* (Chicago: University of Chicago Press, 1969); Ellen Ryerson, *The Best-Laid Plans: America's Juvenile Court Experiment* (New York: Hill and Wang, 1978); Eric C. Schneider, *In the Web of Class: Delinquents and Reformers in Boston, 1810s–1930s* (New York: New York University Press, 1992).

32. Sophonisba P. Breckinridge and Edith Abbott, *The Delinquent Child and the Home: A Study of the Delinquent Wards of the Juvenile Court of Chicago* (1912; repr., New York: Arno Press, 1970), 41, 59.

33. Ibid., 40–41; Randall G. Shelden, "Sex Discrimination in the Juvenile Justice System, Memphis, TN, 1900–1917," in Marguerite Warren, ed., *Comparing Female and Male Offenders* (Beverly Hills, Calif.: Sage, 1981), 55–72; Schlossman and Wallach, "The Crime of Precocious Sexuality," 65–95.

34. Los Angeles County Probation Department, *Annual Report*, 1920, 10; Otto Wilson, *Fifty Years' Work with Girls, 1883–1933: A Story of the Florence Crittenton Homes* (Alexandria, Va.: National Florence Crittenton Mission, 1933), 335–40; Mary Josephine Poggi, "A Study of the Social Activities of the Catholic Church in Los Angeles," (M.A. thesis, University of Southern California, 1916), 41–46.

35. "Improvements at Whittier," *Los Angeles Examiner*, April 7, 1912, and "Legislative Committee of Club Reports," *Los Angeles Tribune*, February 26, 1913, both in Friday Morning Club Scrapbook no. 1, Friday Morning Club Collection; Miriam Van Waters, "Where Girls Go Right: Some Dynamic Aspects of State Correctional Schools for Girls and Young Women," *The Survey* 48 (May 27, 1922): 361–76.

36. Schlossman and Wallach, "The Crime of Precocious Sexuality," 70; Margaret Reeves, *Training Schools for Girls* (New York: Russell Sage Foundation, 1929).

37. Burton J. Rowles, *The Lady at Box 99: The Story of Miriam Van Waters* (Greenwich, Conn.: Seabury Press, 1962); Mennel, "Miriam Van Waters"; Estelle B. Freedman, " 'In the Matter of the Removal of Miriam Van Waters': Female Deviance in Post World War I America," paper presented at the Berkshire Conference on the History of Women, June 1, 1984.

38. Miriam Van Waters, "The Socialization of Juvenile Court Procedure," n.d., 65, copy of article located in box 37, file 465, Miriam Van Waters Papers, Schlesinger Library, Radcliffe College. Van Waters discussed her philosophy of the court and juvenile corrections in numerous other publications, including *Youth in Conflict* (New York: Republic Publishing Company, 1926); "Juvenile Court Procedure as a Factor in Diagnosis," *Publications of the American Sociological Society* 16 (1921): 209–17, located in box 16, file 238, Ethel Sturges Dummer Papers, Schlesinger Library, Radcliffe College; "The Juvenile Court as a Social Laboratory," *Journal of Applied Sociology*, located in box 37, file 465, Van Waters Papers.

39. Van Waters to Ethel Sturges Dummer, October 1922, box 38, file 819, Dummer Papers; Van Waters, "Where Girls Go Right," 374.

40. Van Waters, "Where Girls Go Right," 361–76; *Report of the Los Angeles County Probation Committee on Juvenile Hall and El Retiro*, 21–27; "Industrial Home Ordered," *Los Angeles Times*, April 1, 1919; Van Waters to Ethel Sturges Dummer, July 17, 1921, box 38, file 819, Dummer Papers.

41. Dummer to Van Waters, July 30, 1920, box 37, file 818, Dummer Papers. Van Waters' findings from this survey were published in the article "Where Girls Go Right." Dummer continued to offer Van Waters both emotional and financial support over the next ten years. She corresponded regularly, encouraging Van Waters in her work, and visited El Retiro and the Colony on several occasions. Dummer sent money to help El Retiro through times of financial crisis. She also provided financial support for Van Waters' career by hiring a stenographer to assist her with the *Survey* article and paying her salary when she took time off to write *Youth in Conflict*. Van Waters to Dummer, November 19, 1921, box 38, file 819, Dummer Papers; Van Waters to Dummer, 1924, box 6, file 52, Van Waters Papers.

42. Van Waters, "The Juvenile Court as a Social Laboratory," 12.

43. Rowles, Lady at Box 99, 124–25; Miriam Van Waters to her parents, February 14, 1918, box 5, file 46, Van Waters Papers; Van Waters, "Speeches in Connection with Juvenile Hall Work," 1919, box 33, file 427, Van Waters Papers.

44. Van Waters to Ethel Sturges Dummer, November 19, 1921, box 38, file 819, Dummer Papers; Rowles, Lady at Box 99, 106–17; "College Girl Works Wonders," *Los Angeles Times*, February 3, 1918, 14.

45. On the conservative trend in local and state politics, see Tom Sitton, "The 'Boss' without a Machine: Kent K. Parrot and Los Angeles Politics in the 1920s," *Southern California Quarterly* 67 (Winter 1985): 365–87; Bean and Rawls, *California: An Interpretive History*, chap. 24; Mowry, *California Progressives*, chap. 11.

46. Van Waters to her parents, 1920 (month unknown), box 5, file 48, Van Waters Papers; Van Waters to her parents, April 3, 1921, box 5, file 49, Van Waters Papers; Van Waters to Ethel Sturges Dummer, December 29, 1922, box 38, file 820, Dummer Papers.

47. Van Waters to her father, November 28, 1921, box 5, file 49, Van Waters Papers.

48. Van Waters to Ethel Sturges Dummer, December 4, 11, and 12, 1921, box 38, file 819, Dummer Papers.

49. Van Waters to Ethel Sturges Dummer, September 14 and October 17, 1920, box 37, file 818, Dummer Papers; "El Retiro Girls Stay," *Los Angeles Times*, September 17, 1920; Van Waters to Ethel Sturges Dummer, May 9, 1921, box 38, file 819, Dummer Papers.

50. Van Waters to Ethel Sturges Dummer, January 8, 1922, and March 6, 1921, box 38, file 819, Dummer Papers.

51. Van Waters to Ethel Sturges Dummer, October 28, 1923, box 38, file 820, Dummer Papers.

52. "College Girl Works Wonders," *Los Angeles Times*, February 3, 1918; Van Waters promotes "scientific" methods of examination in "Juvenile Court Procedure as a Factor in Diagnosis," 211–13, and "The Juvenile Court as a Social Laboratory," 12.

53. Case 16936, 1920. (I have changed the original names appearing in case files.)

54. Van Waters, "The Socialization of Juvenile Court Procedure," 67.

55. For a more elaborate discussion of sentencing patterns in the Los Angeles Juvenile Court, see Odem, "Delinquent Daughters," chap. 4.

56. Case 17153, 1920.

57. Van Waters to Ethel Sturges Dummer, August 21, 1927, box 38, file 820, Dummer Papers; "Girl School under Inquiry" *Los Angeles Times*, August 14, 1927; "Girls' School Closing Hinted," *Los Angeles Times*, August 17, 1927; Lusby quoted in "El Retiro Row Brings Retort," *Los Angeles Times*, August 18, 1927.

58. "Girl School under Inquiry"; "Girls' School Closing Hinted"; "Protest in El Retiro Case Filed," *Los Angeles Times*, August 21, 1927; Miriam Van Waters, "Begun in Idealism—Ended in Politics," n.d., box 14, file 163, Van Waters Papers.

59. Lavinia Graham Timmons, President, Los Angeles League of Women Voters, to Hon. R. F. McClellan, President of the Los Angeles County Board of Supervisors, August 15, 1927, box 5, file 7, League of Women Voters of Los Angeles Papers, Urban Archives Center, California State University, Northridge; Van Waters, "Begun in Idealism," 3; "Ask Girl School Hearing," *Los Angeles Times*, August 19, 1927; "File El Retiro Row Retort," *Los Angeles Times*, August 20, 1927.

60. Van Waters to Ethel Sturges Dummer, June 11, 1928, box 38, file 822, Dummer Papers; *Report of the Los Angeles County Probation Committee on Juvenile Hall and El Retiro*.

61. Van Waters to her parents, February 17, 1929, box 6, file 57, Van Waters Papers.

62. Van Waters to Ethel Sturges Dummer, January 23, 1929, and December 27, 1930, box 38, file 822; Dummer Papers; Rowles, *Lady at Box 99*, 202–3; Mennel, "Miriam Van Waters," 710.

PART THREE

Ethnic Dimensions, Ethnic Realities

African-Americans and the Politics of Race in Progressive-Era Los Angeles

Douglas Flamming

Sometime in 1908, progressive leaders in Los Angeles held a meeting to muster financial support for their emergent good government crusade. Attending the meeting was one L. G. Robinson, a recent arrival to the city, who had been attracted to the "Goo-Goos" almost immediately. He had "a profound faith in good government and wanted to make it a reality." When the call for funds came, Robinson stepped to the front and thumped one hundred dollars on the table—the first contribution. As Robinson's biographer had it, this act "electrified the group" and gave the good government crowd "a new spirit for victory." Meyer Lissner and Marshall Stimson, two of the dominant progressives in the state, heralded "this extraordinary sacrifice on the part of a county janitor." Chester Rowell, another leader in California's insurgent movement, penned a laudatory poem entitled "L.G.," which he distributed widely and published in his Fresno newspaper. That a janitor would contribute substantial savings to a political crusade led by affluent professionals was rather unusual. More surprising, though, was that Robinson was an African-American.[1]

Historical accounts of California progressivism have failed to mention L. G. Robinson and his fellow black progressives in Los Angeles. Likewise, studies of black Los Angeles have ignored the politics of progressivism.[2] This essay seeks to bring together African-American history and progressive history in hopes of providing a richer understanding of both. By examining the role that black Angelenos played in reform campaigns, one can also assess how progressivism shaped the development of the black community in the urban West. Although most African-Americans in the city did not abandon the regular Republicans to join the reformers, a substantial number of black leaders did become progressives; even those who never became progressives often adopted progressive rhetoric and embraced some of the reformers' principal aims.

What follows is a preliminary investigation of the relationship between race and politics in Los Angeles during the first two decades of the twentieth century. Drawing principally on qualitative evidence (with the needed statistical analyses of black voting behavior left to the future), this essay endeavors to show that African-American leaders in Los Angeles were intensely interested in the electoral struggles of the Progressive Era, and that white progressives often sought to win black votes and kept their fingers on the political pulse of the black community. As a result, race became an important undercurrent in California progressivism, and, by the 1920s, the political conflicts of the era had fractured black political allegiances and prompted early defections from the Republican party.

African-Americans had been politically engaged in California throughout the nineteenth century, but they had been few in number and were largely concentrated in the northern part of the state.[3] Black political activism in Los Angeles increased sharply during the Progressive Era, because of the growing number of African-Americans moving to the city and the institutional development that accompanied that growth. Between 1900 and 1910 the number of blacks living in Los Angeles nearly tripled, surging from 2,131 to 7,599. If the city's black population for 1910 was substantially less than in some major urban centers—New York with 91,709 blacks, and Chicago with 44,103, for example—it was higher than in some cities that later assumed national importance as African-American centers; Detroit, for instance, had only 5,741 black residents. Of course, the overall population figures for Los Angeles also lurched upward during the first decade of the century. Excluding blacks, the city's population escalated from 100,348 to 311,599, an increase of 211 percent. Blacks comprised only 2.3 percent of the city's inhabitants in 1910, a percentage scarcely different from that in 1890.[4]

Although such figures suggest that African-Americans and other groups simply arrived in similar numbers, that suggestion is misleading and understates the full extent of black migration. To be sure, there was a large increase in the number of whites after the turn of the century, but many of these "newcomers" were actually brought into Los Angeles through the annexation of six communities, a process that more than doubled the size of the existing city. And since the areas annexed between 1900 and 1910 contained virtually no black residents, the influx of new blacks after the turn of the century was proportionally greater than the influx of whites. The same pattern would hold true during the next decade: by 1920, the black population jumped to 15,579 (a 105 percent increase) while the nonblack population rose by 80 percent, to 561,094. The increase among nonblacks occurred partly because the city annexed twenty-one surrounding communities, adding more than 260 square miles to the city. In this sense, black migrants to Los Angeles between 1900 and 1920 were more than simply keeping pace with their nonblack counterparts. This California version of the "Great Migration," which dramatically swelled the black populations of northern cities, clearly and permanently changed the racial composition of Los Angeles.

Black migrants quickly established women's clubs, fraternities, social organizations, and churches, which, together, provided an institutional structure for community action. The churches were especially critical, and in Los Angeles's black community the line between religion and politics was never rigid. The Evangelical Ministers' Alliance, for example, was one of the most influential and outspoken political groups among local blacks. Churches also created more explicitly political organizations that, to outsiders, might have seemed purely secular. One such organization was the Los Angeles Forum. During 1903, several members of the First African Methodist Episcopal Church established the Forum, which soon became a center of political discussion and activism for black Los Angeles. Sunday-afternoon meetings at the Forum created an arena where political ideals and strategies were openly and often heatedly discussed.[5]

For black men, the most important political organization was the Afro-American Council. Part of a statewide association organized in the 1890s, the Los Angeles branch dominated the state council by the early twentieth century. The Los Angeles "subcouncil" had between six hundred and seven hundred members by 1903, and its local leader, James M. Alexander, served as the council's state president from 1906 through the mid-1910s. Among other things, the council pushed for fair treatment from law enforcement agencies and the California penal system. The council also sought patronage positions for politically active blacks. Although the council usually supported Republicans, Alexander encouraged African-Americans to join any political coalition that would serve their interests.[6]

Although women were not allowed to be members of the Afro-American Council until 1912, they created their own traditions of political activism. Many women's clubs became centers for reform and were active in the electoral process (even before California granted women the right to vote in 1911). Black women in Los Angeles were the driving force behind the State Federation of Colored Women's Clubs, an organization lacking neither enthusiasm nor clout within the state's black communities. Like white female activists, politically minded black women were most visible in the realm of social welfare work. During the course of most political campaigns, male views and male politicos received most of the press—even in Charlotta Bass's politically focused newspaper, the *California Eagle,* the leading black paper in Los Angeles. During the mid-1910s, she was the managing editor, in charge of operations, while her husband, Joseph B. Bass, was editor, in charge of the content of the newspaper.[7] But if men dominated black politics, clubwomen were nonetheless well organized and highly visible in the political arena. The Women's Civic League, for example, sponsored meetings at which candidates aired their views and held rallies in favor of the league's preferred candidates.[8]

Even if every black woman and man in the city had been politically active, they could not have realistically expected to make a major impact on the electoral process. Being so few in number compared to white voters, they could not by any means look toward political dominance. At best, they could hope to form an important minority bloc that could be a decisive swing vote in close elections. Nor could they hope to control any political ward or state Assembly District. Los Angeles's black population in 1900 was not highly centralized; and although African-Americans faced increasing concentration (because of restrictive real estate covenants) during subsequent decades, they did not by 1920 comprise a majority of the population in any political district. In 1920, for example, four in ten blacks in Los Angeles lived in the 74th Assembly District, but those African-American residents made up only 14 percent of the total population in that district. White leaders were nonetheless fully aware of the growing political potential of African-American migrants. As early as 1909 the staunchly conservative *Los Angeles Times* devoted an entire section of its Lincoln Day edition to highlighting the successes of the city's emerging black community. Nothing more clearly signaled to all white politicos the arrival of a new player in local affairs. The *Times,* a stand-pat Republican paper that was never friendly to the insurgent-Republican progressives, may well have run the story as an attempt to convince blacks that they could be well represented in city affairs without joining the reformers—that they should remain loyal to the Party of Lincoln. The edition was given to glowing descriptions of black churches, black leaders, and black doctors, all written by local African-Americans, but the more subtle implication of the *Times* was clear: local blacks, though still a relatively small group in the city, could provide a critical swing vote.[9]

For their part, the city's African-Americans never underestimated their political clout—indeed, black leaders usually overestimated it—but there was more involved here than practical politics. Blacks outside the South had reached a critical juncture. No longer content to be merely an emancipated people, they sought to define themselves, to determine who they could and should be, within the nation's rapidly expanding urban society. Black leaders in particular were struggling to strike a proper balance between race consciousness and American consciousness, between group solidarity and individual advancement. The politics of progressivism created the context within which urban blacks in Los Angeles and elsewhere grappled with larger issues of identity and explored new possibilities for themselves and for their race. The politics of progressivism also prompted white politicians to think about the place of African-Americans in the governing process and gave white leaders new opportunities to control black participation in that process. The result was a political era filled with racial conflict, uncertainty, and peculiar alliances.

The lack of available sources makes it difficult to determine how blacks responded to progressive campaigns prior to 1911, but during two elections in that year—the referendum for woman suffrage and the Los Angeles mayoral race—it became clear that the relationship between progressivism and race would be singularly complex. The Los Angeles Woman Suffrage League, organized by progressive-minded Caroline Severance, actually barred black women from the organization. Many African-American women nonetheless supported the suffrage amendment through their own separate organizations. The State Federation of Colored Women's Clubs threw its support to the cause. White suffrage proponents often based their arguments on ideals of superior female virtue, and black women made similar assertions. As one pro-suffrage report had it: "Colored women feel keenly that they may help in civic betterment, and that their broadened interests in matters of good government may arouse the colored brother, who for various reasons has become too indifferent to his duties of citizenship."

For this and other reasons, black women were pro-suffrage. The *Crisis,* monthly journal for the recently formed National Association for the Advancement of Colored People (NAACP), reported that "in California the colored woman bore her part creditably in the campaign for equal suffrage."[10]

In the end, though, male voters had to approve the amendment. Jefferson Lewis Edmond, a founder of the Forum and editor of *The Liberator,* one of the city's struggling black papers, helped make sure they did so. An outspoken and controversial figure, Edmond wrote to leaders of the suffrage movement, including Severance, pledging his support for the cause and, not incidentally, asking for money to keep his newspaper running. He warned Severance that the anti-suffrage coalition was courting the black vote more than the pro-suffragists were. With a one-hundred-dollar donation, he said, *The Liberator* could be in proper condition to gain 5,000 black votes for suffrage. Whether or not Edmond's letter to Severance had the desired effect, the *Crisis* reported one month later that the state's suffrage leaders had "appointed a special worker among the colored people of California." Edmond also made good on his promise to support the cause. "The Negro cannot afford to ally himself with the interests that are opposing woman suffrage," he wrote in *The Liberator.* "While there are doubtless some conscientious men opposing woman suffrage," he continued, "the fact that all the evil combinations of to-day are fighting woman's suffrage is proof of woman's fitness to vote and should bring to the support of the amendment every intelligent man of the State. If the Negro who has the ballot hopes to restore it to his millions of disfranchised brethren, he cannot ally himself with those evil combinations which seek to confine the ballot to the few they can handle, but he will have to vote for every measure looking to the extension of the ballot." How black men actually voted remains unclear, but since the amendment passed by only 3,500 votes statewide, the black male electorate in Los Angeles, which numbered about three thousand, was hardly trivial to the outcome.[11]

In 1911 the city's white male progressives were less concerned about women's suffrage than with the very real possibility that Los Angeles would elect a Socialist mayor. They were shocked and horrified when a Socialist-labor coalition dominated the primary elections. The progressives quickly leaped into an alliance with conservative forces throughout the city in a frantic effort to defeat Socialist mayoral candidate Job Harriman. To some degree, the reformers had created the problem for themselves. In 1910 progressives in Los Angeles, who had recently gained the upper hand in the city council, sought to hinder the progress of organized labor by passing an ordinance that outlawed picketing in the city. Thereafter, outraged labor leaders in the Union Labor Political Club, an all-white group, saw the progressives as enemies and joined with the Socialists to fight the anti-labor reformers. After one of the most bitter mayoral campaigns in the city's history, the election finally was won by the progressive-conservative group. The campaign itself represented a critical moment in the development of African-American politics in the city, for it pushed white progressives to the right and white workers to the left, and placed black Angelenos in the middle, with their vote up for grabs and very much coveted by both desperate coalitions.[12]

Not surprisingly, therefore, both the neoconservative coalition and the Socialist-labor coalition made special appeals to black voters in the 1911 mayoral election. Local African-American leaders made the most of the situation. It was hardly a coincidence that the annual state convention of the Afro-American Council met in Los Angeles during the height of the campaign, offering white contestants a clear chance to bargain with black leaders. One problem for the Socialists was that local labor unions had alienated the African-American community. Trade unions in Los Angeles had been lily-white and had successfully opposed black competition in skilled trades. But in 1911, under pressure from Northern California labor councils and desperate for any political advantage, local union leaders temporarily buried their racism and offered blacks an olive branch. Their appeal seemed to have succeeded when the local Afro-American Council agreed to merge with the Union Labor Political Club to form the Municipal Organization League, which opposed the progressive coalition. Thus, some influential blacks apparently preferred the political left to the neoconservative progressives. The Socialists returned the favor by nominating a black man, G. W. Whitley, for the city council. But local black leaders were hardly united in their support for the Socialist-labor coalition, and some blacks—especially progressive leader Jefferson Edmond—openly fought the trend. The fiery editor voiced considerable displeasure at the leftist movement, recalling that Frederick Douglass had warned against labor unions, pointing out that local unions had turned blacks away, and encouraging workers in the community to "stay out of the union." It is difficult to determine whether black voters followed Edmond's advice. He later claimed they did, but, ironically, he was not happy about it. Edmond came to regret his support for the progressives, and claimed that the insurgent-conservative coalition of 1911 had, by virtue of its anti-Socialist outcry, "hoodwinked the greater portion of Negroes into support of their ticket."[13]

The action of the Afro-American Council nonetheless served notice that some blacks in Los Angeles were willing to explore the possibilities of new biracial coalitions outside of the Republican-progressive framework, a trend that doubtless disappointed the city's white reformers. But political disappointment could run both ways; and in the two years following the 1911 mayoral campaign, some black progressives became bitterly disenchanted with white insurgents, because the Progressive party bungled the issue of race at both the national and local level.

The national election of 1912 marked a turning point in black politics. When the Republican national convention of 1912 approached, the importance of blacks in the party quickly became evident, but in a most unfavorable way. Both Roosevelt and Taft claimed that the other was trying to purchase—literally, with cash—the votes of southern black delegates. By the early twentieth century, there was no effective Republican party in the South, since white Democrats throughout the region had passed a variety of measures disfranchising blacks. Curiously, though, black Republicans from the South maintained their political parties (even though they did not run for office) because they still played a pivotal role in the national GOP convention. Their delegations reflected the size of their state, not the strength of their organizations, and their votes counted at the national convention. This system generated considerable controversy every four years, and by 1912 some white progressives openly fought it. Marshall Stimson of Los Angeles, among others, sought to abolish the votes of southern delegates. He did so as an attack on the corruption inherent in the system, and also to strengthen the hand of western progressives in the convention, but the motion had obvious racial overtones. The motion failed, though, and Roosevelt himself failed to win the southern delegates. Blacks had no faith in Taft, who favored a lily-white Republican party, but many also distrusted Roosevelt, partly because of the abrupt dishonorable discharges he issued to black soldiers involved in the notorious Brownsville affair. When Roosevelt and his followers bolted the Republican convention to form the Progressive party, they paused long enough to castigate Taft for buying the southern vote—a thinly veiled criticism of blacks themselves.[14]

Many African-Americans nonetheless viewed Roosevelt and the Progressive party as their best hope, and they were not shy in their demands. Black politicians were eager to see anti-lynching legislation, the reenfranchisement of southern blacks, and the abolition of Jim Crow laws, and some were advocating federal funding for elementary education, as well as anti-peonage legislation.[15] Anyone thinking the Progressive party would advocate a civil rights program with even half these provisions soon received a jolt at the Bull Moose convention in Chicago. Hoping to lure white voters in the South, Roosevelt outraged blacks everywhere by agreeing to a policy of lily-whitism for southern delegations, all the while trying to maintain the support of blacks from the North and West.[16] Moreover, black activists at the convention were rebuffed when they proposed that a basic civil rights plank be included in the Progressive platform. Even Jane Addams, the strongest white advocate of black equality at the Chicago convention, concluded, not without some feelings of guilt, that "war on behalf of the political status of the colored man was clearly impossible," and that the Progressive party would have to get on its feet before civil rights could seriously be addressed. Blacks, in short, would have to wait. The "Negro question" was erased from the Progressive party's national agenda.[17]

Some blacks in Los Angeles continued to support Roosevelt despite the Chicago debacle, and they received encouragement from the state's white progressives, who did not take the black vote for granted. Governor Hiram Johnson himself told Russ Avery, one of the top progressives in Southern California, that it would be wise for Roosevelt to meet with a black contingent when he campaigned in Los Angeles. Avery called on none other than Jefferson Edmond to draw up a list of black political leaders for the meeting. Avery then notified fellow progressive leader Meyer Lissner of Johnson's concerns and presented Edmond's list. In doing so, Avery stressed the importance of getting the black vote. One of the African-American leaders selected to meet Roosevelt was Dr. J. Alexander Somerville. Dentist, civic leader, and steadfast progressive, Somerville later wrote, "I have always aligned myself with the forces that contended for good government. I was always closely connected with the progressives in this state under the leadership of Governor Hiram W. Johnson . . . in their fight to overthrow the predatory forces that had control of California at that time." Somerville "admired 'The Big Stick' wielded by Theodore Roosevelt, and followed him into the Bull Moose Party." At the meeting with Roosevelt in 1912, he recalled "one member of the committee, a Baptist minister, Reverend J. D. Gordon, asking Roosevelt, 'Well, Colonel, how do you stand on the Negro question?'" According to Somerville, "Mr. Roosevelt puckered his mouth in one of those well-known poses where he showed all his lower teeth and said, 'I feel like cursing whenever anyone asks that question. My record speaks for itself.' " Somerville accepted this comment uncritically, but many blacks thought the record spoke in unfavorable ways.[18]

California's white progressives courted the black vote not because they were troubled by Taft, who was not even on the ballot in their state, but because they were worried about Woodrow Wilson. Wilson was the first Democratic presidential candidate to receive serious consideration from American blacks. Late in the campaign, Wilson sent an open letter to blacks, seeking to reassure them of his intention to see "justice done to the colored people in every matter; and not mere grudging justice, but justice executed with liberality and cordial good feeling." W. E. B. DuBois, who had become editor of the *Crisis*, believed this was as good as American blacks would get in 1912, and, in a historic break with tradition, he and other black leaders threw their support to the Democrats. It is not possible to know how blacks in Southern California voted, but nationally it is estimated that more than 100,000 blacks actually voted Democratic, a total that would have amounted to about one-fifth of the national black vote.[19]

Many blacks who strayed from the old faith in 1912 viewed their defection as a form of liberation. They had become free agents in the political arena, free to pursue their own interests and coalitions without mindlessly following the party of emancipation. The National Negro Congress of 1914 took up the issue explicitly, asking its delegates to determine whether and why to support the Republicans, Democrats, or Progressives. As Charlotta Bass of the pro-Republican *Eagle* later recalled, "this was the first time the Negro was in a position to think and act for himself and for his own best interest."[20] Many historians still assume that black voters remained firm in their loyalty to the Grand Old Party until their dramatic shift toward the New Deal Democrats in the 1930s. A more accurate view suggests that the election of 1912, by dislodging large numbers of the African-American electorate from the Republican party, marked a critical turning point in black politics. The fissures created by the Progressive party facilitated the black Democratic surge a quarter century later. In a 1940s study of Negro political thought, black scholar Elbert Lee Tatum concluded, in revealing language, that "the further the Negro moves in time from 1915 toward the present, the more the Negro ceases to be a slave to any party label." "This attitude and political independence," he added, "is a complete reversal of his passive acquiescence of former days."[21]

In retrospect, the shift away from the Republicans in 1912 and subsequent years might be seen as the politics of desperation, not liberation.

Stand-pat Republicans had all but committed themselves to a lily-white polity, and the Progressive party, after a bit of agonizing, had written off the "Negro Question." The *Crisis* had gloomily supported Wilson, but after the election DuBois worried openly: "it is quite possible that Mr. Wilson, surrounded by counselors who hate us, may never realize what we suffer, how we are discouraged, and the hindrances to our advance." Not only was it quite possible; it was almost guaranteed. Hence, DuBois's anguished letter to Wilson four years later, which stated, "during the last campaign, believing firmly that the Republican Party and its leaders had systematically betrayed the interests of colored people, many of our members did what they could to turn the colored vote toward you. We received from you a promise of justice and sincere endeavor to forward their interests. We need scarcely to say that you have grievously disappointed us." Such appeals had no impact on Wilson's Jim Crow administration. By 1916, every major party had erased African-Americans from the national agenda. Blacks in the urban North and West found themselves without national-level representation. And without any political collateral in Washington, they had precious little with which to build state or local coalitions.[22]

In subsequent years, indeed decades, black Los Angeles would grapple with the ambiguities of party allegiance and nonpartisan politics. Liberation from party labels promised the possibility of new coalitions, but it also threatened to fragment the black vote into political insignificance. Electoral divisions among African-American voters seemed apparent in the local and state elections of 1914. Or, as the *Eagle* put it, "the political pendulum is still swinging." Democrats, Progressives, Socialists, even Prohibitionists—all courted the black vote. Hugh J. Macbeth and William E. Easton, two prominent black leaders in the city, were strong advocates of the Progressive party, and even the pro-Republican *Eagle* was impressed by their activism. A large banner on the front page, on which their pictures were prominently displayed, read, "Negro Progressives Coming into Their Own," and in this case "progressives" meant, literally, Progressive party advocates. Another story in the *Eagle* noted that the two men were "hammering away" at political meetings and had received "quite a few signatures" endorsing their "Progressive principles." The *Eagle*'s own affiliation with the Party of Lincoln seemed less than whole-hearted on occasion. In 1914 the paper actually encouraged blacks to vote in favor of state-level good government reforms—a move that required some explanation. Even as he trumpeted measures that would strengthen nonpartisan politics and called upon African-Americans to "put the government of the state en-

tirely in the hands of the people," Joseph Bass quickly added that being
"non-partisan in state affairs does not mean a blow at your party nationally. You can still be a republican and be a non-partisan in home or
state government." Since blacks had been all but snuffed out of national-
level politics, this concession to political free agency at the state and
local level was no trivial matter for a Republican paper. The following
year, Charlotta Bass would tour California, visiting blacks throughout
the state, and return to Los Angeles convinced "that issues, rather than
party labels, were the things to fight for." Such sentiments from an important Republican leader might well have convinced MacBeth and
Easton that the progressives were winning the war."[23]

Fighting for issues at the local level, black political leaders in Los Angeles scored occasional victories in the years between 1912 and America's entry into World War I. In the process, black activists honed their
skills in the art of minority politics, withdrew further from the Republican party, and consolidated their positions of leadership within the
black community. During these years, blacks became less visible in the
sphere of national politics, and no dramatic political changes occurred
for blacks in California or Los Angeles. But the mid-1910s were nonetheless critical years in the development of black politics in the city.

The mayoral election of 1913 exemplified trends that would characterize black urban politics in Los Angeles for the next generation. In that
campaign a contingent of white progressive leaders, fearful of another
Socialist surge, aligned with local conservatives in an organization
called the Municipal Conference. This group fielded a ticket headed by
mayoral candidate John W. Shenk. As the city attorney, Shenk was, in
George Mowry's words, an "undistinguished conservative."[24] He may
have been just that to whites in the Municipal Conference, but to local
blacks he was something else entirely. He was the perpetrator of the
hated "Shenk Rule" and an enemy of the race. The Shenk Rule stemmed
from an incident in 1912, when C. W. Holden, a black businessman,
went into a local bar with a white friend. The bartender charged the
Caucasian a nickel but tapped Holden for a dollar. Holden called for
authorities to revoke the bartender's license for infringement of civil
rights, but City Attorney Shenk ruled that "it was neither extortion nor
a violation of the Civil Rights Act to charge a negro more for an article
than a white man." Public places that wanted a white-only clientele
seized on this ruling to ward off black customers simply by charging
them unthinkably high prices. Blacks bitterly opposed this trend. Titus
Alexander, a prominent and sometimes volatile black leader, later

threatened violence against shops that discriminated in this way. The black Evangelical Ministers' Alliance publicly denounced Alexander's tactics, but the ministers themselves openly demanded that the authorities enact and enforce basic civil rights statutes.[25]

For Jefferson Edmond, the black progressive who had served faithfully as the principal liaison between white reformers and the black community, Shenk's nomination by the Municipal Conference was a bitter pill. A dissident group of white progressives also abhorred the conservatism of the Municipal Conference and formed a rival progressive organization, the People's Campaign Committee. But both factions of white progressives supported Shenk for mayor. Edmond had advertised *The Liberator* as "A Weekly Newspaper Devoted to the Cause of Good Government and the Advancement of the American Negro." He had seen progressivism and black progress as inseparable. But the candidacy of John Shenk snuffed out that faith. "Shenk for mayor?" asked an astonished Edmond. "By a ruling as city attorney," he wrote, "Mr. Shenk completely nullified the Civil Rights bill in this state. He ruled that a saloon-keeper, or a restaurant-keeper, or any business house can charge a Negro a dollar for an article that he sells to a white man for five cents." "Liberty," the angry editor said, "is worth fighting for—yea, dying for." And he used his paper to fight Shenk, tentatively suggesting that Job Harriman and the Socialists might offer the best hope for black Angelenos, but ultimately throwing his support to the little-known independent candidate, Henry H. Rose.[26]

The veteran progressive Meyer Lissner saw the black backlash against Shenk as a threat to the Municipal Conference campaign, and he tried to repair the damage. Progressive leaders may have portrayed themselves as being above politics, as servants of the public will, but behind the scenes they played the game of interest-group politics as well as any seasoned ward boss. Lissner saw a chance to win back some black support when he learned that W. E. B. DuBois was coming to Los Angeles to celebrate the founding of the local chapter of the NAACP. Lissner instructed Shenk to attend one of DuBois's rallies at the Temple Auditorium in an effort to attract black support. One can glean something of the dynamics of white progressivism by imagining a nervous Shenk, surrounded by people who hated him, trying to woo African-American votes at a meeting held in honor of the nation's most aggressive spokesperson for civil rights.[27]

Shenk won the primary and saw Socialist candidate Job Harriman knocked out of the race, but he did not win a plurality and, surprisingly, was forced to face the independent candidate—Henry H. Rose—in a run-off election. To the Municipal Conference's dismay, Shenk went down to defeat in a close race, and the little-known Rose became mayor. Municipal Conference candidates did not even gain a majority in the city council, winning only five of eleven seats. Some historians have ascribed this neoconservative failure to the Socialists, who apparently threw their support to Rose once Harriman was out of the running. George Mowry also suggested that "a surprisingly large number of businessmen . . . deserted the Good Governmentites once the Socialist threat had been removed." But considering the low Socialist turnout in the primary and the highly conservative nature of the Municipal Conference, neither of these explanations seems sufficient. Did the black vote make the difference for Rose? Black leaders in Los Angeles thought so. Historian Lonnie G. Bunch III has noted that Edmond, seeking to avenge the Shenk Rule, effectively "marshalled the black and disaffected white vote to ensure Shenk's defeat." Whether Edmonds wielded this much political clout is open to question, but other local leaders also claimed that blacks provided the critical swing vote for Rose. As the *Eagle* had it, "our mayor, the Hon. H. H. Rose, . . . graces that position from the fact the Colored voters lined up for him to a man."[28]

The Shenk Rule continued to reverberate through subsequent campaigns, in which the *Eagle* took pains to point out "Jim Crow candidates unworthy of support." One such candidate was Vincent Morgan, a member of the police commission who ran for district attorney in 1914. His place on the commission, which issued licenses for eating and drinking establishments, posed a problem for African-American voters. In response to Shenk's ruling, black leaders had asked the police commission to revoke the license of any establishment that violated state civil rights statutes. The commission denied that request, and African-American leaders held Morgan responsible. Holding back none of his ire, *Eagle* editor Joseph Bass condemned Morgan as one who "countenances the wholesale discrimination that is in vogue in this city at this time against our race and our race only." "If he thinks he can get by without being shown up in this issue by the *Eagle*," the editorial continued, "he is very dull, stupid, and disingenuous." Morgan lost, prompting a bit of merriment from the *Eagle,* which, putting a twist on things, concluded, "the colored voters would not eat crow, Thank You."[29]

The defeat of Shenk and Morgan represented victories for black Angelenos, to be sure, but in retrospect they also symbolized the contraction of political possibilities for African-Americans in the city. In both cases, blacks were punishing enemies, not creating new coalitions for the advancement of meaningful civil rights statutes. It was rearguard action, a defensive strategy to ward off an assault by Jim Crow. Given the situation, the politics of defense made sense and may be seen as a valiant effort on the part of the city's black political leaders. But it could not have been comforting to local blacks that in subsequent years the *Eagle* would support certain candidates for the California assembly because "each session some legislation is introduced that is detrimental to the race."[30]

Sometimes, too, it was difficult to ascertain which white candidates would best serve black interests. Occasionally, a Caucasian candidate, through sheer ineptitude in speaking to black audiences, made the choice easy for blacks, as when Samuel Shortridge spoke to local African-Americans as a candidate for chief justice of the California Supreme Court. "You Negroes are doing well" he said. "You are getting carpet on your floors and are learning to play pianos"—at which point a good portion of the audience made a defiant exit.[31] The careers of Shenk and Rose reveal that white candidates who openly supported civil rights could subsequently turn against the black community and that Anglo officeholders who offended black voters could learn from their mistakes and change their approach to racial politics. Shenk eventually redeemed himself within the black community, while Rose soon assumed the mantle of villain. In 1914, a local black named Charles W. Wilson ran for assemblyman in the 74th district. He lost but called for a recount, a move contested by his white opponent. Shenk, however, supported Wilson's right to a recount, and the votes were tallied for a second time. Wilson lost anyway, but the *Eagle* praised Shenk's efforts and noted, "we are glad to commend and stand up for a man who stands for a square deal for all as Judge Shenk did in this case."[32] Shortly thereafter, it was Mayor Rose who found himself mired in racial controversy. First he rebuffed a delegation of black women who asked him to investigate "discrimination in public places." Then he scoffed at the local NAACP and the Evangelical Ministers' Alliance when those groups protested against the showing of *The Birth of a Nation* in Los Angeles. The *Eagle* spared nothing in blasting the city's chief executive, condemning him as a liar and "an ingrate," and later had the pleasure of announcing, in a large front-page banner in 1915, "Mayor H. H. Rose Wisely Decides Not to Seek Re-election." Recalling the Shenk-Rose campaign in 1913, the *Eagle* lamented "the irony of fate." "We have been slain in the house of our friends. We were valiant soldiers and shared in the march of Mayor Rose to a glorious victory. We have, as a result thereof, been denied even the smallest solace of comfort, for any of the things that were an uplift or stood for progress."[33]

One way for blacks to avoid the guile of white politicians was to run for office themselves. By the mid-1910s the idea was clearly in the air. In early 1913, when one member of the city council died in mid-term, the *Los Angeles Times* asked, "Will the new member of the City Council . . . be a negro?" "This is a new question injected into the situation, and if the 15,000 negro voters of Los Angeles have any influence with present members of the Council, they will cause the subject to be given serious consideration." Unless the census figures grossly underestimated the number of African-Americans living in the city in 1910 and 1920, there were nowhere near 15,000 black voters in Los Angeles in 1913. Perhaps, though, the perception that black voters were a force to be reckoned with was significant enough. No black was appointed to fill the vacancy in 1913, but two years later Sidney P. Dones, later heralded as the father of the Central Avenue business district, made a bid for the council. Dones appealed to African-American voters by pointing to the Shenk Rule and the police commission's efforts to uphold it, to the showing of *The Birth of a Nation,* and to the fact that blacks had almost no access to city jobs. The best remedy, he said, was to elect one of their own. An ecstatic *Eagle* boosted his candidacy. The Women's Civic League held a rally on his behalf at Wesley Chapel. But Dones lost badly in the primary.[34]

Some black leaders openly blamed the black masses for Dones's calamity. In a letter to the *Eagle,* Seaborn B. Carr of Pasadena put it bluntly: "Before the primaries were held they claimed that there were 30,000 colored voters in Los Angeles and the motto was 'Sidney P. Dones will and must win,' and he received less than 2,000 votes. What became of the other 28,000 votes?" The editors of the paper were no less critical. Their election report complained that "the Colored voters failed absolutely to turn out and as a result of the timidity the Colored councilmanic candidate suffered defeat. The Colored people certainly missed one golden chance to place upon the ticket a member of their own race." Such views were not entirely new. In 1914, when Charles Wilson sought to become the first black assemblyman in California, black elites criticized the rank-and-file electorate for the lack of enthusiasm. Under the heading "Disorganized as Usual," the *Eagle* moaned that "the colored man in the pending campaign is not more in evidence [because of] his antipathy to organization." Wilson, the paper had predicted earlier, needed only two-thirds of the black vote to win in the 74th Assembly District, an area of the city in which the black population was growing rapidly. But as the election approached, the *Eagle* stated that the absence of collective effort "has created an apathy among our people which borders close to no interest in the campaign." Nearly half a century later, when Charlotta Bass thought back about blacks in Los Angeles politics during the 1910s, she concluded, "the great trouble and hurdle to progress then, . . . as it is today, was the apathy and indifference of the people to anything they termed 'politics.' "[35]

Such sentiments are understandable, given the depth of political commitment demonstrated by the city's black leaders. *The Liberator* and the *Eagle*, the Afro-American Council and the Women's Civic League—these newspapers and political organizations, and others like them, devoted considerable time and energy in their efforts "to uplift the Race" through political agitation. Unlike their fellow blacks in the South, African-Americans in Los Angeles could vote and campaign freely. Black voters faced no legal or social obstacles to full participation in the political arena. But throughout the 1910s, poorly attended political meetings and sagging election statistics left black activists exasperated and uncertain. To some degree, the city's African-American leaders set themselves up for a fall by inflating local population statistics and exaggerating the potential electoral strength of the black citizenry. They were urban boosters, and, as American boosters will, they set impossible goals for the people they claimed to represent.

Virtually no records survive to reveal the political ideals and electoral strategies of the vast majority of black Angelenos in the Progressive Era. It is difficult to determine whether they took an active part in the 1911 mayoral election, what they knew about the Progressive party convention in 1912, how often they read the *Eagle,* or whether they cared about Sidney Dones's bid for the council. One of the enduring puzzles of the Progressive Era was that as the reform impulse increased, mass political participation declined. Progressives often said they were returning politics to the people, but the political world that the progressives created was one in which the bulk of ordinary voters participated less than ever. In the South, voter turnout plummeted because of de jure disfranchisement of blacks and poor whites. But even outside the South, voter turnout fell as traditional party allegiances gave way to nonpartisan politics. When the political leaders of the black community liberated themselves from the Party of Lincoln, did rank-and-file blacks lose interest? Did poor black voters come to feel, as their poor white counterparts apparently did, that politics had slipped into the hands of an affluent few? That Marcus Garvey's program of black nationalism became so popular among ordinary blacks in Los Angeles during the early 1920s suggests that many working-class blacks had indeed become alienated from co-alitional politics. By the 1930s, the Forum, which had always been open to everyone and which was viewed by many blacks as the most demo-cratically run black political organization, had begun to decline in in-fluence. The NAACP and the Urban League emerged as the political cat-alyst of the community. As one old-timer later noted, "The NAACP was run by the aristocrats. . . . And the Urban League was the most aristo-cratic . . . the upper group."[36]

Black leaders may have branded the black masses as sluggards, and ordinary African-Americans may have scoffed at their "aristocratic" leaders, but blacks of all classes knew there was more to the defeat of Sidney Dones than black apathy or black elitism. The fundamental problem was that white party bosses would not nominate African-Americans for office, and white voters seldom voted for black candi-dates. One exception was the Socialist Party of Los Angeles, which nom-inated G. W. Whitley for city council in 1911 and gave him full party support at the polls in a losing effort. None of the other political coa-litions of the day seemed eager to place blacks in office. Throughout the 1910s, white progressives wanted black votes but not black officials or even black advice. Jefferson Edmond, disdainful of the Municipal Con-ference in 1913, explained the patterns of progressive-conservative ex-clusion of blacks: "Last week a call was issued for two hundred citizens to . . . arrange for indorsing municipal candidates. To that conference no Negroes were invited. That conference appointed a committee of twenty-five to name a ticket, but no Negro was made a member of the ticket-making twenty-five. This means that the Negroes, in spite of their number and loyalty, are to be absolutely ignored, as [they have] been by the Lissner-Stimson-Alexander bunch hereto-fore. Given no consider-ation in the selection of candidates, he is to have no consideration after said candidates are elected." Moreover, he said, black progressives who sought their party's nomination were turned away. Black candidates therefore ran as independents in search of a coalition, as Dones did in 1915. Without party backing in an at-large city primary, Dones never had a chance. Any black voter casting a ballot that year had to decide whether to vote for a potential winner or to vote for Dones, a sure loser, out of principle. Dones pursued the only strategy possible for turning out an unusually large black vote on his behalf—he campaigned on a strong civil rights platform. In doing so, however, he no doubt frightened away whatever white support he might have won by campaigning as a successful, moderate businessman. Such was the political dilemma of black Los Angeles during the Progressive Era, and for African-American politicians in the city that dilemma has never completely dissolved.[37]

For the city's black leaders the Progressive Era marked a period of political excitement and, within the realm of the black community, of political empowerment as well. For the black middle class and those who aspired to it, the political battles of the 1910s served as an initiation into modern urban affairs. The emerging political elite in black Los Angeles sharpened its political skills, built stronger organizations, made lasting connections with white leaders, and explored new coalitional strategies. Too often, of course, black campaigns were studies in frustration. In 1916, for example, political free agency in the black community seemed to degenerate into factional squabbling. In that year, too, ballots in Los Angeles were printed with instructions for election officials to "Tear off the corner [of the ballot] if the voter is a Negro," an affront checked only by the outraged reaction of blacks on the election board. In the aftermath of the 1916 elections, the *Eagle* could only conclude that "the Colored Race is just where they started before the campaign—no more nor less."[38] But for all their frustration, the city's black political activists emerged from the Progressive Era as a core of experienced community leaders. Thereafter the black middle class of Los Angeles would maintain its privileged position in Afro-American society and would persevere in the political arena.

Its efforts were rewarded in 1918, when Frederick M. Roberts of Los Angeles succeeded in becoming the first black assemblyman in California. Roberts won in the 74th District, the "Black Belt of Los Angeles," as local African-Americans had come to call it. At the time of Roberts's election, though, the "Black Belt" District was still majority white, and Roberts won by campaigning as a regular Republican candidate with the support of the Republican party. One historian has written that "with the arrival of Frederick Roberts on the scene, there was the first evidence that blacks in California were preparing to shape western history and not be passively shaped by it." Another has argued that Roberts's successes gave life to black political activism in Los Angeles, prompting local African-Americans to set aside "the idealistic optimism and insularity of the earlier period." Such views ignore the political activism of blacks in the Progressive Era. A more accurate interpretation is that Roberts was able to win precisely because black Angelenos had been vigorously trying to shape their political history in the decade prior to his election.[39]

In succeeding as a Republican party regular, Roberts was exceptional among local blacks, for during the 1920s black leaders in Los Angeles grew increasingly nonpartisan in their search for a biracial coalition that could further their civil rights agenda. In 1921 leaders of the Republican-dominated Forum supported Titus Alexander in an election bid, even though he had moved squarely into the Democratic party. More remarkably, in 1922 the California State Colored Republican League actually threw its support to the Democratic gubernatorial candidate, Thomas Lee Woolwine. Headed by none other than Joseph Bass, the league was the most influential black Republican organization in the state and, unlike white Republican organizations, was explicit in its demands for civil rights. After interviewing Woolwine about his views on race relations, the league sent him a remarkable letter pledging every effort on his behalf. "Let me add," the league secretary insisted, "that your party affiliation does not enter into this matter with us; if we as a people were ever indebted to the Republican Party for what they have done for us, we feel that we have long since paid that debt by our faithful service and loyalty with compound interest, long, long ago; and from now henceforth we expect to vote for the man and measures, and not the Party." Few statements so powerfully underscored the depth to which progressive sentiments had permeated the state's African-American political community. Perhaps the Colored Republican League saw the roots of its nonpartisanship in political expediency, not progressive ideology, but such rhetoric clearly pointed up how influential the California progressives—black and white—had been in transforming the political world of black Republicans. Not until the presidential election of 1936 would it be certain on the national level that the mass of American blacks had finally abandoned the Party of Lincoln. But in California, as early as 1922, the most important black Republicans in the state, most of whom were civic leaders from Los Angeles, had all but tendered their resignation to the Grand Old Party.[40]

By the end of the 1930s, blacks had become an integral part of the New Deal coalition. A foreshadowing of the new dispensation came in 1934, when Augustus F. Hawkins, a New Deal Democrat and black Angeleno, ousted Republican Frederick Roberts from the statehouse. Hawkins replaced Roberts as the only black in the state legislature, and he remained the only African-American in the Assembly for more than a decade. Most black voters shifted to the Democratic party and thereafter maintained a strong allegiance to it. African-American demands for civil rights remained essentially unchanged from the previous generation, but black leaders now perceived the liberal wing of the Democratic party as their best hope for a better world. And with the phenomenal black exodus from the South during and after World War II, the Democratic party evolved into a multiracial coalition in which blacks assumed ever-increasing influence.

The possibility of such a development—of African-American political clout within a liberal Democratic party—would have seemed highly unlikely to black Angelenos during the Progressive Era. Yet, in significant ways, African-American leaders in the Progressive Era laid the groundwork for what followed. By insisting that empowerment was possible within an overwhelmingly white political system and by wilingly exlporing a variety of political alliances to advance black interests, they created an ethnic political culture that later flowed easily into the New Deal coalition.

In the final analysis, African-American leaders probably had very little impact on the major political battles that were fought in Progressive-Era California. But the reverse was clearly not true. The politics of reform had a significant influence on the black community. Progressivism emerged as a force in western life at the same time that Los Angeles's black community was beginning to coalesce. The electoral confrontations of the period served as a training ground for the city's emerging black leaders. The politics of progressivism allowed the new African-American elite to establish relationships with influential white politicians, consolidate their positions of leadership in the black community, and learn the intricacies of modern urban politics. Their efforts ultimately engendered a black political culture that inspired subsequent generations of African-American activists. In the 1920s, however, black leaders in Los Angeles must have looked back on the Progressive Era with considerable ambivalence. Politics, they had found, was an indispensable but often untrustworthy companion.

NOTES

1. Baxter S. Scruggs, *A Man in Our Community: The Biography of L. G. Robinson of Los Angeles, California* (Gardena, Calif.: Institute Press, 1937), 76–77. My estimate of the date of the meeting is based on Robinson's biography and the history of the mainstream progressive movement.

2. On progressivism in California, two standard works are George E. Mowry, *The California Progressives* (Berkeley: University of California Press, 1951), and Spencer C. Olin, Jr., *California's Prodigal Sons: Hiram Johnson and the Progressives, 1911–1917* (Berkeley: University of California Press, 1968); see also Robert M. Fogelson, *The Fragmented Metropolis: Los Angeles, 1850–1930* (Cambridge, Mass.: Harvard University Press, 1967).

On blacks in Los Angeles during the early twentieth century, see J. Max Bond, "The Negro in Los Angeles" (Ph.D. diss., University of Southern California, 1936); Rudolph M. Lapp, *Afro-Americans in California* (San Francisco: Boyd and Fraser, 1987), chaps. 3–4; Emory J. Tolbert, *The UNIA and Black Los Angeles* (Los Angeles: Center for Afro-American Studies, 1980); Lawrence B. De Graaf, "The City of Black Angels: Emergence of the Los Angeles Ghetto, 1890–1930," *Pacific Historical Review* 39 (1970): 323–52; James A. Fisher, "The Political Development of the Black Community in California, 1850–1950," *California Historical Quarterly* 50 (September 1971): 265–66. E. Frederick Anderson, *The Development of Leadership and Organization Building in the Black Community of Los Angeles* (Saratoga, Calif.: Century Twenty One Publishing, 1980), does not grapple with progressivism, but chaps. 3 and 4 offer useful data on black politics in Los Angeles prior to World War I.

Daniel T. Rodgers, "In Search of Progressivism," *Reviews in American History* 10 (December 1982): 112–32, remains a compelling review of the revisionist historiography of the 1970s. Ironically, some of the "old" historians of progressivism actually dealt more with blacks than the revisionists have. See, for example, Dewey W. Grantham, Jr., "The Progressive Movement and the Negro," *South Atlantic Quarterly* 54 (October 1955): 461–77; and Arthur S. Link, "The Negro as a Factor in the Campaign of 1912," *Journal of Negro History* 32 (January 1947): 81–99.

3. Rudolf M. Lapp, *Afro-Americans in California*, 1–34, and "Negro Rights Activities in Gold Rush California," in Roger Daniels and Spencer C. Olin, Jr., eds., *Racism in California: A Reader in the History of Oppression* (New York: Macmillan, 1972); Fisher, "Political Development"; and Philip S. Foner and George E. Walker, eds., *Proceedings of the Black State Conventions, 1840–1865* vol. 2 (Philadelphia: Temple University Press, 1980).

4. Population figures for this paragraph and the next are taken, or calculated, from Bond, "Negro in Los Angeles," 38–103b; and De Graaf, "The City of Black Angels." On annexations see Fogelson, *Fragmented Metropolis,* 224–27.

5. Anderson, *Leadership,* 34–35, 51–80.

6. See the "Afro-American Council" correspondence file in the papers of Governor George Pardee, Bancroft Library; James Alexander's "Appeal to Reason" pamphlet (1906) is especially enlightening and filled with mainstream progressive ideals. *Pasadena News,* August 18, 1903, has information on delegates to the Afro-American Council's annual convention; for more on that conference, see also the issues dated August 19, 20, and 21, 1903.

7. Charlotta A. Bass, *Forty Years: Memoirs from the Pages of a Newspaper* (Los Angeles: Charlotta Bass, 1960). Charlotta Bass, though leaving editoral decisions to her husband, was extremely politically active throughout her life, as

her memoirs indicate. After the death of her husband in the 1930s, Charlotta Bass managed both the business and the editorial ends of the *Eagle* until it ceased publication in the mid-1960s.

8. *The Crisis*, May 1912; *Eagle*, May 1, 1915. California's Afro-American Council first admitted women to membership in 1912 (see *Crisis*, October 1912).

9. *Los Angeles Times*, February 12, 1909, sec. 3.

10. *Crisis*, September 1912. More generally on black women's organizations during the Progressive Era, see Cynthia Neverdon-Morton, *Afro-American Women of the South and the Advancement of the Race, 1895–1925* (Knoxville: University of Tennessee Press, 1989).

11. J[efferson] L. Edmond to Caroline Severance, September 29, 1911, box 16, Caroline M. Severance Papers, Huntington Library. Edmond's name is inconsistently spelled in the press, often being presented as Edmonds. *Crisis*, October, November (*The Liberator* quoted) 1911; Joan M. Jensen and Gloria Ricci Lothrop, *California Women: A History* (San Francisco: Boyd and Fraser, 1987), 61–65, 69–70.

The size of Los Angeles's black electorate in 1911 must be estimated. In 1913 black political leaders in Los Angeles claimed that African-Americans could marshal up to 15,000 voters in the city (they estimated 10,000 male and 5,000 female, without explaining why men voters would outnumber women voters by 100 percent), but this figure seems impossible given that the official census counted only 15,579 blacks in the entire city as late as 1920. A better estimate can be garnered from census materials. There were about 2,641 males of voting age in 1910. The estimated rate of population growth among blacks in Los Angeles from 1910 to 1911 was 12 percent. Those figures (2,641 plus 12 percent growth) suggest that there were about 2,958 voting-age males in Los Angeles in 1911. The census usually underrepresented blacks in the city, but, at the same time, probably not all black males were registered to vote—so the two problems of adjustment cancel each other out. Consequently, an estimate of about 3,000 black male voters is a safe bet. Calculations made from data taken from the aggregate population figures for 1900 and 1910 from published U.S. Census reports and from Bond, "The Negro in Los Angeles," 55 (table VIII).

12. Fogelson, *Fragmented Metropolis*, chap. 10, especially 213–15; Grace H. Stimson, *Rise of the Labor Movement in Los Angeles* (Berkeley: University of California Press, 1955), chap. 21; Mowry, *California Progressives*, 49–56.

13. Stimson, *Rise of the Labor Movement*, 336–37; Lapp, *Afro-Americans in California*, 61; *Crisis*, October 1911. On Edmond's views, see Seaborn B. Carr's eulogy for Edmond in *Eagle*, January 16, 1915; and Edmond's own recollections of 1911 in *The Liberator*, April 4, 1913, copy in John Randolph Haynes Papers, Special Collections, University of California, Los Angeles. On Socialists and the issue of race, see David W. Southern, *Malignant Heritage: Yankee Progressives and the Negro Question, 1901–1914* (Chicago: Loyola University Press, 1967), 72–73. Marshall Stimson's autobiography, *Fun, Fights, and Fiestas in Old Los Angeles* (n.p.: 1966), which often provides intricate detail on Progressive-Era politics, not only fails to mention the Socialist-Labor party in the 1911 election but even gets the year wrong (calling it the election of 1912). He makes no mention of the black vote.

14. *Crisis*, July 1912, reporting the mud thrown between Taft and Roosevelt, states, "While this merry recrimination went on the colored delegates for the most part proved to be an unusually high class of men and for the most part unbribable" (Marshall Stimson Scrapbooks, vol. 3, Huntington Library). More generally on southern blacks and the national Republican party convention, see McMillen, *Dark Journey*, 57–71; and Paul D. Casdorph, *Republicans, Negroes, and Progressives in the South, 1912–1916* (University: University of Alabama Press, 1981). For the record, the South sent 252 voting delegates to the national convention (Casdorph, *Republicans*, 2) even though it was a forgone conclusion that the Democrats would sweep the South.

15. *Crisis*, August 1912.

16. Ibid., September 1912; McMillen, *Dark Journey*, 62–64; John Dittmer, *Black Georgia in the Progressive Era, 1900–1920* (Urbana: University of Illinois Press, 1987), 104–9; Southern, *Malignant Heritage*, 73–78.

17. Black views on Roosevelt, Taft, Wilson, and the election are usefully reported in *Crisis*, July–December 1912; Jane Addams's explanation of the decisions made in Chicago and her plea for the black vote are in "The Progressive Party and the Negro," *Crisis*, November 1912. Her article was originally penned for *McClure's* magazine but was rejected because of its "controversial" subject matter (see *Crisis*, December 1912).

18. Russ Avery to Meyer Lissner, September 10, 1912, box 12, Meyer Lissner Papers, Special Collections, Stanford University (my thanks to Tom Sitton for this reference); Dr. J. Alexander Somerville, *Man of Color: An Autobiography* (Los Angeles: Lorrin L. Morrison, 1949), 83–84.

19. See the *Crisis* throughout 1912; Wilson quoted in John Hope Franklin, *From Slavery to Freedom: A History of Negro Americans* (New York: Knopf, 1974), 334; and, less precisely, in W. E. B. DuBois to Henry Morganthau, April 10, 1916, box 2, W. E. B. DuBois Collection, Special Collections, Fisk University Library.

20. Bass, *Forty Years*, 39–41.

21. Elbert Lee Tatum, "The Changed Political Thoughts of Negroes of the United States, 1915–1940," 1. This is a manuscript version of an article published in the *Journal of Negro Education* 16 (Fall 1947): 522–33, located in box 203, folder 22, Charles S. Johnson Papers, Special Collections, Fisk University Library. The date 1915 seems to have been arbitrarily chosen by Tatum, who gives little attention to the 1912 election.

22. *Crisis*, December 1912; W. E. B. DuBois to the President of the United States, October 10, 1916, and (a more forceful and angry letter) W. E. B. DuBois to Henry Morganthau, April 10, 1916, both in box 2, DuBois Collection.

23. *Eagle*, September 12, October 17 and 24, 1914, and September 25, 1915; Bass, *Forty Years*, 41.

24. Mowry, *California Progressives*, 205–10, quote on 206.

25. A brief account of the Shenk Rule is related in Lonnie G. Bunch III, "A Past Not Necessarily Prologue: The Afro-American in Los Angeles since 1900," in Norman M. Klein and Martin J. Schiesl, eds., *20th Century Los Angeles: Power, Promotion, and Social Conflict* (Claremont, Calif.: Regina Books, 1990), 105–6. On the controversy sparked by Titus Alexander and the response by the Ministers' Alliance, see *Eagle*, December 13, 1913.

26. *The Liberator*, April 4, 1913, copy in Haynes Papers.

27. Meyer Lissner [on Municipal Conference stationary] to John Shenk, April 25, 1913, box 4, John W. Shenk Papers, Special Collections, Stanford University (my thanks to Tom Sitton for this reference). On DuBois's visit see Anderson, *Leadership*, 38; Lapp, *Afro-Americans*, 38–39; and Tolbert, *UNIA*, 33–34.

28. On the black vote against Shenk, see *Eagle*, February 6, 1915; and Bunch, "A Past" (citing nothing, but apparently basing his statement on a surviving copy of *The Liberator*), 129, n.20. On the campaign generally, see Fogelson, *Fragmented Metropolis*, 216–17, which offers no explanation for Shenk's demise; Mowry, *California Progressives*, 205–10; and Marshall Stimson Scrapbooks, vol. 3, Stimson Papers. Stimson's autobiography (*Fun, Fights, Fiestas*, chap. 23) seeks to lay to rest the bitterness of the progressives' internal strife during 1913 (even though the news clippings in Stimson's Scrapbooks are filled with that bitterness). Stimson supported the Municipal Conference; Edwin T. Earl, editor of the progressive *Express*, opposed it as a sellout to the conservative powers. In a careful bit of understatement, Stimson states that Earl "felt that a compromise was being made with forces that were inimical to the city's best interest. I think he was mistaken, but the matter is open to question" (*Fun, Fights, Fiestas*, 216). Stimson does not mention the black vote or the Socialists.

29. *Eagle*, August 22 and 28, 1914.

30. Ibid., August 19, 1916.

31. This story related in Bass, *Forty Years*, 40.

32. On Wilson's candidacy, see *Eagle*, August 22, 1914; on Schenk and the recount, *Eagle*, October 3, 1914.

33. Ibid., February 6 and 20, 1915.

34. *Los Angeles Times*, March 1, 1913; *Eagle*, April 3 and May 1 and 8, 1915.

35. Quotes in *Eagle*, May 15 and May 8, 1915, October 17, 1914, and Bass, *Forty Years*, 39.

36. Tolbert, *UNIA*; quote in Anderson, *Development of Leadership*, 71–72.

37. Edmond quoted in *The Liberator*, April 4, 1913, copy in Haynes Papers.

38. On the 1916 campaign see *Eagle*, March 10, April 8, and May 6, 1916.

39. Roberts's career has been badly neglected by historians and demands serious study. For a brief introduction, see the entry for Frederick Madison Roberts in Rayford W. Logan and Michael R. Winston, *Dictionary of American Negro Biography* (New York: Norton, 1982), 526–27; Roberts's obituary in *Los Angeles Times*, July 20, 1952; and Michael Goldstein, "The Political Careers of Fred Roberts and Tom Bradley: Political Style and Black Politics in Los Angeles," *Western Journal of Black Studies 5* (Summer 1981): 139–46. The first historical interpretation of Roberts presented in this paragraph is from Lapp, *Afro-Americans*, 47; the second is from Anderson, "Development," 66. In 1920, the 74th District had the highest concentration of blacks of any Assembly district in the county, with a total number of 6,251 blacks in that district. But that total amounted to only 14.1 percent of the overall population in the "Black Belt." By 1930, the Assembly district lines had been redrawn, and the old 74th had been incorporated into the 62nd District, the population of which was 36.5 percent

black. Population figures and Assembly district maps in Bond, "Negro in Los Angeles," 75–85. The earliest reference I have seen to the 74th District's being the "Black Belt of Los Angeles County" is in *Eagle*, August 19, 1916.

40. Lapp, *Afro-American*, 47, gives the conventional view, stating, "In these years [between 1919 and the mid-1930s] professional black politicians were still attached to the party of Lincoln. . . . Most blacks in the United States saw only the rope of the lynch mob and the cloak of the Ku Klux Klan in the Democratic party. Not until the presidency of Franklin Delano Roosevelt did that feeling change." On Titus Alexander see Anderson, *Development of Leadership*, 67; on Woolwine see C. H. Alston [Secretary, California State Colored Republican League] to Thomas Lee Woolwine, August 8, 1922; see also letters exchanged between Alston and Woolwine, June 14 and August 9, 1922, all in Thomas Lee Woolwine Collection, Huntington Library.

The "New Nationalism," Mexican Style

Race and Progressivism in Chicano Political Development during the 1920s

George J. Sanchez

When Zeferino Ramírez stood up in front of his fellow residents of Belvedere, an unincorporated area east of the city of Los Angeles, he had long since been recognized as a leader among the Mexican immigrants there. That Sunday-night meeting on June 12, 1927, was called to focus on a community crisis, and it was no surprise that Ramírez, a local businessman, had been asked to preside over the discussion. At issue was a plan to incorporate the area into a full-fledged municipality, a move that would certainly make it more difficult for Mexican settlement in the district. At least three plans for incorporation had been submitted to Los Angeles County officials within the year by real estate and manufacturing interests in Belvedere. Their strategy was to significantly increase the taxes of local residents to pay for city services, thereby forcing the largely working-class people of the community to sell their property in a depressed market. The area in dispute could thereby be resold to middle-class Anglo-Americans, forcing up property values in neighboring communities and making a tidy profit for real estate companies.[1]

In conspicuous attendance at this most important community meeting were Anglo-American leaders recognized by many for their solid progressivism. The head of this delegation, for example, was John Perry Wood, a Pasadena attorney who had secured a national reputation battling California utility companies before being elected judge of Los Angeles County Superior Court in 1911. To him and other Anglo-American leaders in attendance, this was just another case of large corporate interests attempting to disempower "the people." Marco

Hellman, one of the largest bankers in Southern California and a major landowner in Belvedere, was the most visible enemy in this case, having initiated the latest incorporation effort.[2]

The Anglo-American progressives at this Belvedere meeting counseled the largely immigrant audience to apply quickly for naturalization, arguing that those Mexican immigrants without first papers would be unable to vote against incorporation, if the issue ever appeared in an election. But Mexican community leaders had other priorities. Zeferino Ramírez joined the Spanish-language newspaper *La Opinión*, the Mexican consulate representative, and every other Mexican leader in warning against this advice. To him and to the others, the negation of Mexican citizenship would have been a larger crime than that being perpetrated on the residents of Belvedere.[3]

Although the meeting had brought together leaders from two distinct communities, this incident clearly indicates a divergence in thinking between the Mexican community leadership of Southern California and the remnants of the Anglo-American progressive movement. Outside observers might conclude that the progressive movement had little, if anything, to do with Mexican political development during the 1920s, at least as represented by this community leadership. On the surface, progressivism seems an ideology that emerged from outside the largely immigrant community, especially when it manifested intolerant efforts such as Americanization.

George Mowry, in his 1951 classic study of the California progressives, defined progressivism in the state as an exclusively upper-middle-class movement emerging from urban battles in 1906 to wrest political control from the corrupt hands of the Southern Pacific Railroad. According to Mowry, progressives were largely young, college-educated journalists, attorneys, and independent businessmen, born in the Protestant Middle West, who were as likely to attack organized labor as organized capital when either sought to control the political institutions in the state. They saw themselves as neutral arbitrators on the political scene, attempting "to recapture and reaffirm the older individualist values" in the face of an increasingly industrialized and bureaucratized social, political, and economic world now dominated by the large monopolistic corporation and the threatening class forces from below.[4]

Although Mowry saw the progressive movement waning in the state after 1916, other authors have pointed to the continuation of the progressive tradition well into the 1920s. Although anti-progressive forces came back strongly in California after World War I, historian Jackson

Putnam pointed to the continued strength of the progressive movement in the election of C. C. Young to the governorship in 1926.[5] Wrapped in this story of the continuation of progressive impulses in the 1920s was the confusion over the central tenets of progressive social thought. To illustrate the heterogeneity of progressive ideology, Daniel Rodgers described three "languages" employed by progressives: the rhetoric of anti-monopolism, an emphasis on social bonds, and the language of social efficiency.[6] Not surprisingly, each of these languages had a history before the progressive period, and each retained its impact in social and political discourse into the 1920s. In the historiography of the period, progressivism became less of a "movement," with discernible actors and goals, and more of an "impulse," with commonality emerging only from a widespread attempt to find order in the modern world out of the chaos of industrialization.

In Southern California, as in other parts of the nation, this progressive "impulse" took on a decidedly nationalist fervor after the World War I period. Foreigners increasingly were viewed as a threat to the social bonds that united communities. Although anti-Asian sentiments were part of the progressive tradition in the state from the start, the 100 percent American movement of the war period shifted this nativist impulse toward all "foreigners."[7] While some in the progressive movement turned to advocating severe immigration restriction, others attempted to assimilate the immigrants already in their communities with programs designed to promote the abandonment of native cultures and the rapid adoption of American ways.[8] Both these efforts indicate that progressivism in the 1920s became ever more equated with American nationalism for Anglo-Americans in Southern California.

Ethnic communities in California, however, dealt with the shifting ideological tenets of Anglo-American progressivism in a variety of ways. There is some indication that the Italian and Jewish communities of San Francisco, for example, adopted strategies that mirrored this stress on Americanization, joining with native-born whites in developing assimilative programs aimed at their most recent newcomers.[9] More often, however, ethnic residents are depicted as simply resisting these efforts at Americanization, either as organized entities or as individuals; such a depiction places these groups wholly outside of the progressive tradition. In my research on the Mexican immigrant community of Los Angeles, I have come to recognize many ideological strains of the progressive "impulse" shared by immigrant leaders and Anglo-Americans alike: an "impulse" to find a rational order in society and government in the face of increasing industrialization and class strife. In this sense, progressivism existed in cultures and touched peoples beyond the narrow boundaries of the United States.[10] A recognition of this shared impulse, I believe, should lead to a new understanding of the global meanings of this search for order and sheds light on the intellectual traditions of immigrants in California in the period.

According to recent scholarship on the Mexican Revolution, the ideas of the leadership elite that came to power in Mexico after 1917 had much in common with certain tenets of American progressivism. Discussing Alvaro Obregón, who assumed the Mexican presidency in 1920, historian Ramón Ruiz compares his views on capital-labor relations to the views of Wilsonian progressives, who were "enlightened perhaps but certainly not radical." Obregón believed that government should function as a "neutral arbitrator" between labor and capital, "giving business and industry the opportunity to earn a just profit, and in the process, to provide labor with adequate wages and a decent standard of living." Despite the violent character of the revolution and his coming to power, Obregón as early as 1915 expressed the belief that, of all reforms needed in Mexico, the "most important were moral in character."[11]

With a line of leaders that stretched from Francisco Madero to Venustiano Carranza and to Alvaro Obregón, Mexico's revolution had failed to bring into power leaders such as Emiliano Zapata, who espoused radical proposals for reform. Instead, a growing middle class, frustrated for decades by the intransigence of dictator Porfirio Díaz, took control of the country. Grown weary of military action, political maneuvering, and near anarchy, which marked the period from 1914 to 1917 following the overthrow of Adolfo de la Huerta, these individuals increasingly backed Carranza's constitutionalist forces when faced with the unpredictable Francisco Villa in the north and the agrarian revolt of Zapata in the south. In the United States, this newfound perspective on politics and society would best be reflected by the Mexican government's representatives in this country: the consuls. These consuls, and the local expatriates who worked with them, exposed the largely working-class population of Mexican immigrants to a "progressive" rhetoric.

The signing of the 1917 constitution brought stability to Mexico and increased professionalization of the Mexican diplomatic corps in the United States. In addition, during the 1920s a younger generation of consular and diplomatic officials came to dominate these consulates. Although most major positions continued to be handed out as political rewards, the shared experiences and collective ideology of these consular officials made them distinct from previous generations of officials.[12] Unlike their predecessors, most had taken an active part in the Mexican Revolution, although not usually as front-line military or political participants. They most often had been students who consciously opposed Porfirio Díaz and backed Francisco Madero's middle-class revolution against dictatorial powers.

For the individuals who would assume positions in Mexico's diplomatic corps in the 1920s, the government produced by the 1917 constitutional convention in Querétaro represented stability and order and their own political coming-of-age. Future Los Angeles consul Rafael de la Colina, for example, served as a messenger during the Querétaro constitutional convention, remembering it as an "extraordinary experience."[13] The delegates were clearly representative of the emerging Mexican middle class as described by historians Michael Meyer and William Sherman:

> The delegates of Querétaro represented a new breed of Mexican politician and, in a sense, constituted a new social elite. Unlike the Convention of Aguascalientes, military men constituted only 30 percent of the delegates. Over half had university educations and professional titles. The large majority were young and middle class; because they had been denied meaningful participation during the Porfiriato, many were politically ambitious.[14]

After 1917, but particularly with Alvaro Obregón's ascendancy to the Mexican presidency in 1920, this ideology of order and control came to be represented in Mexican communities in the United States by the Mexican consuls. Obregón encouraged consulates to expand their efforts to protect Mexican nationals already working in the United States. In Los Angeles, given the volume of migration from Mexico and the lack of a significant Mexican-American middle class, the consul emerged as the central organizer of community leadership.[15] Although the Mexican government's position toward emigrants had long been ambivalent, during the 1920s the government began to realize that these immigrants could provide considerable expertise if they could be convinced to return to Mexico. Therefore, the programs initiated by the Mexican consulate sought to preserve the cultural integrity and patriotism of Mexican emigrants and to encourage their ultimate return to Mexico.

These efforts were to be carried out largely by the organization of Honorary Commissions made up of members of expatriate communities affiliated with the consulate offices. Though the members of these commissions received no pay from the Mexican government, consuls repeatedly assured them of their importance to their native country, and they became key spokespersons in their respective communities.[16] In Los Angeles, the Comisión Honorífica, in conjunction with the consulate office, sponsored patriotic celebrations, organized community-wide alliances and educational conferences, and initiated a plan for alternative schools where children could learn the Spanish language and Mexican history.

While members of Mexico's diplomatic corps were quintessential representatives of Mexico City's elite, those gathered to participate on Honorary Commissions were a more diverse group. Although outlying nonurban areas of Southern California were often served by respected blue-collar workers, the Honorary Commission of central Los Angeles was limited almost exclusively to middle-class businessmen and professionals. Nonetheless, the members of this commission did not constitute a homogeneous group by any means. Many were political refugees who had fled the Mexican Revolution and, depending on who was in power in Mexico, could be either in or out of favor with the consulate. Most had come from Mexico with professional credentials and became the barrios' first doctors, lawyers, and pharmacists. Only a relative few were small entrepreneurs who had moved up the social ladder after arriving in the United States.[17]

These individuals shared a conservative worldview and differentiated themselves from the Mexican masses on the basis of race, class, urban background, and education. In Mexico, they had feared the volatile nature of the mestizo peasant led by a Zapata or a Villa, but in the United States they found themselves cast together with the lower classes through the common thread of nationality and the racism of Anglo-American society, which rarely distinguished between rich and poor Mexicans. Through their affiliation with the Mexican consulate, they were able to cultivate a tenuous leadership role in a mostly working-class population.[18] If the Mexican community had a middle class in the progressive tradition, this was it.

Zeferino Ramírez was one of the few who had risen from humble surroundings in the United States to assume a position of respect and authority among the Mexican community of Los Angeles. He had come to Los Angeles during the decade of the revolution and was forced to live in an insect-infested room with fellow Mexicans unable to find work. Returning to Mexico briefly to bring over his wife and children, he finally managed to save enough to return to Los Angeles and buy a small home in Belvedere. For seven years he worked as a highway laborer. In the mid-1920s, with the help of Protestant missionaries, he started a business of his own, opening an undertaking establishment after taking an embalming class. As one of Belvedere's first Mexican businessmen and a founder of the Mexican Chamber of Commerce, he quickly earned the respect of his neighbors. He spearheaded efforts to establish a Mexican school in Belvedere with the help of the consulate and always took pride in his Mexican nationality.[19]

More typical of the sort of individual who made up the Honorary Commissions was Juan B. Ruiz, a pharmacist and manager of Ruiz Pharmacy, the oldest drugstore in Los Angeles. Born in Culiacán, Mexico, in 1896, Ruiz was the son of a large rancher and mine operator in that state who had taken a neutral position in the revolution. Having been forced to flee to the mountains during 1913, Ruiz took a government job under Carranza after attending medical school in Mexico City. Although offered a position in the Department of Education under Obregón, Ruiz decided to move to Los Angeles in 1920 and was able to invest $500 in the purchase of a drugstore on Main Street. During the 1920s, his establishment became known as one of the most important sites for political hobnobbing; Ruiz played host to Mexican politicians from Alvaro Obregón to José Vasconcelos. Ruiz himself served as campaign manager for Vasconcelos when he made his unsuccessful bid for the Mexican presidency in 1928.[20]

Others in the inner circle of the Mexican consulate had similar, if not as exciting, stories of emigration and ascendancy. Mauricio Calderón was the main businessman responsible for the growing Spanish-language music industry of Los Angeles in the 1920s. As proprietor of Calderón Music Company, he had been active in Mexican social circles since his arrival in Los Angeles in 1915, having fled the revolution in Chihuahua. Physicians R. J. Carreón, Rafael Martin Del Campo, and Camilo Servin all arrived in Los Angeles in the 1920s to attend medical school or to begin practices serving the ever-expanding Mexican immigrant community. These doctors would consistently involve themselves in social welfare work and the establishment of clinics under the auspices of the Mexican consulate, in addition to becoming prominent members of the Honorary Commissions.[21]

These individuals saw themselves as operating between the masses of working-class Mexican immigrants, often as "guardians" of their "race," and the Anglo-American power brokers in the city, particularly the capitalists who employed Mexican labor. But, unlike Anglo-American progressives in the 1920s, these leaders developed a progressive ideology in the context of *Mexican,* not American, society. Whereas Anglo-American reformers increasingly sought either to Americanize the foreigners or to exclude them, the Mexican progressives tried to encourage continued loyalty to mother Mexico.

Ironically, Mexican progressives during the 1920s often shared some of the same negative attitudes toward Mexican immigrants as those expressed by Anglo-American progressives who advocated naturalization and Americanization. The Mexican progressives encouraged return migration partly because they believed that life in the United States had "civilized" the part-Indian peasant migrant; no longer provincial villagers, these immigrants had developed national—rather than regional— pride. In the United States, workers learned new skills and a work discipline that Mexican leaders believed was desperately needed for Mexico's own development. Mexican nationals who had experienced life in the United States were believed to be potentially more productive and refined than the typical mestizo villager.

This attitude had as its counterpart in Mexico the ideology of *indigenismo,* which sought to exalt the native Indian of Mexico while destroying his culture and land base. Part of the larger effort to institutionalize the Mexican state and legitimize it throughout the population, *indigenismo* reflected the contradiction of an institutionalized revolution dedicated to constructing a sense of unifying nationalism among a diverse and often unwieldy population. As one scholar has put it, "the ultimate and paradoxical aim of official *indigenismo* in Mexico was thus to liberate the country from the dead weight of its native past.[22] While in Mexico only urbanization and government intervention could hope to modernize the Indian, in the United States American society itself was seen as aiding the effort.[23]

Moreover, during the 1920s the middle classes used nationalism to disarm revolutionary sentiment among the mestizo and Indian populations while legitimizing their own rule by emphasizing their claim to the revolutionary heritage. At the 1924 commemoration of Emiliano Zapata's death, for example, Obregón's hand-picked successor, Plutarco Elias Calles, claimed that "Zapata's agrarian program is mine." This was an amazing act of co-optation on the part of Calles, who had fought Zapata while alive and had hitherto failed to implement even the mildest land reform. When the municipal government of Mexico City formed an Official Committee of Patriotic Commemorations in 1925, it did so to ensure ideological uniformity in public ceremonies and to circulate propaganda that closely reflected the policies of the federal government.

During the 1920s the Mexican government was able to circumvent many strikes by accusing unruly labor leaders of being unpatriotic and counterrevolutionary.[24]

In the United States, the Honorary Commissions also organized official celebrations of Mexican national holidays. In September of 1921, to celebrate the one hundredth anniversary of Mexico's independence from Spain, the newly formed Mexican Committee of Patriotic Festivities organized a month-long program, which included a parade of citizens of Mexican states, a beauty contest, Mexican music concerts and film exhibits, and a public ceremony culminating in the traditional *grito,* or "yell." This was the first year that the Mexican independence activities were directly sponsored by the Mexican consulate office, working largely through the Los Angeles Honorary Commission.

But tension and mistrust often lurked behind the supposed unity of the Mexican community at these events. A small organization made up largely of American-born Chicanos, the Sociedad Hispano Americana, had sponsored Mexican independence celebrations for many years prior to 1921 and refused to step aside when the new Committee of Patriotic Festivities was organized by the Mexican consulate. The editor of a consulate-sponsored newspaper, *El Heraldo de México,* called on the renegade organization to give way to the newly formed committee, since it was "genuinely Mexican." The editor did acknowledge, however, that these "semi-compatriots, sons of beautiful California," also had a right to honor Mexican heroes. No doubt another factor in raising *El Heraldo*'s ire was that the official Mexican Committee of Patriotic Festivities maintained its headquarters at the newspaper's offices.[25]

As the decade progressed, other, more ambitious projects were undertaken by the Los Angeles Honorary Commission working in conjunction with the consulate. During the mid-1920s, for example, Spanish-language libraries were established in Southern California, with books donated by the Mexican government and by local Mexican book dealers. This effort represented an attempt to educate the masses of Mexican immigrants about the country they had left, along with ensuring that adults would not lose their native tongue. Concern about the Americanization efforts clearly moved the Mexican government officials and middle-class leaders of the immigrant community to take seriously the threat of changing cultural loyalties among laborers.

By the late 1920s, directors of Mexicanization efforts, like their Americanizing counterparts, increasingly focused on the children of immigrants. In 1927 and 1928, grandiose plans for about fifty schools for

Mexican children were developed in the offices of the Mexican consul general in Los Angeles. In a program consciously patterned after Japanese and Hebrew schools, Mexican children attended classes from 4 to 6 P.M., after a full day in the American public school system. Study included instruction in the Spanish language and in Mexican geography, history, and native arts. As one student remembered, "the teachers were the old fashioned kind who taught by 'rote'—you did things over and over until you got them right."[26]

The clear intent of these schools was to instill in the pupils a love of Mexico, a land that many of them had not seen. Fundamentally, many immigrant parents were concerned about their children's inability to speak Spanish and felt that this extra instruction would keep the children connected to their own native tongue. But the schools also attempted to foster an emotional attachment to the Mexican nation, in the hope that these children of immigrants would look upon their condition as somewhat tragic but temporary. For example, Beatrice Palomarez, the daughter of Zeferino Ramírez, recalled this poignant moment in the Mexican school of Belvedere: "The last 15 minutes of class were so special. Everyone would close his books and settle down and Mrs. Robles would read us a chapter from a book that told the story of a little boy's travels from the old world to the new. Sometimes we would see Mrs. Robles, as she closed the book, brushing a tear from her eyes, carried away with the pathos of the story."[27]

The effort to establish Mexican schools throughout Southern California is evidence that many of the projects sponsored by the Honorary Commissions were able to combine the interests of the Mexican government with those of large sections of the Mexican immigrant population. That does not mean, however, that those interests were identical. The Mexican government, for its part, wanted the immigrants and their families to remain loyal to the Mexican nation, to refuse American citizenship, and eventually to return to Mexico. Working-class Mexican immigrant parents, on the other hand, valued the maintenance of ties to Mexico's culture and language as the most important aspect of Mexicanization efforts.

In 1928, the Mexican government sent representatives from the Secretariat of Education to unify the various efforts made by local communities in Southern California to establish schools. Some members of the Los Angeles Mexican community, however, were afraid that the schools would thereby become entangled with political and religious questions that were consuming the Mexican nation. *La Opinión* urged that the schools be organized on principles that "have nothing to do with the internal or direct political interests of the government," and that the government should "categorically and sincerely [proclaim] that, in its heart, it shall work only toward the progress and the culture of the race." This editorial writer noted that "although in Mexico the attacks will not cease between one group and another . . . here within the educational systems . . . neutrality, tolerance, and unity shall reign absolute."[28] Local Mexicans, therefore, were asking the Mexican government to fund an effort without using it for political means.

Despite an enormous amount of time and energy expended on the establishment of Mexican schools in the late 1920s, no more than ten schools were founded. Mexico could hardly have been expected to build a great number of schools for its citizens in the United States when it was unable to provide an adequate education for the children within its own borders. Some in Los Angeles, however, accused the Mexican government of lukewarm support for these efforts. One editorial writer demanded that the government cease to sponsor "useless festivities and banquets, ceremonies in which nothing beneficial results." Noting the schools' continued financial difficulties, he advocated additional funding for them.[29] No amount of pleading, however, could alter the funding priorities of the Mexican government.

In promoting Mexican nationalism, Mexican government officials were not simply altruistically striving to provide a positive national identity for Mexicans in the United States. As mentioned, their intent was to convince emigrants to return to Mexico.[30] The Mexican government realized that the past and present siphoning off of many hard-working citizens hampered its recovery from the ravages of revolution, particularly in the northern states, which lacked an adequate labor supply. The presence of so many Mexican citizens in the United States was also an embarrassment to leaders who had fought a nationalistic revolution against the pro-American dictator, Porfirio Díaz. When Americanization programs called for Mexicans to become citizens and abandon their native country and customs, Mexican leaders worried that the United States would steal away its most potentially productive nationals.

When the Great Depression hit Los Angeles with full force in 1930, therefore, consul Rafael de la Colina jumped at the chance to repatriate Mexican nationals and their often American-born children. Working closely with local American officials, he arranged for county-sponsored trains to return Mexicans living in Los Angeles and on relief back to

Mexico. When members of the Mexican Chamber of Commerce complained that the deportation raids launched by the Immigration Service disrupted the local community, they were criticizing the chaotic nature of the raids, which made residents afraid to shop or work, not repatriation itself. The Comité de Beneficencia Mexicana, a committee of the Los Angeles Honorary Commission, changed its own focus in 1931 from supporting indigent Mexicans in the city with food, clothes, and medical care to paying for railroad passage back to Mexico for those who could not afford it. The repatriation efforts of the middle-class leadership, therefore, were not simply a reaction to initiatives formulated by racially inspired Anglo officials, but the culmination of efforts begun in the early 1920s to keep Mexicans in the United States loyal to their mother country.[31]

Ultimately, support for repatriation ended the reign of the Mexican progressives who had been leaders in Los Angeles's Chicano community. The exit of approximately one-third of the city's 150,000 Mexican residents during the repatriation period of the early 1930s ushered in a new type of leadership: American-born Chicano leaders more affiliated with their working-class communities and organized labor backgrounds. After 1935, the Mexican consulate would never again play as crucial a role in organizing local leadership around goals formulated in Mexico City. Increasingly, the Mexican-American community would see its own political future as wrapped in the context of American civil rights and the fulfillment of the promises of U.S. citizenship.

Even Zeferino Ramírez, long considered a leader in this "México de afuera," community, would change his perspective. Although he never officially changed his citizenship, a trip to the interior of Mexico in the late 1920s did convince him never to return to live permanently in his native country. Visiting Mexico with the intent of moving his business, he decided that "everything there [was] still very backward and very disorganized."[32] By 1945, at the conclusion of World War II, his daughter Julia urged him to become involved in the construction of a monument to the Mexican-American soldiers who had died in the war. After forming a committee and convincing the Los Angeles City Council of the worthiness of the project, Zeferino himself contributed the final $4,000 toward the cost of the monument. Still standing at the triangle formed by Lorena, Brooklyn, and Indiana streets, this monument also marks the dividing line between the city and county of Los Angeles and the entrance to Belvedere, the adopted home of Zeferino Ramírez. More emphatically for the purposes of this story, it also marks the transition from a Mexico-centered leadership to a leadership focused on political and social advancement in U.S. society.[33]

Despite this eventual turn, the political generation that emerged in Los Angeles during the 1920s reflected both Los Angeles progressive politics at the time and the institutionalized revolution of the Mexican state. These leaders intended to impose order on the chaos of the Mexican Revolution and the turbulence of the Mexican situation in the United States, while retaining Mexican national pride and progress. While trying to change Mexico from afar, they also encouraged working-class Mexicans to see their future intertwined with a middle-class leadership of professionals and businessmen. For these leaders, the bonds of race could help maintain social control in an otherwise divisively hierarchical political and economic order. The story of these progressive Mexican community leaders suggests the need to expand our definitions of "progressivism," question assumptions that this movement was purely an American phenomenon, and search for new ways of incorporating the thinking of leaders of various ethnic groups into a multicultural perspective of the past.

NOTES

1. *La Opinión*, June 10–13, 1927. Ironically, incorporation of this area would later be taken up as a strategy of empowerment by East Los Angeles Chicanos. See Jorge García, "Forjando ciudad: The Development of a Chicano Political Community in East Los Angeles" (Ph.D. diss., University of California, Riverside, 1986); and Reynaldo F. Macias, Guillermo Vicente Flores, Donaldo Figueroa, and Luis Aragon, *A Study of Unincorporated East Los Angeles,* Monograph no. 3, Aztlán Publications (Los Angeles: Chicano Studies Center, University of California, Los Angeles, 1973).

2. "John Perry Wood" and "Marco H. Hellman," in *Who's Who in Los Angeles County, 1927–1928* (Los Angeles: Chas J. Lang Publisher, 1928), 16, 239; "Clifford John Shepherd," "Marco H. Hellman," and "Lloyd Mowat MacDonald," in *Who's Who in California: A Biographical Dictionary, 1928–29* (San Francisco: Who's Who Publishing Company, 1929), 16, 43, 459.

3. *La Opinión*, June 10–13, 1927, especially the editorial on June 11, 1927.

4. George E. Mowry, *The California Progressives* (Berkeley: University of California Press, 1951), especially 55, 86–104. See Richard Hofstadter, *The Age of Reform: From Bryan to FDR* (New York: Knopf, 1955), for a similar analysis of progressives on a nationwide scale. Robert Wiebe, on the other hand, would see the progressives emanating from the very bowels of the modern organization in a quixotic "search for order." See *The Search for Order* (New York: Hill and Wang, 1967).

5. Jackson K. Putnam, "The Persistence of Progressivism in the 1920s: The Case of California," *Pacific Historical Review* 35 (November 1966): 396–98.

See also Arthur Link, "What Happened to the Progressive Movement in the 1920s?" *American Historical Review* 64 (1959): 833–51.

6. Daniel T. Rodgers, "In Search of Progressivism," *Reviews in American History* 10 (December 1982): 113–32.

7. For anti-Asian sentiment among California progressives, see Spencer C. Olin, Jr., *California's Prodigal Sons: Hiram Johnson and the Progressives, 1911–1917* (Berkeley: University of California Press, 1968), 80–90; and Roger Daniels, *The Politics of Prejudice: The Anti-Japanese Movement in California and the Struggle for Japanese Exclusion* (Berkeley: University of California Press, 1962), 46–64.

8. See George J. Sanchez, " 'Go After the Women': Americanization and the Mexican Immigrant Woman, 1915–1929," in Ellen Carol DuBois and Vicki L. Ruiz, eds., *Unequal Sisters: A Multicultural Reader in U.S. Women's History* (New York: Routledge, 1990), 250–63.

9. See David G. Herman, "Neighbors on the Golden Mountain: The Americanization of Immigrants in California. Public Instruction as an Agency of Ethnic Assimilation, 1850 to 1933" (Ph.D diss. University of California, Berkeley, 1981), 594–611.

10. See, for example, James T. Kloppenberg, *Uncertain Victory: Social Democracy and Progressivism in European and American Thought, 1870–1920* (New York: Oxford University Press, 1986), for a study that sees similar "impulses" on both sides of the Atlantic.

11. Ramón Eduardo Ruiz, *The Great Rebellion: Mexico, 1905–1924* (New York: Norton, 1980), 179–81; Dr. Atl, "Obregón y el principio de la renovación social," in Editorial Cultura, *Obregón: Aspectos de su vida* (México, 1935), 71.

12. For a cogent analysis of earlier consular relations with the Mexican immigrant community, see Juan Gómez-Quiñones, "Piedras contra la Luna, México en Aztlán y Aztlán en México: Chicano-Mexican Relations and the Mexican Consulates, 1900–1920," in James W. Wilkie, Michael C. Meyer, and Edna Monzón de Wilkie, eds., *Contemporary Mexico: Papers of the IV International Congress of Mexican History* (Berkeley: University of California Press, 1976), 494–527.

13. Rafael de la Colina, *Una vida de hechos*, Archivo Histórico Diplomático Mexicano, Serie Testimonios 1. (Mexico City: Secretaria de Relaciones Exteriores, 1989), 27.

14. Michael C. Meyer and William L. Sherman, *The Course of Mexican History*, 2nd ed. (New York: Oxford University Press, 1983), 542. See also Peter H. Smith, "La política dentro de la Revolución: El congreso constituyente de 1916–1917," *Historia Mexicana* 22 (1973): 363–95.

15. This is a social structure quite unlike that in San Antonio, Texas, as described by Richard A. García in *Rise of the Mexican American Middle Class: San Antonio, 1929–1941* (College Station: Texas A&M University Press, 1991). García's San Antonio had two well-developed upper classes—an exiled Mexico-focused group of elites and a dual-focused Mexican-American middle class—competing for the leadership of the large working-class population in the 1920s and 1930s.

16. Lawrence A. Cardoso, *Mexican Emigration to the United States, 1897–1931: Socio-economic Patterns* (Tucson: University of Arizona Press, 1980), 106, 116.

17. See George J. Sanchez, "Becoming Mexican American: Ethnicity and Acculturation in Chicano Los Angeles, 1990–1943" (Ph.D. diss., Stanford University, 1989), 266–67, for a description of the social backgrounds of the Mexican immigrant elite in Los Angeles during the 1920s.

18. See Gómez-Quiñones, "Piedras contra la Luna," for a similar perspective on this relationship.

19. Interview with Zeferino Ramírez, "Biographies and Case Histories" folder 2, Z-R5, Manuel Gamio Collection, Bancroft Library, University of California, Berkeley; Zeferino Ramírez, "Origins of the Ramírez Family, from What I Remember," trans. Jean Ramírez, ed. Beatrice R. Palomarez (unpublished manuscript, Ramírez family papers, 1983); interview with Beatrice R. Palomarez, October 15, 1990.

20. Eustace L. Williams, "Racial Minorities Survey—Mexican: Juan B. Ruiz," May 6, 1937, and Walton D. Fore, "American Guide: Cultural Centers-LA-265.2: Mexican," 287–88, Federal Writers Program Collection, MS 306, Department of Special Collections, University Research Library, University of California, Los Angeles.

21. Fore, "American Guide," 285–89.

22. David A. Brading, "Manuel Gamio and Official Indigenismo in Mexico," *Bulletin of Latin American Research* 7, no. 1, (1988): 88.

23. See Alan Knight, "Racism, Revolution, and *Indigenismo*: Mexico, 1910–1940," in *The Idea of Race in Latin America, 1870–1940* (Austin: University of Texas Press, 1990); Henry C. Schmidt, *The Roots of Lo México: Self and Society in Mexican Thought, 1900–1934* (College Station: Texas A&M University Press, 1978), 77–84, 97–123.

24. Ilene V. O'Malley, *The Myth of the Revolution: Hero Cults and the Institutionalization of the Mexican State, 1920–1940* (Westport, Conn.: Greenwood, 1986), especially chap. 3; *La Opinión,* November 26, 1926.

25. *El Heraldo de México,* September 15, 20, and 29, 1921; *Los Angeles Times,* September 7, 1921. The amount of coverage and publicity given the independence celebrations was extraordinary in *El Heraldo:* a front-page story on the planning and fruition of the festivities appeared every day through the month of September.

26. Cardoso, *Mexican Emigration,* 107–9; *La Opinión,* November 26, 1926, February 17 and November 12, 1927, September 1, 1929; Beatrice R. Palomarez, "Escuela México" (unpublished paper, n.d.).

27. Palomarez, "Escuela México."

28. *La Opinión,* May 10, 1928.

29. C. Trejo y Lerdo de Tejada, Secretaria de Educación Pública, to Secretario de Relaciones Exteriores, October 4, 1930, and Rafael de la Colina, Los Angeles Consul de México, to Secretario de Relaciones Exteriores, November 26, 1930, folder IV-264-1, Archives of the Secretariat of Foreign Relations, Mexico City; *La Opinión,* June 21, 1930.

30. This had been a long-standing objective, ever since President Obregón established the Department of Repatriation within the Secretariat of Foreign Relations in May 1921 and allocated funds for those wishing to return. See Alfonso Fábila, *El problema de la emigración de obreros y campesinos mexicanos* (Mexico City: Talleres Gráficos de la Nación, 1929), for the most extreme anti-emigration sentiments by a Mexican government official of the period.

31. Francisco E. Balderrama, *In Defense of La Raza: The Los Angeles Mexican Consulate and the Mexican Community, 1929 to 1936* (Tucson: University of Arizona Press, 1982), 15–32; Abraham Hoffman, *Unwanted Mexican Americans in the Great Depression: Repatriation Pressures, 1929–1939* (Tucson: University of Arizona Press, 1974), 38–115.

32. Interview with Zeferino Ramírez, Manuel Gamio Collection.

33. Ramírez, "Origins of the Ramírez Family," 39.

PART FOUR

The Legacy of Reform

The Progressive Legacy in California

Fifty Years of Politics, 1917–1967

Jackson K. Putnam

To the historian of politics one of the most fascinating consequences of political upheaval is the phenomenon of the unintended result. When a set of reformers sweep their enemies from the field and triumphantly put their program into place only to see it perform far differently than they intended, such an outcome reinforces the historian's belief in the essential mysteriousness and uncontrollability of human affairs. In some respects the record of the California progressives serves nicely as a case in point.[1] Although Hiram Johnson and his fellow insurgents were remarkably successful in achieving most of their specific goals, it can nevertheless be asserted that their most prized objective eluded them.

This goal was fundamental political reform. Convinced that a corrupt and sinister collection of "interests" had gained control of the political system, progressives sought to deprive these forces of political power and return that power to "the people," where it supposedly belonged. The basic villain, they believed, was the political party, which they deliberately sought to weaken or even destroy because it seemed the primary vehicle of special interests' political power.[2] Although much of their program to expand the power of the people—direct primaries, direct legislation, recall, women's suffrage, presidential primaries, and direct election of U.S. senators—gained wide acceptance, their efforts to weaken the party and to institutionalize nonpartisanship had results that were sometimes bizarre and usually far different from those intended.

The progressives made four major assaults on the political party in California. First, they sought to make judicial and local governmental elections mandatorily nonpartisan, requirements that came into effect in 1911 and 1913.[3] Second, they placed a host of incremental restrictions on party organizations—restrictions that made these organizations large, unwieldy, and powerless, particularly when they were deprived of the right to endorse primary candidates.[4] Third, they instituted the notorious cross-filing law of 1913, which allowed candidates to file on any and all party tickets regardless of party affiliation.[5] Fourth, in 1915 they attempted to make all state offices nonpartisan. Although a pro-Johnson legislature passed such a law, the voters defeated it in a referendum election the same year.[6] Thus, the political party survived as an institution in California, but only in a much weakened condition.

The ironic consequence of California's weak party system was that the power of the supposedly sinister special interests was enhanced, not reduced. In retrospect this result is not surprising, and if the California progressives had been less zealous and more realistic, they might have realized that they were throwing out the baby with the bath when they sought to destroy the political party. For the party in California as elsewhere had often served to moderate, regulate, and forestall the demands of special interests as well as to implement them. Also, it often served as a source not only of funds but of social ideas and programs that were often at odds with the demands of special interests. Thus, the party provided a shield for the officeholder against the undue influence of the lobbyist. Now deprived of such direction and support, the officeholder found himself heavily dependent on lobbyists for the funding and social information and direction previously supplied by the party. In the eyes of one observer, the California legislature became a large "commodity market," where legislators mainly concerned themselves with passing or blocking legislation supported or opposed by their alleged masters, the lobbyists for special interests.[7] According to this interpretation, this system reached its highest (or lowest) stage of development in the 1930s and 1940s, when master lobbyist Artie Samish forced legislators to do his bidding and became in his own words the "governor of the legislature."[8]

Although this mordant scenario embodies much historical truth, it contains many distortions as well. It vastly exaggerates the degree of political corruption in the state, for California under the progressives became and remained mainly free of the bribery, boodling, and treasury raiding that was typical of the machine politics of other states where the political party remained strong.[9] In fact, Samish's payoffs to compliant legislators seemed always to be for small-scale personal gratification ("food, booze, and broads") and money for reelection campaigns that, by today's standards and even by those of the 1930s, seem remarkably inexpensive. The system seemed to work well for lobbyist and legislator alike, and neither apparently had much sense of having corrupted the process that they came to control.

Surprisingly, the system seems also to have worked well for the general public. Here we encounter the primary paradox of California progressivism. In their blundering but well-intentioned zeal to reform politics, the progressives crippled the political party and inadvertently enhanced the power of "the interests," but at the same time they fashioned a new nonpartisan political culture which served the state well for more than half a century. Deprived of the party shield and support, the California officeholder had to face directly the complex and often contradictory pressures of his constituents as well as his own inchoate ethical urges to serve the "public good." In short, officeholders, especially governors and legislators, had to formulate policies based on their familiarity with practical realities and to judge their own effectiveness by actual results.[10] It soon dawned on them that social realities were invariably more complex than ideological constructs and partisan rhetoric, and from this awareness flowed three other guides to political action: that systematic fact gathering was a necessary prelude to policy formation; that sustained political experience was superior to partisan preconception; and that trial and error was often the most reliable method of social problem solving. In other words, with the rise of nonpartisanship pragmatism supplanted ideology in the public arena.

Closely related to the institutionalization of pragmatism, and rivaling it in importance, was the replacement of political extremism with political moderation. For as the politician directly confronted interest groups in formulating public policies, he found them extraordinarily diverse and divided—not composed solely of selfish businessmen and corrupt labor bosses, as early progressive propagandists would have it. These lobbyists came from all segments of society and represented worthy causes as well as ignoble ones. Caught up in a perpetual political scramble of conflicting demands, the new progressive governors and legislators learned to shape programs by reconciling opposing interests through negotiation and compromise more than by ineffectually attempting to implement policies drawn up in party caucuses or political conventions. Conceived in conflict and delivered through compromise, such programs were bound to be moderate, "half-a-loaf" solutions to social problems, and although held in contempt by partisan ideologues and doctrinaires, they became the standard product of progressive politics in the state.

Third, the new nonpartisan style of political behavior replaced laissez faire with institutionalized activism. California, it should always be remembered, was and is constantly in a state of boom, expansion, contraction, emergency, and flux; and neither politician nor citizen could reasonably expect government to be passive or quiescent under such conditions. The quiet Jeffersonian dogmas about "governing best by governing least" found little actual acceptance in the state; instead, California constituents expected their officials to perform, and those who learned to shape policies to serve social needs were usually the accepted and successful political leaders. Action became a byword in California politics.

This cluster of political practices and attitudes—nonpartisanship, pragmatism, moderation, and activism—which I call "neoprogressivism" did not materialize immediately or without irony. In fact, during Hiram Johnson's administration they seem to have emerged only in part. Johnson, though the primary exponent of nonpartisanship, was both vociferously partisan and ideological in the way that he espoused partisanship, castigating his enemies in both the Republican old guard and in the Democratic party as evil tools of the special interests. On the other hand, he and his henchmen were classically pragmatic in their reliance on expert opinion and systematic studies of social conditions in devising public policies.[11] Furthermore, though Johnson often was outrageously immoderate in his rhetoric, he and his supporters were capable practitioners of political moderation when it came to shaping legislation through compromise. And the enormous volume of legislation passed by the Johnsonians leaves little doubt that they were political activists.

In the reign of Johnson's successor, William D. Stephens (1917–1922), the neoprogressive style seemed to hit its natural stride, and it became the dominant pattern of political behavior in the state for the next half-century.[12] Although he was somewhat of a dark horse of California progressivism—suffering from Johnson's paranoid dislike of him, which kept him out of the governor's office until the last possible moment in 1917—Stephens gained election to the governorship on a cross-filing fluke the following year.[13] Stephens nevertheless fought off the gathering anti-progressive forces and established the neoprogressive system on a sound and lasting foundation. Like all progressives, he wrapped him-self in the mantle of nonpartisanship; but for the next decade and more, the term tended to lose meaning in the state, because the California Democratic party became practically extinct and the major political battles were fought in the primary elections between progressive and conservative Republicans.[14]

Stephens was also a thoroughgoing pragmatist. Like Johnson before him, he appointed numerous fact-gathering commissions to study public problems, and he based policy recommendations on their findings rather than on ideological preconceptions. His most imaginative action was his government reorganization policy, in which he consolidated most of the new progressive state agencies into a streamlined system of departments modeled on the modern business corporation, which was finding great favor in the public eye during the 1920s. This policy enabled him to de-scribe himself to the public as the state's "business manager," which served nicely to counteract the old-guard conservative rhetoric depicting progressives as impractical visionaries and/or corrupt politicians who were allegedly opposed to the reemergent business ethos of the decade.

In line with the neoprogressive formula, Stephens also showed him-self to be both an activist and a moderate. He expanded many state ser-vices and established new ones, and he financed this enlargement of gov-ernment activity by a 35 percent increase in corporation taxes (the controversial King Bill of 1921). The state's biennial budget more than doubled during his administration, but it did not become unbalanced, and he further demonstrated his essential moderation when he vetoed a number of progressive bills that he thought too expensive.

By 1922, however, Stephens had acquired much adverse political bag-gage, and his reelection campaign of that year revealed a basic weakness of the neoprogressive approach to politics: it made for good adminis-tration but bad campaigning. The pragmatic component is probably most at fault, because pragmatism, by deemphasizing ideology and dull-ing the edges of clear-cut moral and emotional appeals, places the can-didate at a disadvantage before an opponent who uses such appeals. In the California experience this disadvantage has proved especially deadly in intraparty squabbles. During the period under study every elected in-cumbent governor seeking reelection who encountered significant oppo-sition in the primary election invariably suffered defeat. Governor Stephens began this process in 1922, when his primary opponent, con-servative state treasurer Friend W. Richardson, attacked him for his al-legedly radical and spendthrift policies and retired him to private life.

Although Governor Richardson (1923–1926) was a sworn enemy of progressivism and made a mighty effort to destroy every remnant of it, he was in the end undone by the very neoprogressive forces that he had at first defeated.[15] Specifically opposed to the neoprogressive style—ideological rather than pragmatic, extremist rather than moderate, and laissez-faire rather than activist—he launched a full-scale anti-progressive program during his first two years in office. He vigorously cut many state services, reduced the budget by several millions of dollars, vetoed more than 50 percent of the bills passed by the legislature, and continuously harangued his opponents in the press as "spendthrifts," "radicals," "socialists," and "parasites." The progressives fought back strenuously, however. They organized the highly activist Progressive Voters League (PVL), regained working control of the legislature in 1924, sharply increased the budget, and laid the foundation for the recapture of the statehouse two years later.[16]

The leader of this neoprogressive counterattack was Lieutenant Governor C. C. Young. The primary election of 1926 provided the California voters with a clear-cut choice of continuing with the conservative mode of politics or reverting to a neoprogressive approach, and they chose the latter. While Richardson continued his free-wheeling attacks on the progressives in his battle for the Republican renomination, Young, the PVL candidate, unambiguously articulated the rhetoric of progressivism. He admitted that his proposed program of expanded state services would cost money and require higher taxes, but in a remarkably candid display of neoprogressive doctrine, he went on to make two corollary assertions. First, he argued that California's rapid population and economic growth (the state's population increased by more than 60 percent in the 1920s) made a corresponding governmental growth in state services essential. Second, he said that genuine economy in government, which Richardson was agitating for, would consist of efficient management and fiscal accountability rather than lower taxes and state budgets. A more candid clash between conservative and neoprogressive principles could hardly be imagined, and when the voters nominated and elected Young, they seemed to be making a clear choice.[17]

Nor did Governor Young (1927–1930) disappoint his constituents after he took office. True to his promise, he raised taxes and approximately doubled the budget. Programs for the state's indigent and handicapped were substantially expanded, and the first comprehensive old-age pension law in the country was passed. Other innovations included the establishment of the state park and agricultural pest control systems as well as the first tentative steps toward water impoundment for flood control, irrigation, and hydroelectricity production under state auspices.[18] Alert to the danger of being identified as a spendthrift radical, Young sought to project the image of a pragmatic moderate instead. Like Stephens earlier, he referred to himself as California's "business manager," and he not only completed the process of government reorganization but inaugurated other policies that won for him a reputation as an outstanding administrator. For example, he established a cabinet system to oversee all governmental operations, implemented a comprehensive budget and accounting system, and revised the state's statutes into a modern code system. Also, like Governor Stephens and other neoprogressives, he relied on information derived from state-sponsored studies to formulate policies instead of basing them on ideology. Finally, he closed his administration with a treasury surplus, which he insisted should be used for improvements of state institutions and as a fund for future emergencies rather than be made a basis for tax cuts. This record in office seemed to secure his reputation as a pragmatic-moderate-activist administrator without peer among recent governors in the state.[19]

Young also resembled Stephens as governor when he failed to get renominated. His failure seems paradoxical in view of his record, but in truth he had acquired a panoply of political negatives by the time of the 1930 elections. As with Stephens, his pragmatic approach to politics made for uninspiring campaign rhetoric, a situation made worse by his colorless personality. The Great Depression was beginning to be felt in the state, and Young, like political incumbents elsewhere, was partly blamed for it. The prohibition issue proved his main undoing, for he had to share the "dry" vote with a crusading Los Angeles prosecutor; as a result, the popular "wet" candidate, Mayor James Rolph, Jr., of San Francisco, won the nomination and the governorship.[20]

In the California political arena, where the main battles were waged between conservatives and neoprogressives, Governor Rolph (1931–1934) is a hard man to classify.[21] Having defeated the dean of California progressivism (Governor Young), he was identified in the public mind as a conservative. In many ways this designation was accurate, though in other ways it was not. He did not by any means reflect the neoprogressive style, lacking both the understanding and the experience to be a pragmatist, the will to be an activist, and the consistency to be a moderate. He did do a number of progressive things, however. For instance,

he spent much of Governor Young's treasury surplus on relief for the
depression's unfortunates; he established a program of youth conservation camps that somewhat anticipated the New Deal's Civilian Conservation Corps; and he successfully pushed for the Central Valley Project
Act in the teeth of private power company opposition, which (as with a
similar proposal in 1922) castigated it as an exercise in socialism.

On other issues, however, the governor seemed to be a committed reactionary, even a kind of proto-fascist. He cut budgets drastically. He
attempted to return relief and other functions to counties and local ju-
risdictions already bankrupt because of their dependence on the property tax. To solve the problem of increased spending on old-age pensions, he advocated that the eligibility age be raised to seventy-five. He
vetoed an income tax bill, signed a bill establishing a sales tax, and condemned anyone who advocated increased corporation taxes as an "enemy of the people." He also endorsed mob violence against agricultural
strikers in the Imperial Valley and congratulated a lynch mob in San Jose
for hanging two kidnap-murder suspects.[22] Through it all, he insouci-
antly maintained a public air of innocent optimism and glad-handing
frivolousness. He had been elected on a slogan of "smile with sunny
Jim," and he maintained his glued-on gubernatorial grin throughout his
tenure in office while the somber effects of the deepening depression
seemed to make it more and more ludicrously inappropriate. Even many
conservatives were seemingly embarrassed by his antics and probably relieved in their "heart of hearts" when cardiac arrest carried him off to
his reward in June 1934.

Rolph left behind a political system in much disarray. As usual, a
gaggle of Republican politicians competed for their party's gubernatorial nomination; but now, for the first time since 1910, they also had to
worry about serious opposition from a revitalized, New Deal–oriented
Democratic party. Fortunately for the Republicans, the Democrats fool-
ishly forfeited their opportunity by engaging in an exceedingly sangui-
nary political brawl over the gubernatorial nomination; in the end, they
selected the sensational but unelectable ex-Socialist Upton Sinclair,
who stood on his famous but impractical "EPIC" platform. The ultimate beneficiary of the imbroglio was acting governor Frank Merriam,
who defeated a slate of opponents (including former governor C. C.
Young) in the Republican primary and went on to win the general election against Sinclair.[23]

Governor Merriam (1934–1938) was a political surprise. A deeply
experienced Republican conservative who emerged from a campaign

that had smeared Sinclair mercilessly and mendaciously as a sinister "red," he was expected to perform as an old-guard Republican fighting off the encroachments of the New Deal. Although many New Dealers and some historians have argued that he did play that role, it seems more accurate to assert that he actually helped to bring the New Deal to California and, in the process, adopted the politics of neoprogressivism more than the politics of conservatism. Although he was an old-line Republican who had long espoused the rhetoric of conservatism, he shrewdly adopted the mantle of nonpartisanship. This was an astute move, because he governed at a time of Democratic resurgence in the state, with the Democrats gaining majority party status there during his administration and winning control of the state Assembly.[24]

With nonpartisanship adopted, pragmatism, activism, and moderation soon followed. Merriam's pragmatism was revealed as early as the 1934 campaign, when he recognized the popularity of the New Deal and endorsed it in all but name and also supported the more controversial but wildly popular Townsend movement.[25] After being elected, he worked closely with the legislature, including the "EPIC Democrats" led by state senator Culbert Olson, to establish state programs of all sorts (especially for relief and old-age security) and make the state eligible to receive federal grants-in-aid. Merriam was also a very activist governor: he increased both taxes and budgets precipitously; he signed bills establishing the state's first income tax and increasing levies on banks, corporations, liquor, and insurance; he made the sales tax less regressive by exempting groceries; and he even attempted unsuccessfully to pass a severance tax on oil, thereby earning the furious animosity of Artie Samish, who represented the oil companies. Merriam also proved himself a moderate by successfully opposing other taxes in the second half of his administration and by resisting the demands of Senator Olson and his EPIC Democrats, who espoused a much more sweeping New Deal program.[26]

Despite this seemingly creditable record, Merriam too learned about the perils of neoprogressivism when running for reelection. Unlike his predecessors, he did win renomination, but at a heavy price. Alleging that the governor had become too liberal, Samish persuaded Lieutenant Governor George Hatfield to oppose Merriam on behalf of Republican conservatives; and liberal Republican Raymond J. Haight entered the primary because he considered Merriam too conservative. Although Merrim defeated both, he was identified in the public eye as colorless and "wishy-washy"—as pragmatists usually are, especially when confronted with a dynamic and ideological opponent in the general election.[27] Culbert Olson was that kind of opponent. And when he dazzled the electorate with his ringing but misleading slogan of "Bring the New Deal to California," he brought the Democrats to power after forty years in the political wilderness and retired the aged but effective governor to private life.[28]

If Frank Merriam demonstrated the disadvantages of the pragmatic approach to politics in campaigning for reelection, Governor Olson (1939–1942) revealed the shortcomings of the ideological approach in trying to govern. His political zeal blinded him to the difficulties of trying to "bring the New Deal to California" when (1) much of the New Deal was already there; (2) the New Deal had ended on the national scene; (3) the Democratic party was divided in the state between conservative and New Deal factions; and (4) the Republican party still controlled the state Senate. Oblivious to such obstacles and totally lacking in finesse in negotiating with the legislature, Olson shaped his program largely according to his liberal-left ideology and then attempted to drive it through the legislature. At the same time, he delighted doctrinaire liberals and infuriated ideological conservatives by courageously pardoning labor martyr Thomas Mooney and supporting the actions of the congressional La Follette Committee in its exposure of civil liberties violations in the state, mainly by agribusiness concerns.[29]

These tactics earned him plaudits from the left, the undying enmity of the right, and ineffectuality in the legislature. In the first legislative session, nearly the entire Olson program was defeated or pigeonholed; in the second, Olson endured a repeat of that process plus a party revolt that placed both houses of the legislature in the hands of his opponents. The remaining two years of his term saw no real improvement in his political fortunes, especially since the onset of World War II and the waning of the depression seemed to make his "New Deal" program irrelevant.[30] Olson's crowning humiliation came in the 1942 primary, when, facing negligible opposition from candidates in his own party, he barely beat off the challenge of Republican candidate Earl Warren, who cross-filed on the Democratic ticket. This, of course, was a prelude to his devastating defeat in the fall election.[31]

Viewed in retrospect, Olson's political failure in office can be attributed at least in part to his failure to adhere to the neoprogressive formula. Although he was an activist, he was a most ineffective one. But instead of being a pragmatist, he was largely an ideologue; and rather than being moderate, he was more of an extremist. Ironically, he resembled Friend W. Richardson more than any other governor under study here. Although they came from opposite ends of the political spectrum, they were similar in deviating from the neoprogressive approach to politics. They were even more similar in their ineffectiveness.

If neoprogressivism declined under Olson, it made a mighty comeback in the reign of his successor. All the neoprogressive "buzz words"—nonpartisanship, pragmatism, moderation, and activism—seem made-to-order to depict the administrations of Governor Earl Warren (1943–1953). Nonpartisanship came naturally to him, since as a young man he identified himself with the Hiram Johnson progressives and embraced their emphasis on "the man, not the party" as an article of faith. But by the 1940s this appeal had changed from a slogan to a necessity for survival, since the Republicans were now the minority party. The remarkable fact that they continued to dominate California government for a quarter of a century after losing their majority (except for Culbert Olson's ineffectual interlude) is a tribute to their finesse. Warren contributed importantly to this achievement in at least three ways. First, as the main founder of the California Republican Assembly (CRA), he enabled the Republicans to get around the legal restrictions placed on party organization and activity by providing them with a formally private organization but actually a shadow party that was subject to none of these restrictions. Dominated by Republican bigwigs, the CRA coordinated party activities, raised funds, selected candidates, and performed a host of other actions that kept the Democrats off balance until they finally learned how to do the same thing in 1953.[32]

Second, Warren and others continually and with devastating effectiveness played their trump card—cross-filing. By benefiting incumbents because of their greater name familiarity, this device originally helped to "kill" the state Democratic party in the 1920s, when its registration fell to less than 25 percent. Now, though revived in the matter of registration, it remained electorally "dead" or at least debilitated, since Republican incumbents constantly cross-filed on Democratic tickets and defeated the Democrats in the primaries. Warren, as incumbent attorney general, came close to defeating Democrat Olson in the 1942 primary; in 1946 he became the only governor in the history of the state to pull off this trick and enjoyed the luxury of winning reelection with no significant opposition whatsoever.[33]

Finally, Warren played the nonpartisan role by living it. A genuinely charismatic personality full of warmth and geniality, Warren was also sincerely concerned with social issues, eager to work with anyone regardless of party label to realize his objectives, and more than willing to compromise in attaining them. As a result, he was able to get more than 90 percent of his program through the legislature. He also remained on good terms with his fellow Republicans; even though many of them regarded his program as anathema, they never presented him with any serious opposition in his three gubernatorial primaries. Warren's personality, like Dwight Eisenhower's, has long been recognized as one of his most valuable political assets, and in a very real sense it was a nonpartisan personality.[34]

Likewise, pragmatism came naturally to Earl Warren. In his memoirs he constantly used the word *pragmatic* to describe his policies and actions, and it is probably true that no modern governor was less concerned with strict ideological questions than he.[35] Governing at a time when California was probably more beset by turmoil and the problems of growth than at any other time in history, he was mainly concerned with devising policies that answered the state's needs. Well aware that doctrinaire formulas were inadequate to the task, he came increasingly to rely on "citizens' committees" to investigate problems and recommend solutions as well as to provide grass-roots support for such policies after he proposed them.[36]

The many problems and the many proposed solutions made Warren one of the most activist governors in the history of the state. Increased revenues brought on by wartime prosperity enabled him to provide additional outlays for social services of all kinds, and although he signed a bill providing for some temporary tax reductions, he earmarked most of the surplus for upgrading education, roads, state institutions, and the like; and he used these spending programs as "shock absorbers" in easing the transition to a peacetime economy. Furthermore, he insisted that rapid wartime and postwar growth necessitated the expansion of a host of state services, especially for higher education institutions, public hospitals, and a new mental health system, which became the major beneficiaries of increased spending.[37]

Warren's activism carried him into new fields as well. Faithful to his political roots as a public prosecutor, he recognized crime as a major problem of the modern era, and he made a modest effort to deal with it where it was probably least menacing but most embarrassingly close to him—among lobbyists and legislators.[38] Nor did he shrink from taking on powerful interest groups when he deemed it necessary. He fought oil companies to a standstill in his victorious demand for higher gasoline taxes to finance his highway program. He was less successful in his struggle with electric companies over the public power issue in connection with the Central Valley Project. And he was thoroughly beaten by the California Medical Association (CMA) when he attempted to secure passage of a state health insurance program modeled on the federal Social Security program. Although he later secured some of the program through the "back door" by expanding the unemployment insurance system, Warren was largely defeated by the CMA's shrill cry of "socialized medicine," amplified by the campaign firm of Whitaker and Baxter, who ironically had handled Warren's election campaign. Historical hindsight indicates that Warren was defeated on this issue because he was too far ahead of his time.[39]

The same was true of his stance on racial issues. Although he was often tarred with the brush of racism because of his leadership role on the Japanese incarceration issue, Warren became acutely aware of the problems of racial minorities in the state, especially of blacks who flocked there to work in the war industries. In 1945 he astounded the legislature and numerous lobbies when he proposed the creation of a state commission to protect minorities from employment discrimination by employers and labor unions. This proposal was too radical for the legislature, which defeated it, and also for the electorate, which voted down a similar initiative measure the following year. It put Warren in the vanguard of the civil rights movement, however, and foreshadowed his role on the United States Supreme Court in the next decade.[40]

On all these controversial issues, whether he won or lost, Warren usually took a moderate rather than a radical position. There were always those who wanted to go further than he did, and he always showed a willingness to compromise if he could salvage some of his program. In no other issue did he show himself to be more effectively moderate than on the explosive "subversion" controversy. In the era of McCarthyism in California, the anti-Communist hysteria had three major foci: in the state legislature, where Senator Jack B. Tenney held sway on the state's Un-American Activities Committee; in Hollywood, where moguls blacklisted uncooperative screenwriters and actors before hostile congressional committees; and in the state university, where the Board of Regents sought to impose a special loyalty oath. Warren took courageously vociferous stands against anti-Communist extremism in all three places, and he could do so effectively because his own anti-Communist credentials were well known. He had attacked Communists and left-wing extremists long before it became politically popular to do so; by attacking right-wing extremism with equal energy, the popular governor staked out a middle-of-the-road position on the issue, and the vast majority of the California electorate followed him there. By isolating and marginalizing the extremists on both sides of the issue, he rendered them relatively powerless. The advantages of political moderation were probably never more clearly demonstrated.[41]

The lesson was clear to Warren's successor, Lieutenant Governor Goodwin J. Knight. Governor Knight (1953–1958), originally a progressive Republican, had turned articulately conservative in the 1930s and 1940s as a Los Angeles Superior Court judge and remained something of a conservative foil to Warren's liberal persona as lieutenant governor after 1946. Now he saw fit to swing back into a moderate-liberal stance, in hopes of picking up as much as possible of Warren's enormous constituency. Adopting the motto "Moderation is best. Avoid all extremes," and asserting that the major reality of California public life in the 1950s was its "almost unbelievable growth," he soon became an adroit practitioner of the neoprogressive mode of politics. Picking up much of the labor vote in 1954 by adamantly opposing a "right-to-work" initiative, he almost defeated the Democrats' Richard Graves by cross-filing in the gubernatorial primary of that year and easily defeated him in the fall election.[42]

Serving now as an elected governor, Knight settled more comfortably into his pragmatic-activist-moderate position. He signed bills expanding traditional liberal programs, such as old-age pensions, workers' compensation, unemployment insurance, and disability insurance, and he presided over the birth of an innovative program in child care and the much-admired Short-Doyle Mental Health Act. Knight also secured positive changes in the laws dealing with crime control and the regulation of alcoholic beverages, and he substantially increased higher education appropriations. He called for the establishment of a statewide water plan, but did nothing to implement it because of costs. Knight remained very much of a moderate in fiscal affairs, increasing expenditures when tax receipts increased but resisting the passing of new tax legislation.[43]

With this creditable record Governor Knight happily anticipated reelection in 1958, which would put him in a good position for a presidential bid when Eisenhower would mandatorily retire in 1960. The trouble was that other California Republican "big guns," especially Vice President Richard Nixon and U.S. Senate minority leader William F. Knowland, also coveted the presidency, and both could capitalize on the dim view that Republican party leaders and financiers were taking of

Knight's increasingly liberal politics. The outcome of this struggle was, of course, the ludicrous "musical chairs" imbroglio of 1958, whereby the Republicans forfeited control of the state government and gave the Democrats an opportunity to don the mantle of neoprogressivism, which the Republicans had deliberately discarded.[44]

The Democrats, under the leadership of Governor Edmund G. "Pat" Brown (1959–1966), wasted no time in doing so. As the only Democrat holding statewide office in 1950, Brown had used his position as attorney general to help rebuild the party in that decade. Other factors— such as the emasculation of the cross-filing law in 1952 and the formation of the California Democratic Council (CDC), which played the same role in the party that the CRA did for the Republicans—contributed to the process.[45] The Democrats soon began winning many more legislative and congressional seats than ever before, and when Pat Brown led them to victory in 1958 by gaining control of the legislature and all but one of the statewide constitutional offices, some predicted the dawning of an age of Democratic dominance equaling the sixty-year era of Republican rule in the state (1898–1958). Although this prediction proved premature, Governor Brown plunged into a major effort to make it come true.

Although lacking Warren's charisma, Brown was every bit as pragmatic and knowledgeable about the political system, and being personally friendly with Warren, he learned much from him about the tactics of moderation and compromise in dealing with the legislature. He was a typical neoprogressive activist with an extensive legislative agenda to meet the needs of a rapidly growing state, and he was aware of the advantage of "hitting the ground running" while his public support was still strong after his decisive election victory. He immediately pushed through large tax increases on incomes, inheritances, banks, insurance companies, race tracks, beer, and cigarettes (to his chagrin the oil companies again defeated severance taxes), and he began the process of sharply increasing the state budget, which more than doubled during his tenure. As usual, many of these expenditures went to the expansion of existing social services of all kinds, but he was genuinely innovative in other areas, such as consumer protection and smog control.[46]

Perhaps Brown's most significant innovation was in the racial field, and here he succeeded where Warren had failed. Pushing through a law prohibiting employment discrimination based on race and setting up the Fair Employment Practices Commission (FEPC) to enforce it, Brown also signed bills prohibiting racial discrimination in other aspects of public life (restaurants, public accommodations, and elsewhere), and in 1963 he successfully backed the passage of the landmark Rumford Fair Housing Act, which, more than any other, helped to put California in the vanguard of the civil rights revolution just getting under way in the country.[47]

In some ways even more innovative was the implementation of the California Water Project. Although pundits had long called for a massive investment in water impoundment, storage, and transfer technology to bring surplus water from the humid North to the water-starved South, a Byzantine tangle of political jealousies and regional rivalries had always operated to block such plans. Using his political talents of negotiation (including threats, punishments, and payoffs), in 1959 Brown managed to secure passage of the Burns-Porter water bonds legislation, which got the project started. Eventually, some two million acre-feet of water annually were transferred, and although second-guessers nowadays fault it on ecological grounds, perhaps justifiably, it was nevertheless a political achievement of a high order.[48]

Similar plaudits are characteristically accorded Governor Brown for his improvements in higher education. The Fisher Act of 1961, requiring every prospective public school teacher to have an academic major, was applauded by many; but the Donahoe Act of the previous year is Brown's chief claim to fame in this field. By establishing the famous Master Plan for higher education, the law provided a rational framework for the state's junior colleges (now called community colleges), state colleges (now called state universities), and the University of California system by allocating funds, students, and functions according to a well-defined mission for each. It was designed according to an ideal of making a college education available to every citizen capable of profiting from one, and although it has since come under attack for falling short of its goals, it has probably come closer to this ideal than any other higher education system in the country.[49]

Like Warren, Brown also sought to improve the health care system and perhaps with slightly more success. He poured money into the medically indigent program and the state mental hygiene system, and in 1965 signed the Medi-Cal Act. Although the latter is primarily federally funded, for a time it looked as though California was moving toward the comprehensive care system that Warren had attempted twenty years earlier.[50] Needless to say, it has not materialized.

Brown also found it necessary to make a major foray into the field of government reorganization. The state government had grown enormously since Governor C. C. Young's last major reorganization, and although Warren had made some piecemeal changes, Brown proposed a comprehensive restructuring. The legislature cooperated in passing Brown's streamlining proposal in 1961; moreover, under the leadership of Assembly speaker Jesse Unruh in 1965–66, it impressively reorganized itself. By vastly expanding and professionalizing legislative staffs, establishing annual year-round sessions, increasing legislative salaries, and assisting in reapportioning the state Senate according to the one-man, one-vote formula, Unruh helped to upgrade the legislature to number-one status in the nation and gained a national reputation for himself.[51]

Unruh not only secured the passage of much liberal legislation on his own but also acted as Brown's chief ally in getting the governor's program enacted. The two were never close, but until their furious falling-out in the mid-1960s, the neoprogressive system had never worked better than when these two dominated the executive and legislative branches of the California government and devised and implemented public policies for the public good.[52]

Brown's career also demonstrated again the maxim that a creditable administrative record is no guarantee of continued political success. Although he had fairly easily won reelection in 1962 against another Republican heavyweight, Richard Nixon, his negatives were accumulating rapidly by the mid-1960s. The Democratic disarray in the 1964 election; the eruption on the campuses; racial upheavals, including the Watts riot; and the poisonous controversy over the Vietnam War—all served to polarize the party into right and left extremes and left the governor pitifully exposed to the condemnation of both camps when he tried to maintain his typical moderate position on all issues.[53] Again the pragmatic moderate found himself helpless before the onslaught of ideological opponents; and when one of them, Mayor Samuel Yorty of Los Angeles, opposed him in the 1966 primary, his days were numbered. Although Brown won renomination, Yorty polled almost a million votes and once again demonstrated the fatal weakness of the neoprogressive incumbent when confronted with serious opposition in the primary. In the November election Ronald Reagan not only defeated him, the last neoprogressive, but began the process of destroying the neoprogressive system itself.[54]

Thus it was that the California progressives created a political system very different from what they intended. But it can be argued that they "builded better than they knew." The neoprogressive order served the state's needs for at least half a century and probably served them better than the system that has come to replace it.[55]

NOTES

1. For good accounts of the development of progressivism in California, see George Mowry, *The California Progressives* (Berkeley: University of California Press, 1951), especially chap. 6, "Harvest Time." See also Spencer C. Olin, Jr., *California's Prodigal Sons: Hiram Johnson and the Progressives, 1911–1917* (Berkeley: University of California Press, 1968); and Michael P. Rogin and John L. Shover, *Political Change in California: Critical Elections and Social Movements, 1880–1966* (Westport, Conn.: Greenwood, 1970), chaps. 2 and 3.

2. Olin, *Prodigal Sons*, 44 ff.; Grant McConnell, *Private Power and American Democracy* (New York: Knopf, 1966), 40–43.

3. McConnell, *Private Power*, 43; Olin, *Prodigal Sons*, 441; Eugene C. Lee, *The Politics of Nonpartisanship: A Study of California City Elections* (Berkeley: University of California Press, 1960). The Office of Superintendent of Public Instruction was also made nonpartisan.

4. A good description of the progressive weak party system in California can be found in Charles G. Bell and Charles M. Price, *California Government Today: Politics of Reform* (Homewood, Ill.: Dorsey Press, 1980), chap. 8. In 1989 the U.S. Supreme Court invalidated the ban on primary endorsements in statewide races, but in 1991 it reinstated it for local and judicial elections on narrow procedural grounds. *Los Angeles Times*, June 18, 1991, 3, 20.

5. James C. Findley, "Cross Filing and the Progressive Movement in California Politics," *Western Political Quarterly* 12 (Sept. 1959): 691–711; Dean McHenry, "Cross Filing of Political Candidates in California," *Annals of the American Association of Political and Social Science* 248 (November 1946): 226–31; Franklin Hichborn, "The Party, the Machine, and the Vote: The Story of Crossfiling in California Politics," *California Historical Society Quarterly* 38 (December 1959): 349–57; and Robert Pitchell, "The Electoral System and Voting Behavior: The Case of California's Cross-Filing," *Western Political Quarterly* 12 (June 1959): 459–84.

6. Olin, *Prodigal Sons*, 111–12; McConnell, *Private Power*, 43.

7. Carey McWilliams, *California: The Great Exception*, rev. ed. (Santa Barbara, Calif.: Peregrine Smith, 1976), 207–13.

8. Ibid., 198–209, 213; McConnell, *Private Power*, 49; Lester Velie, "The Secret Boss of California," *Collier's*, August 13 and 20, 1949; Arthur H. Samish and Bob Thomas, *The Secret Boss of California: The Life and Good Times of Art Samish* (New York: Crown, 1971).

9. Mowry, *California Progressives*, 300–301.

10. This essay deals primarily with governors rather than legislators, because, although the latter were important, they also tended to deal with specialized subjects, and except for the ones who became governors themselves (C. C. Young, Frank Merriam, and Culbert Olson) they did not ordinarily develop a comprehensive overall approach to the state's politics. The great exception was Jesse Unruh, who is discussed later.

11. For a thoughtful appraisal of this aspect of progressivism in California, see Olin, *Prodigal Sons*, 172–73.

12. The following account of the Stephens administration is based primarily on two studies by the author. See Jackson K. Putnam, "The Persistence of Pro-

gressivism in the 1920s: The Case of California," *Pacific Historical Review* 35 (November 1966): 399–404, and *Modern California Politics*, 3rd ed. (San Francisco: Boyd and Fraser, 1990), 2–9. See also H. Brett Melendy and Benjamin F. Gilbert, *The Governors of California* (Georgetown, Calif.: Talisman Press, 1965), 322–34.

13. H. Brett Melendy, "California's Cross-Filing Nightmare: The 1918 Gubernatorial Election," *Pacific Historical Review* 32 (August 1964): 317–30.

14. For a good account of this era of Democratic decline, see Robert E. Hennings, *James D. Phelan and the Wilson Progressives of California* (New York: Garland, 1985), chaps. 12–14.

15. Putnam, "Persistence of Progressivism," 404–8, and *Modern California Politics*, 8–10; Melendy and Gilbert, *Governors of California*, 336–47.

16. Putnam, "Persistence of Progressivism," 406–7; Russell M. Posner, "The Progressive Voters League, 1923–1926," *California Historical Society Quarterly* 36 (September 1957): 251–61; John L. Shover, "The California Progressives and the 1924 Campaign," *California Historical Quarterly* 51 (Spring 1972): 58–74; and Daniel P. Melcher, "The 1924 Election in California," *Southern California Quarterly* 60 (Summer 1968): 155–82.

17. Another issue, mainly extraneous to the conservative-progressive struggle, affected the 1926 election. This was a quarrel between the Bank of Italy, soon to become the Bank of America, and independent banks over the question of branch banking. See Russell M. Posner, "The Bank of Italy and the 1926 Campaign in California," *California Historical Society Quarterly* 37 (September 1958 and December 1958): 267–75, 347–58; and two articles in *Journal of the West* 23 (April 1984): William Hively, "The Italian Connection and the Bank of America's First Million," and Lynne P. Doti, "Banking in California: The First Branching Era," 56–64, 65–71.

18. Jackson K. Putnam, *Old-Age Politics in California: From Richardson to Reagan* (Stanford, Calif: Stanford University Press, 1970), 20–26; Putnam, "Persistence of Progressivism," 409–10, and *Modern California Politics*, 11; Donald J. Pisani, *From Family Farm to Agribusiness: The Irrigation Crusade in California and the West, 1850–1931* (Berkeley: University of California Press, 1984), chap. 12.

19. Putnam, "Persistence of Progressivism," 410–11, and *Modern California Politics*, 12–13; Melendy and Gilbert, *Governors of California*, 348–61.

20. Putnam, *Modern California Politics*, 12–13; Royce D. Delmatier, Clarence F. McIntosh, and Earl G. Waters, eds., *The Rumble of California Politics, 1848–1970* (New York: Wiley, 1970), 217–19.

21. On Rolph see Delmatier, *Rumble of California Politics*, 219–20; Putnam, *Modern California Politics*, 14–16; Melendy and Gilbert, *Governors of California*, 363–78; Herbert L. Phillips, *Big Wayward Girl: An Informal Political History of California* (Garden City, N.Y.: Doubleday, 1968), chap. 10; Duncan Aikman, "California's Sun God," *Nation* 132 (January 1931): 35–37; Herbert G. Goldbeck, "The Political Career of James Rolph, Jr." (M.A. thesis, University of California, Berkeley, 1936).

22. Duncan Aikman, "Governor Lynch and His Mob," *Nation* 137 (1933); Brian McGinty, "Shadows in St. James Park," *California History* 57 (Winter 1978/79), 290–307.

23. Rogin and Shover, *Political Change*, 124–47; Charles E. Larsen, "The Epic Campaign of 1934," *Pacific Historical Review* 27 (May 1958): 127–47; Leonard Leader, "Upton Sinclair's EPIC Switch: A Dilemma for American Socialists," *Southern California Quarterly* 62 (Winter 1980): 361–85; Russell M. Posner, "A. P. Giannini and the 1934 Campaign in California," *Quarterly of the Historical Society of Southern California* 39 (June 1957): 190–201; Bob Barger, "Raymond L. Haight and the Commonwealth Progressive Campaign of 1934," *California Historical Society Quarterly* 43 (September 1964): 219–30; Walton Bean, "Ideas of Reform in California," *California Historical Quarterly* 51 (Fall 1972): 213–26; Fay M. Blake and H. Morton Newman, "Upton Sinclair's EPIC Campaign," *California History* 63 (Fall 1984): 305–12. Gregg Mitchell, *The Campaign of the Century: Upton Sinclair's Race for Governor of California and the Birth of Media Politics* (New York: Random House, 1992).

24. Putnam, *Old-Age Politics*, 73; Robert E. Burke, *Olson's New Deal for California* (Berkeley: University of California Press, 1953), 5–24.

25. Putnam, *Old-Age Politics*, 39–41, and *Modern California Politics*, 21–22.

26. Putnam, *Modern California Politics*, 22–23, and *Old-Age Politics*, 73; Samish and Thomas, *Secret Boss*, 44–46; Burke, *Olson's New Deal*, 21–22.

27. Samish and Thomas, *Secret Boss*, 70–72; California Secretary of State, *Statement of Vote*, Primary Election, August 30, 1938 (Sacramento: California Secretary of State, 1938), 5–7.

28. Burke, *Olson's New Deal*, chap. 3.

29. Ibid., chaps. 4–5; Putnam, *Old-Age Politics*, 115–17, and *Modern California Politics*, 25–26; Richard H. Frost, *The Mooney Case* (Stanford, Calif.: Stanford University Press, 1968), chaps. 27–28.

30. Burke, *Olson's New Deal*, chaps. 7–14.

31. Ibid., 214–29.

32. Putnam, *Modern California Politics*, 32; Lee Katcher, *Earl Warren: A Political Biography* (New York: McGraw-Hill, 1967), 82–86.

33. John D. Weaver, *Warren: The Man, the Court, the Era* (Boston: Little Brown, 1967), 101, 148; Earl Warren, *The Memoirs of Earl Warren* (Garden City, N.Y.: Doubleday, 1977), 159, 171; Janet Stevenson, *The Undiminished Man: A Political Biography of Robert Walker Kenny* (Novato, Calif.: Chandler and Sharp, 1980), chap. 7. Warren came close to repeating the triumph in 1950. Although James Roosevelt managed to secure the Democratic nomination against the cross-filing Warren, 969,443 to 719,468, Warren lambasted him in the general election by about 1,100,000 votes, the largest margin in history for a contested election, and carried every county in the state. California Secretary of State, *Statement of Vote*, Primary Election, June 6, 1950 (Sacramento: California Secretary of State, 1950), 4–5; Katcher, *Earl Warren*, 262.

34. Katcher, *Earl Warren*, 6–7, 56, 161–65, 196, 232; Jack Harrison Pollack, *Earl Warren: The Judge Who Changed America* (Englewood Cliffs, N.J.: Prentice-Hall, 1979), 94–96.

35. Warren, *Memoirs*, chap. 7.

36. Ibid., 193, 199–200, 206–7; Richard B. Harvey, *Earl Warren: Governor of California* (Jericho, N.Y.: Exposition, 1969), 70–80.

37. Warren, *Memoirs*, 164, 174–75, 177–86, 226–27 ff.

38. Katcher, *Earl Warren*, 242–46.

39. Ibid., 186–90, 209–13; Warren, *Memoirs*, 187–89; Harvey, *Earl Warren*, 119–32.

40. Katcher, *Earl Warren*, 193–97; Warren, *Memoirs*, 187–89; Harvey, *Earl Warren*, 119–32.

41. Katcher, *Earl Warren*, 94–99, 117–21, 132–33, 154–56, 196–97, 200, 203, 213–15, 218–19, 231, 252–54, 275–76, 281–82; Warren, *Memoirs*, 218–23; Putnam, *Modern California Politics*, 39–41. On the subversion issue in general, see Ingrid W. Scobie, "Jack B. Tenney and the 'Parasitic Menace': Anticommunist Legislation in California, 1940–1949," *Pacific Historical Review* 43 (May 1974): 188–211; Edward L. Barrett, Jr., *The Tenney Committee: Legislative Investigation of Subversive Activities in California* (Ithaca, N.Y.: Cornell University Press, 1951); Robert L. Pritchard, "California Un-American Activities Investigations: Subversion on the Right?" *California Historical Society Quarterly* 49 (December 1970): 309–28; Edward R. Long, "Earl Warren and the Politics of Anti-Communism," *Pacific Historical Review* 51 (February 1982): 51–70.

42. Delmatier, *Rumble of California Politics*, 328–33, 335; Melendy and Gilbert, *Governors of California*, 427–33; Putnam, *Modern California Politics*, 41–43; Phillips, *Big Wayward Girl*, 158–62.

43. Delmatier, *Rumble of California Politics*, 333–36; Melendy and Gilbert, *Governors of California*, 432–34. On the Short-Dolye Act see Gale Cook, "A Promise Unfulfilled" *California Journal* 20 (May 1989). 194–97.

44. The "musical chairs" campaign, also known as the "big switcheroo," occurred when Senator Knowland decided to run for governor, forcing Knight to run instead for Knowland's vacated U.S. Senate seat. Both lost along with most other California Republican statewide officeholders. See Totton J. Anderson, "The 1958 Election in California," *Western Political Quarterly* 12 (March 1959): 276–300; Delmatier, *Rumble of California Politics*, 434–36; Phillips, *Big Wayward Girl*, chap. 26; Gladwin Hill, *Dancing Bear: An Inside Look at California Politics* (Cleveland: World, 1968), chap. 11. Kurt R. Schuparra, "Freedom versus Tyranny: The 1958 California Election and the Origins of the State's Conservative Movement," *Pacific Historical Review* (forthcoming, 1994).

45. In 1952 the cross-filing law was amended by an initiative requiring cross-filing candidates to indicate their party affiliations after their names on the ballot. This requirement proved a boon to the Democrats, who repealed the law completely in 1959. Nonpartisanship did not come to an end in the state, however, since the laws requiring large, ineffective party organizations and nonparty local elections remained on the books. Governor Brown also continued nonpartisanship in his dealings with the legislature and with the general public. On the CDC see Francis Carney, "The Rise of the Democratic Clubs in California," in Eagleton Institute of Practical Politics, *Cases on Party Organization* (New York: McGraw-Hill, 1963), 32–63. Jacqueline R. Braitman, "Elizabeth Snyder and the Role of Women in the Postwar Resurgence of California's Democratic Party," *Pacific Historical Review* 62 (May 1992): 197–220.

46. Melendy and Gilbert, *Governors of California*, 442–44 ff.; Delmatier, *Rumble of California Politics*, 342 ff., Phillips, *Big Wayward Girl*, 188; Putnam, *Modern California Politics*, 48, 50.

47. Putnam, *Modern California Politics*, 49, 54; Delmatier, *Rumble of California Politics*, 341–42, 349–51. The Rumford Act was repealed by initiative in 1964 but was reinstated by the state Supreme Court the following year. On the political effectiveness of Brown's race relations program, see Roger Rapoport, *California Dreaming: The Political Odyssey of Pat and Jerry Brown* (Berkeley: Nolo Press, 1982), 75.

48. Rapoport, *California Dreaming*, 14, 57–60; Delmatier, *Rumble of California Politics*, 343; Phillips, *Big Wayward Girl*, 195–98; Putnam, *Modern California Politics*, 49–50; Hugo Fisher, "Water: Life-Blood of the West," in *California: The Dynamic State* (Santa Barbara, Calif.: McNally and Loftin, 1966), 107–21.

49. Louis H. Heilbron, "Higher Education for the Millions," in *California: The Dynamic State*, 122–45; Delmatier, *Rumble of California Politics*, 345.

50. Putnam, *Modern California Politics*, 54, and *Old Age Politics*, 135–36.

51. Putnam, *Modern California Politics*, 52–53; Melendy and Gilbert, *Governors of California*, 446–47; Delmatier, *Rumble of California Politics*, 348, 355–57. A stimulating critique of Brown's reorganization plan was made by Ron Seyb, "It's Ideas That Count: Pat Brown Reorganizes California's Executive Branch," paper presented at the annual meeting of the Western Political Science Association, Seattle, March 21, 1991.

52. Delmatier, *Rumble of California Politics*, 348–49. On Unruh see also Ed Gray, "Jesse Unruh, 'Big Daddy' of California," *Nation* 196 (March 9, 1963): 199–207; Helen Fuller, "The Man to See in California," *Harper's* 242 (April 1971): 64–72; James R. Mills, *A Disorderly House: The Brown-Unruh Years in California* (Berkeley: Heyday, 1987); and Phillips, *Big Wayward Girl*, chap. 31.

53. In 1964 U.S. senator Clair Engle suffered an eventually fatal brain tumor. Governor Brown and the CDC endorsed state controller Alan Cranston to succeed him, but the Unruh forces backed Pierre Salinger. When Salinger defeated Cranston in the primary but lost to Republican George Murphy in the general election, both factions were angry and discredited. When Brown decided to run for a third term two years later, Unruh's break with him became permanent. Delmatier, *Rumble of California Politics*, 351–59; Phillips, *Big Wayward Girl*, chap. 30.

54. Totton J. Anderson and Eugene Lee, "The 1966 Election in California," *Western Political Quarterly* 20 (June 1967): 535–54.

55. For a brief overview of that system, see Jackson K. Putnam, "The Pattern of California Politics," *Pacific Historical Review* 61 (February 1992): 23–52. Although the story is complex, suffice it to say that Governor Reagan undermined the neoprogressive system more in rhetoric than in action; Jerry Brown weakened it by inconsistency, hostility, and inattention; and George Deukmejian sought deliberately to destroy it and largely succeeded. Whether Pete Wilson has the will, the desire, or the ability to revive it is problematical.

Index

Compositor:	BookMasters, Inc.
Text::	10/13 Sabon
Display:	Sabon
Printer:	Maple-Vail Book Mfg. Group
Binder:	Maple-Vail Book Mfg. Group